Lecture Notes in Computer Science 2140

Edited by G. Goos, J. Hartmanis and J. van Leeuwen

T0230325

Springer
Berlin
Heidelberg
New York
Barcelona
Hong Kong
London
Milan
Paris
Tokyo

Isabelle Attali Thomas Jensen (Eds.)

Smart Card Programming and Security

International Conference
on Research in Smart Cards, E-smart 2001
Cannes, France, September 19-21, 2001
Proceedings

Springer

Series Editors

Gerhard Goos, Karlsruhe University, Germany
Juris Hartmanis, Cornell University, NY, USA
Jan van Leeuwen, Utrecht University, The Netherlands

Volume Editors

Isabelle Attali
INRIA Sophia Antipolis
BP 93, 06902 Sophia Antipolis Cedex, France
E-mail: Isabelle.Attali@inria.fr

Thomas Jensen
IRISA/CNRS
Campus de Beaulieu
35042 Rennes, France
E-mail: Thomas.Jensen@irisa.fr

Cataloging-in-Publication Data applied for

Die Deutsche Bibliothek - CIP-Einheitsaufnahme

Smart card programming and security ; proceedings / International
Conference on Research in Smart Cards, E-Smart 2001, Cannes, France,
September 19 - 21, 2001. Isabell Attali ; Thomas Jensen (ed.). - Berlin ;
Heidelberg ; New York ; Barcelona ; Hong Kong ; London ; Milan ; Paris ;
Tokyo : Springer, 2001
   (Lecture notes in computer science ; Vol. 2140)
   ISBN 3-540-42610-8

CR Subject Classification (1998): C.3, C.2, D.3.2, D.4.6, E.3, F.3, K.6.5, K.4.4

ISSN 0302-9743
ISBN 3-540-42610-8 Springer-Verlag Berlin Heidelberg New York

Springer-Verlag Berlin Heidelberg New York
a member of BertelsmannSpringer Science+Business Media GmbH

http://www.springer.de

' Springer-Verlag Berlin Heidelberg 2001

Typesetting: Camera-ready by author, data conversion by DA TeX Gerd Blumenstein
Printed on acid-free paper   SPIN 10840169   06/3142   5 4 3 2 1 0

Foreword

The E-smart 2001 international conference on research in smart cards was held in Cannes, France on 19–21 September. The conference was jointly organized by the Java Card Forum, Eurosmart and INRIA, and received helpful financial support from the Conseil Régional Provence-Alpes-Côte d'Azur.

The intention with E-smart is to provide a forum for discussion and exchange of results on smart card development, security, and applications. This year's program was established by an international program committee that examined 38 papers submitted and selected 20 of these for presentation. The list of topics of this year's presentations includes biometrics, cryptography and electronic signatures on smart cards, hardware and software solution for smart card security, formal methods for smart card evaluation and certification, architectures for multi-applications and secure open platforms, middleware for smart cards and novel applications of smart cards. The conference also featured an invited talk by Simon Moore from the University of Cambridge.

Isabelle Attali
Thomas Jensen
E-smart 2001 program committee co-chairs.

Organization

Program Committee

Isabelle Attali, INRIA
Dominique Bolignano, Trusted Logic
Bertrand du Castel, Schlumberger
Wolfgang Effing, Giesecke & Devrient
Christian Goire, Bull CP8
Pieter Hartel, University of Twente
Peter Honeyman, University of Michigan
Thomas Jensen, IRISA / CNRS
Pierre Paradinas, Gemplus
Joachim Posegga, SAP AG
Peter Ryan, CERT
Jean-Paul Thomasson, ST Microelectronics
Yasuyoshi Uemura, ECSEC

Thanks are due to the following people for their help with the refereeing of papers: Thomas Genet, Valerie Viet Triem Tong, Stefan Friedich, Harald Vogt, Jaap-Henk Hoepman, Neil Henderson, Adam Field, and Jordan Chong.

Table of Contents

Protecting Consumer Security Devices
The Next 10 Years

Simon Moore

University of Cambridge, Computer Laboratory
Simon.Moore@cl.cam.ac.uk

Extended Abstract

In this talk, I will speculate about the likely near-term and medium-term scientific developments in the protection of low cost consumer security devices.

The mass adoption of embedded computing devices (mobile phones, PDAs, smartcards, etc) is moving us rapidly into the ubiquitous computing age. If these devices are too be a boon rather than a bane then robustness is going to be increasingly important. Security will be increasingly important, not only for traditional roles like payment mechanisms and access control, but also for peer to peer transactions and new business structures.

Peer to peer transactions between ones own devices need to be transparent and robust. Transactions between your devices and others needs more control to ensure that communication only takes place at your convenience. This requires robust authentication mechanisms (e.g., the *Resurrecting Duckling Protocol*[1]) coupled with a simple, elegant and intuitive user interface.

Novel business models arise from low cost embedded security devices. For example, per use leasing arrangements in a variety of guises, e.g. washing machines and other home appliances, software, videos, pay TV, public bicycles and car pools.

In practice we have seen how invasive attacks (reverse engineering), litigation attacks (abusing the legal discovery process) and business process failures have resulted in design discovery. Thus, inline with Kerckhoffs' principle, the security of a consumer security devices should only lie in keeping the key secret.

Extracting a key must be kept economically unattractive. Invasive attacks (probing the chip) to obtain key information are simpler than full reverse engineering attacks. These attacks tend to leave tamper evidence which limits their scope for some applications, but is a significant risk in any environment where identical copies of the same security device are useful (e.g. current PayTV systems).

Non-invasive attacks, on the other hand, extract information by analysing side channel information like electromagnetic emissions and power consumption, which leave little tamper evidence. As part of the G3Card European project (IST-1999-13515) we have been advancing attack techniques to better understand threat models. This knowledge is being used to guide the development of novel circuit and software techniques to make non-invasive attacks more difficult.

---

[1] see http://www.cl.cam.ac.uk/users/rja14/duckling.html

I. Attali and T. Jensen (Eds.): E-smart 2001, LNCS 2140, pp. 1–1, 2001.
© Springer-Verlag Berlin Heidelberg 2001

Jakarta:
A Toolset for Reasoning about JavaCard

G. Barthe, G. Dufay, M. Huisman, and S. Melo de Sousa*

INRIA Sophia-Antipolis, France
{gbarthe,gdufay,mhuisman,sdesousa}@sophia.inria.fr

1   Introduction

JavaCard [22] is a dialect of Java that enables Java technology to run on new generation smart cards and other devices with limited memory. As JavaCard is becoming increasingly popular, there has been a strong interest, both from academics and industrials, to reason formally about the JavaCard platform.

This paper reports on preliminary results with Jakarta, a toolset for specifying and reasoning about the JavaCard platform. The main ingredients of the toolset are:

1. the Jakarta Specification Language (JSL), a front-end for producing highly readable executable specifications;
2. the Jakarta Transformation Kit (JTK), a program to manipulate and transform JSL specifications;
3. the Jakarta Prover Interface (JPI), a compiler that translates JSL specifications into proof assistants;
4. the Jakarta Automation Kit (JAK), a toolset to support reasoning about executable specifications within proof assistants.

The main slogan behind Jakarta's design is that:

> a dedicated specification language is not only useful to achieve readable executable specifications that are easy to animate and debug, but it also can have a dramatic positive impact on formal verification.

To support this slogan, the benefits of this approach over using a proof assistant directly, as done in our previous work [3], are illustrated.

1.1   Background

Formal Methods for Smart Cards   With the increasing popularity of Java and JavaCard, there has been a spate of efforts, both by academics and industrials, to develop formal models for the Java and JavaCard platforms, see *e.g.* [3,6,9,16,20,21,27,28,31].

---

* On leave from University of Beira Interior-Portugal, and partially supported by the Portuguese research grant sfrh/bd/790/2000.

I. Attali and T. Jensen (Eds.): E-smart 2001, LNCS 2140, pp. 2–18, 2001.

In earlier work [3], we report on CertiCartes, a formalisation in Coq [2] of a large part of the JavaCard platform. With over 15,000 lines of Coq scripts, our formalisation constitutes to date the most in-depth machine-checked account of the JavaCard platform. CertiCartes contains a formal executable specification of the (defensive) JavaCard Virtual Machine JCVM, and a formal executable specification of the JavaCard ByteCode Verifier BCV, with its correctness proof.

This BCV has been constructed in a systematic way, by abstraction, from the specification of the virtual machine. First an abstract virtual machine has been constructed, describing the computational behaviour of bytecode verification. This abstract virtual machine is obtained systematically from the concrete virtual machine by defining a notion of abstract state, a function α mapping states to abstract states, and by adapting the semantics of each instruction to abstract states. It has been shown that the abstraction function "commutes with" execution (up to subtyping). Next, a data flow analyser has been build, that computes from the abstract virtual machine the BCV as a predicate on programs, and it has been shown that this data flow analyser terminates.

The methodology followed to specify and prove the correctness of the BCV is very appealing, in that it provides a systematic approach to the design and validation of static analyses for JCVM programs. Indeed, we are keen on applying a similar methodology for analysing object initialisation, information flow *etc.* However, our experiences with proving the correctness of the BCV suggest that Coq and more generally current proof assistants are not completely adapted for such endeavours: the specification of the virtual machine is cluttered, proofs are tedious and the level of automation is low.

Prototyping Environments and Proof Assistants Many of these difficulties can be solved by using a dedicated prototyping environment that supports some/most administrative aspects of formal semantics. A number of tools have been designed for this purpose, including ASF+SDF [15], Centaur [10], Letos [18] and RML [30]. These tools are rather diverse in their design and functionalities, but they all provide:

– a readable format for giving a formal semantics to programming languages;
– support to execute the semantics, which in particular allows to check that the semantics reflects the intended behaviour of the language.

However, prototyping environments lack functionalities to reason formally about the semantics, in contrast to proof assistants such as Coq [2], Isabelle [29] or PVS [32], which feature advanced type systems that support precise specifications and sophisticated reasoning.

In order to deal with real-size programming languages, there is thus considerable interest in integrating prototyping environments and proof assistants. Despite preliminary work in this direction, see Section 6.1, we still lack a tool that reflects manipulations in the specification environment of prototyping systems directly into the reasoning environment of proof assistants.

1.2   This Paper

The Jakarta toolset is an attempt to overcome the difficulties encountered in CertiCartes through the design of a suitable bridge between a prototyping environment and a proof assistant. The main goal of Jakarta is to provide *support for refinements and abstractions*. Through JTK, Jakarta offers interactive support to define a function $f' : \sigma' \to \sigma'$ from a previously defined function $f : \sigma \to \sigma$. The process, which operates at the level of rewrite rules, can be used if (1) σ' is less specific than σ, in which case the process requires an abstraction function $\alpha : \sigma \to \sigma'$ or; (2) σ' is more precise than σ, in which case the process requires a refinement function $\alpha : \sigma' \to \sigma$. Currently, Jakarta supports abstractions, refinements will be future work. In the context of reasoning about the JavaCard platform, abstraction is useful to construct *e.g.* the BCV from the JCVM.

To improve the support for refinement and abstractions, the Jakarta toolset has been designed with the following objectives.

- *Clarity of specifications*: Jakarta specifications are written in JSL, a front-end for producing executable specifications. The JSL language is a first-order, polymorphically typed system which features polymorphic datatype declarations and function definitions by conditional rewrite rules. The formalism is reasonably neutral and leads to specifications that are easy to read, extend and manipulate.
- *Tool independence*: the JSL specification language is minimal and JSL specifications are thus easy to embed into other formalisms. We have developed a compiler JPI that translates JSL specifications into an intermediate representation language JIR, and then from JIR to proof assistants, prototyping environments and programming languages. Due to the limited format of JSL rewrite rules, JSL specifications are close to their compiled counterpart, which ensures that what you specify (in JSL) is what you reason about (*e.g.* in Coq).
- *Proof automation*: the limited format of JSL makes it possible to develop customised tools to reason about JSL specifications. For example, JAK generates for every JSL function f an inversion principle, which is based on an analysis of JSL rewrite rules. Given a predicate ϕ, relating f's input to its output, an application of the inversion principle reduces the task of proving $\forall \boldsymbol{x} : \boldsymbol{\sigma}. \; \phi \, (\boldsymbol{x}, \; f \, \boldsymbol{x})$ to several simpler subtasks. This has shown particularly useful in proving the correctness of the BCV.

A further pay-off of the independence of proof assistants is that JSL supports *partial functions*, such as the head of a list. While such partial functions cannot be compiled into the specification language of proof assistants, they can be transformed automatically via JTK into a specification based on total functions, which can be translated to proof assistants.

The Jakarta toolset is implemented in Objective Caml [24]. Figure 1 summarises its basic architecture. In its standard use, the Jakarta toolset takes JSL specifications as input. The Jakarta Transformation Kit (JTK) can transform a JSL specification into a more abstract one. The Jakarta Prover Interface (JPI)

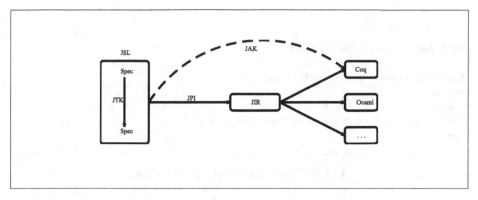

Fig. 1. Jakarta Architecture

translates JSL specifications into a format that is readable for *e.g.* a proof assistant or a prototyping environment, via an intermediate language (JIR). The Jakarta Automation Kit (JAK) generates appropriate proof strategies in the proof assistant, based on the JSL specification.

1.3   Organisation of the Paper

The remaining of the paper is organised as follows: Section 2 introduces JSL and presents the specification of the JCVM in JSL. Section 3 gives an overview of JPI, and Section 4 describes the functionalities that will be provided by the JTK. Section 5 is concerned with JAK, and discusses its usefulness in establishing the correctness of the BCV. Section 6 concludes with related work and directions for future research.

2   The Jakarta Specification Language

Jakarta's input language JSL is a minimal language (Figure 2 gives a flavour of JSL, below a larger example of a JSL specification is discussed):

- JSL types are first-order polymorphic types;
- JSL expressions are standard first-order algebraic terms;
- JSL functions are defined by conditional rewrite rules.

Having a restricted framework is useful to abstract or refine specifications and to compile and reason about them in proof assistants.

JSL Expressions JSL expressions are first-order terms built from variables and constant symbols. The latter are either constructor symbols, introduced by datatype declarations, or defined symbols, introduced by function definitions. Formally, expressions are defined as follows.

```
data nat = Zero | Succ of nat.

function plus : nat -> nat -> nat :=
begin
  m -> Zero    => plus m n -> n;
  m -> Succ y => plus m n -> Succ (plus y n);
end.
```

Fig. 2. Example of JSL specification

Definition 1.

– A signature Σ *consists of a set* $\mathcal{C}$ *of* constructor symbols, $\mathcal{D}$ *of* defined symbols *and an* arity *function* $\mathsf{ar} : (\mathcal{C} \cup \mathcal{D}) \to \mathbb{N}$.
– *Let* Σ *be a signature and let* $\mathcal{V}$ *be a fixed set of* variables. *The set* $\mathcal{E}$ *of* expressions *(over* Σ*) is defined by the abstract syntax:*

$$\mathcal{E} := \mathcal{V} \mid \mathcal{E} == \mathcal{E} \mid c \, \boldsymbol{\mathcal{E}} \mid f \, \boldsymbol{\mathcal{E}}$$

where c *ranges over* $\mathcal{C}$, f *ranges over* $\mathcal{D}$, *and in the last two clauses it is assumed that* $\boldsymbol{\mathcal{E}}$ *is of length* $\mathsf{ar}(c)$ *and* $\mathsf{ar}(f)$ *respectively.*
For every $f \in \mathcal{D}$, *we let* $\mathcal{E}_d(f) \subset \mathcal{E}$ *be the set of expressions with head symbol* f, *i.e. we let* $\mathcal{E}_d(f) = \{f \, t \mid t \in \boldsymbol{\mathcal{E}}\}$. *Moreover, we let* $\mathcal{E}_d$ *denote* $\mathcal{V} \cup (\bigcup_{f \in \mathcal{D}} \mathcal{E}_d(f))$.

JSL provides concrete syntax for records. Internally they are represented as inductive datatypes with a single constructors, as is done in Coq, thus no abstract syntax has to be defined for them explicitly.

We assume the reader to be familiar with standard notions such as subterms, occurrences, substitutions, and the associated notations, see *e.g.* [23].

JSL Rules Defined function symbols are specified by rewrite rules. In term rewriting jargon, our formalism is a restriction of constructor-based oriented conditional rewriting with extra variables! More precisely, the semantics of a defined function symbol is described by a set of oriented conditional rewrite rules of the form

$$l_1 \twoheadrightarrow r_1, \ \dots \ , l_n \twoheadrightarrow r_n \Rightarrow g \to d$$

The novelty of JSL rules is that we require that the right-hand sides of conditions are patterns with fresh variables. This restriction yields a formalism that is closely related to pattern-matching.

Definition 2 (Rewrite rule). *Let* Σ *be a signature.*

– *The set $\mathcal{P}$ of patterns is defined by the abstract syntax*

$$\mathcal{P} := \mathcal{V} \mid c\,\mathcal{P}$$

where in the second clause it is assumed that patterns have pairwise disjoint sets of variables (in other words, patterns are required to be linear).
– *An f-rewrite rule is a compound R of the form*

$$l_1 \twoheadrightarrow r_1, \ \ldots \ , \ l_n \twoheadrightarrow r_n \Rightarrow g \rightarrow d$$

where:
- $r_1 \ldots r_n \in \mathcal{P}$, $l_1 \ldots l_n \in \mathcal{E}_d$ *and* $d \in \mathcal{E}$;
- $g = f\,\boldsymbol{x}$ *where* $\boldsymbol{x} \in \mathcal{V}$ *are pairwise distinct;*
- *for* $1 \leq i \leq n$, $\mathsf{var}(l_i) \subseteq \mathsf{var}(g) \cup \mathsf{var}(r_1) \cup \ \ldots \ \cup \mathsf{var}(r_{i-1})$;
- *for* $1 \leq i, j \leq n$ *with* $i \neq j$, $\mathsf{var}(r_i) \cap \mathsf{var}(g) = \emptyset$ *and* $\mathsf{var}(r_i) \cap \mathsf{var}(r_j) = \emptyset$;
- $\mathsf{var}(d) \subseteq \mathsf{var}(g) \cup \mathsf{var}(r_1) \cup \ \ldots \ \cup \mathsf{var}(r_n)$.
– *The* domain $\mathsf{dom}(R)$ *of a rewrite rule R is defined as*

$$\mathsf{var}(g) \cup \bigcup_{1 \leq i \leq n} \mathsf{var}(r_i)$$

– *The set of rewrite rules is denoted by $\mathcal{R}$, so $\mathcal{R} \subseteq \mathsf{List}\ (\mathcal{E}_d \times \mathcal{P}) \times (\mathcal{E}_d \times \mathcal{E})$.*
– *The set of rewrite systems is denoted by $\mathbb{R}$, so $\mathbb{R} = \mathsf{PowFin}\ \mathcal{R}$.*

JSL rewrite rules have a restricted format, but the Jakarta toolset provides some syntactic sugar, *e.g.* to allow more complex structures in the rewrite rules, and to provide means to define constants and records. For example, `record foo = {one : nat; two : bool;}` defines a record with two entries, labelled `one` and `two`. An instance in this record type is created as `{one = Zero; two = False}`. Entries in the record can be accessed using the dot notation, *e.g.* `x.one` returns the value of the `one` entry in the record `x`, and updated using the `with` notation, *e.g.* `x with {two = True}` replaces the `two` entry in the record `x` with the value `True`. Rewrite rules using this syntactic sugar internally are transformed into pure JSL rules.

JSL Execution Model As pointed out by [5], the notion of rewriting for conditional rules is defined inductively. Figure 3 illustrates the execution model for JSL rules. Formally this is defined as follows.

Definition 3. *Let $\mathcal{R}$ be a set of rewrite rules. An expression s $\mathcal{R}$-rewrites to t, written $s \rightarrow_{\mathcal{R}} t$, if there exists a rule $R \in \mathcal{R}$*

$$l_1 \twoheadrightarrow r_1, \ \ldots \ , l_n \twoheadrightarrow r_n \Rightarrow g \rightarrow d$$

a position p of s and a substitution θ with domain $\mathsf{dom}(R)$ such that:

– $s\,|_p = \theta g$ *and* $t = s[p \leftarrow \theta d]$;
– *for* $1 \leq i \leq n$, $\theta l_i \twoheadrightarrow_{\mathcal{R}} \theta r_i$;

where $\twoheadrightarrow_{\mathcal{R}}$ is the reflexive-transitive closure of $\rightarrow_{\mathcal{R}}$.

```
n -> Succ m, l -> Cons hd tl => take n l -> Cons hd (take m tl);
```

- The first condition simplifies the function argument n, checks whether this is non-zero and introduces its predecessor as the fresh variable m;
- The second condition uses the function argument l, checks whether it is a non-empty list and introduces its head as the fresh variable hd and its tail as the fresh variable tl;
- The result is expressed using the fresh variables introduced in the conditions.

Fig. 3. Semantics of a JSL rule

Application: JSL Specification of the JavaCard Virtual Machine To illustrate JSL, we take the formalisation of the JCVM as an example. This application has been the initial motivation for the work on Jakarta. The JSL specification of the JCVM is derived automatically from the CertiCartes formalisation of the JCVM in Coq.

Basically, the JCVM is described as a state transformer: execution of an instruction modifies the internal state space. The virtual machine takes as input the initial state space, and a program (in cap-format) and executes the appropriate code. The state that is produced by an instruction is tagged with a label Normal or Abnormal. If the state is tagged with Abnormal, this means that something bad has happened: either an exception has been thrown (and not been caught), or there is an error in the bytecode, noticed by the virtual machine. These errors in the bytecode normally are found by a bytecode verifier. That we are still checking for these kind of errors makes our virtual machine defensive, *i.e.* we do not expect the input program to be certified. By making different abstractions of a defensive virtual machine, one can construct different bytecode verifiers.

To illustrate the virtual machine, we give the semantics for the negation instruction NEG. Its CertiCartes definition reads as follows.

```
Definition NEG := [t:type_prim][state:jcvm_state]
Cases state of
(sh, (hp, (cons h lf))) =>
  Cases (head (opstack h)) of
    (value x) => (* if the value pushed from the stack is typed by t *)
                 (* then the NEG operation is performed *)
      Cases x of ((Prim tx), vx) =>
        (if (beq_primitive_type t tx)
         then (update_frame
                 (update_opstack (cons ((Prim t), (t_minus t ZERO vx))
                                       (tail (opstack h)))
                              h) state)
         else (AbortCode opstack_error state)) |
```

```
                  _ => (AbortCode opstack_error state)
     end|
   error => (AbortCode opstack_error state)
  end |
_ => (AbortCode state_error state)
end.
```

This instruction assumes that there is a primitive value on the top of the operand stack, and replaces it with its negated value. The Jakarta toolset transforms this into the following JSL rewrite rules[1].

```
function neg : type_prim -> state -> returned_state :=
begin
  s -> {static = sh; heap = hp; stack = Nil}
  => neg p s -> Abnormal s Error;

  s -> {static = sh; heap = hp; stack = Cons f lf},
  f.opstack -> Nil
  => neg p s -> Abnormal s Error;

  s -> {static = sh; heap = hp; stack = Cons f lf},
  f.opstack -> Cons o os,
  o -> {data_type = Ref r; value = k}
  => neg p s -> Abnormal s Error;

  s -> {static = sh; heap = hp; stack = Cons f lf},
  f.opstack -> Cons o os,
  o -> {data_type = Prim p'; value = k},
  p == p' -> false
  => neg p s -> Abnormal s Error;

  s -> {static = sh; heap = hp; stack = Cons f lf},
  f.opstack -> Cons o os,
  o -> {data_type = Prim p'; value = k},
  p == p' -> true
  => neg p s ->
     Normal (s with
             {stack := Cons (f with {p_count := Succ (f.p_count);
                                     opstack := Cons ({data_type = Prim p;
                                                       value = k}) os})
                       lf});
end.
```

Notice how these rules systematically consider all possible cases.

A more complicated instruction to describe formally is invoke_virtual, which contains more different cases that might cause an exception or an error. Below we give the rewrite rule for the normal termination case, the complete formalisation also contains rules for all complementary cases. Exceptions are thrown if this instruction is called with a null pointer argument or if there is

---

[1] Notice that we have changed some tuples to labelled tuples or records.

a security problem, signalled by the function test_security_invokevirtual. In all other cases, an error in the bytecode is signalled. The JSL specification closely follows the JCVM specification. The reader is not expected to understand all the details of this formalisation, but hopefully appreciates how the rewrite rule encodes the evaluation order in a natural way. Again, this formalisation is derived from our earlier work on CertiCartes.

```
function invoke_virtual : nat -> class_method_idx -> state ->
                          capprogram -> returned_state :=
begin
  s -> {static = sh; heap = hp; stack = Cons f lf},
  nargs -> Succ n,
  nth_func f.opstack nargs -> {data_type = Ref r; value = vx},
  vx == null -> False,
  nth_func hp vx -> ob,
  nth_elt cap.classes (get_obj_class_idx ob) -> c,
  get_method c cm_id -> m,
  take nargs f.opstack -> l,
  drop nargs f.opstack -> l',
  test_security_invokevirtual f ob -> True,
  signature_verification (datalist_to_typelist l)
                         m.domain cap -> True
=> invoke_virtual nargs cm_id s cap ->
   Normal (s with
           {stack := (Cons {opstack = Nil;
                            locvars = make_locvars l m.local;
                            method_loc = m.method_id;
                            context_ref = get_owner_context ob;
                            pc = Zero}
                           (Cons (f with {opstack := l'})
                                 lf))});

end.
```

3   The Jakarta Prover Interface

Proof assistants such as Coq support the definition of total, terminating recursive definitions through the combination of fixpoint definitions and case analysis. Under suitable circumstances, which we describe below, it is possible to compile JSL functions into recursive definitions à la Coq. In order to target several proof assistants, prototyping environments and programming languages, we translate JSL specifications first into an intermediate language JIR (Jakarta Intermediate Representation language), supporting such recursive definitions.

The Jakarta Intermediate Representation language (JIR) The Jakarta Intermediate Representation Language is a mild extension of JSL with case expressions.

Definition 4. *Let Σ be a signature.*

- *The set $\mathcal{E}^+$ of JIR expressions (over Σ) is defined by the abstract syntax:*

$$\mathcal{E}^+ := \mathcal{V} \mid \mathcal{E}^+ == \mathcal{E}^+ \mid c\ \mathcal{E}^+ \mid f\ \mathcal{E}^+ \mid \text{case } \mathcal{E}^+ \text{ of } \{\mathcal{M}\}$$

where the set $\mathcal{M}$ of matches is defined as:

$$\mathcal{M} := \langle\rangle \mid \mathcal{M}|p \Rightarrow \mathcal{E}$$

- *A JIR rewrite rule is a rewrite rule of the form*

$$f\ \boldsymbol{x} \to e$$

where $\boldsymbol{x} = (x_1, \ldots, x_n)$ are pairwise distinct variables and $e \in \mathcal{E}^+$ verifies $\text{var}(e) \subseteq \{x_1, \ldots, x_n\}$. The set of JIR rewrite rules is denoted by $\mathcal{R}_{\text{JIR}}$.

Compiling JSL Specifications The Jakarta Prover Interface JPI transforms deterministic JSL functions into JIR functions. The transformation may fail, for example if the rewrite system is not deterministic. If it succeeds, it transforms a set of f-rewrite rules into a recursive function definition à la Coq. The function K is defined thanks to an auxiliary recursive function K' which transforms a set of rewrite rules into a single case expression.

Definition 5.

- *We define $K' : \mathbb{R} \rightharpoonup \mathcal{E}^+$ as follows:*

$$K'(\{([], (e, d))\}) = d$$
$$K'(X_1, \ldots, X_k) = \text{case } t \text{ of}$$
$$\{p_1 \Rightarrow K'\ (X_1') \mid$$
$$\cdots$$
$$p_k \Rightarrow K'\ (X_k')\}$$

where in the last clause it is assumed that $p_1, \ldots, p_k$ are pairwise distinct (for the decomposition to be unique) and:
- *for every $1 \le i \le k$ and $R \in X_i$, head $(\pi\ R) = (t, p_i)$;*
- *for every $1 \le i \le k$, $X_i' = \{(\text{tail}\ (\pi\ R), \pi'\ R) \mid R \in X_i\}$.*
- *We define $K : \mathbb{R} \rightharpoonup \mathcal{R}_{\text{JIR}}$ as follows:*

$$K(\bigcup_{1 \le i \le k}\{C_i \Rightarrow f\ \boldsymbol{x} \to r_i\}) = f\ \boldsymbol{x} \to K'(\bigcup_{1 \le i \le k}\{C_i \Rightarrow f\ \boldsymbol{x} \to r_i\})$$

where it is assumed that $\boldsymbol{x} = (x_1, \ldots, x_s)$ are pairwise distinct.

In other words, K proceeds by checking that all the left-hand sides of the rewrite rule coincide before calling the auxiliary function K'. The function K' proceeds by first partitioning the set of rewrite rules on the right-hand side of the first condition, and then making recursive calls on the partitions, leaving out the first condition.

Note that in practice, the function is parameterised by a predicate ϕ which ensures that the resulting function is of a suitable shape; for example, the predicate ϕ can be used to enforce that the resulting function is total (case expressions must be exhaustive and treat all the possible cases) and unambiguous (the patterns of a case expression must be non-overlapping).

JIR expressions can easily be transformed into input for a specific proof assistant or programming language (to provide execution). Currently our tool supports the proof assistant Coq and the programming language OCaml and we are extending it to support other tools.

We have also implemented a decompiler which transforms case expressions into rewrite rules. The decompiler can be used to translate Coq formalisations to JSL. Notice that the decompiler J is the inverse of the compiler K.

Definition 6. *We define* $J : \mathcal{R}_{\text{JIR}} \to \mathbb{R}$ *as follows:*

$$J(f \ \boldsymbol{x} \to e) = \{((\langle\rangle, (g, e))\}$$
$$\textit{if } e \textit{ is not a case-expression}$$

$$J(f \ \boldsymbol{x} \to \mathsf{case} \ M \ \mathsf{of} \ \{p_1 \to e_1 \mid \ \ldots \ \mid p_k \to e_k\}) =$$
$$\bigcup\nolimits_{1 \le j \le k} \{((M, p_j) : (\pi \ R), \ \pi' \ R) \mid R \in J(f \ \boldsymbol{x} \to e_j)\}$$

4   The Jakarta Transformation Kit

The core of Jakarta's functionality is the Transformation Kit, which provides interactive support for abstractions. As emphasised in the introduction, the constrained format of JSL facilitates (1) manipulation of JSL specifications, and (2) development of automatic transformation procedures for this purpose. Below, we will sketch how JTK provides support for abstractions, the support for refinements will be similar.

The user of Jakarta specifies an abstraction function (in JSL), describing how the abstract state is constructed from the concrete one. For example, the so-called 'type' abstraction, which removes all values, will contain the following rewrite rule (among others, that propagate this abstraction to the level of states):

```
x -> {data_type = t; value = v} => abs_type x -> {data_type = t}
```

The user can tell the JTK to apply this abstraction to a particular JSL function. The JTK performs a syntactical transformation, applying the abstraction function to every component of the rewrite rules, defining the function. For example, applying the type abstraction to `invoke_virtual` (as defined in Section 2) will change the 3rd condition into:

```
nth_func f.opstack nargs -> {data_type = Ref r},
```

After applying this abstraction, the toolset will signal that there are problems with several conditions, and with the right-hand side of the conclusion of the rewrite rule, because variables are used which have not been introduced before (conflicting with the 3rd condition on rewrite rules, Definition 2). *E.g.*, the 4th condition uses the variable vx, which is not introduced in the abstracted version of the 3rd condition.

The user analyses the outcome of the syntactical abstraction and determines what should be changed. For example, in the case of the invoke_virtual instruction, the 6th condition describes the lookup of the dynamic type of an object. In the abstract virtual machine, there are no values, and one can only lookup the static type of a variable. Therefore, the user specifies how this condition should be replaced, by another condition, introducing the variable c. These replacements identify the crucial steps in the abstraction.

Finally, the JTK performs some cleaning, removing conditions which still depend on variables that have not been introduced before. The abstraction process, including replacements, is stored in a so-called *abstraction script*, in order to guide the correctness proof of the abstraction.

5   The Jakarta Automation Kit

As emphasised in the introduction, the constrained format of JSL facilitates (1) reasoning about JSL specifications (2) developing automatic proof procedures for this purpose. We are currently developing a repository of tools to generate proof rules and tactics to reason about executable specifications. This repository, which is called the Jakarta Automation Kit, is tool-specific and oriented towards Coq. However, its underlying principles are applicable to other proof assistants.

One of the proof techniques to reason about JSL functions is the so-called inversion principle. For every function f, an associated inversion principle is derived, based on an analysis of the rewrite rules defining f. Given a predicate ϕ, relating f's input to its output, application of the inversion principle breaks down the proof of $\forall \boldsymbol{x} : \boldsymbol{\sigma}. \; \phi \; (\boldsymbol{x}, \; f \; \boldsymbol{x})$ into several smaller subgoals. For each rewrite rule defining f, a subgoal is generated with the following format: assuming that all left-hand sides of the conditions can be rewritten in their right-hand sides, and assuming that $f \; \boldsymbol{x}$ rewrites into an expression d (as specified by the rewrite rule), one shows that $\phi \; (\boldsymbol{x}, \; f \; \boldsymbol{x})$ holds.

For example, to show the correctnes of the bytecode verifier, one has to show that for every instruction, execution commutes with the abstraction function. Suppose we have a predicate P specifying this. Then, in particular we have to show in Coq:

```
(nargs:nat)(cm_id:class_method_idx)(s:state)(cap:jcprogram)
    (P nargs cm_id s cap (invoke_virtual nargs cm_id s cap))
```

(where invoke_virtual is described in Section 2). Application of the inversion principle reduces this goal to several subgoals (one for each defining rewrite rule), including the following subgoal:

```
(nargs:nat)(cm_id:class_method_idx)(s:state)(cap:jcprogram)
(sh:sheap)(hp:heap)(f:frame)(lf:stack)(n:nat)(r:type_ref)(vx:Z)
(ob:obj)(c:Class)(m:Method)(l,l':(list valu))
    (s = (Build_state sh hp (Cons f lf)))
->  (nargs = (S n))
->  ((Nth_func (opstack f) nargs) = (Build_data (Ref r) vx))
->  ((vx = Null) = False)
```

```
->   ((Nth_func hp vx) =  ob)
->   ((Nth_elt (classes cap) (get_obj_class_idx ob)) = c)
->   ((get_method c cm_id) = m)
->   ((take nargs (opstack f)) = l)
->   ((drop nargs (opstack f)) = l')
->   ((test_security_invokevirtual f ob) = True)
->   ((signature_verification (datalist_to_typelist l)
                             (domain m) cap) = True)
->   ((invoke_virtual nargs cm_id s cap) =
       (update_stack (Cons (Make_frame Nil
                                       (make_locvars l (local m))
                                       (method_id m)
                                       (get_owner_context ob)
                                       0)
                    (Cons (update_opstack l' f ) lf)) s))
->   (P nargs cm_id s cap (invoke_virtual nargs cm_id s cap)).
```

Using rewriting, this subgoal can be simplified further.

   We have proven the commutation property before, without using the inversion principle, and in our experience, using the inversion principle is very useful: by pulling out all the different cases at once, it allows to simplify the goals by applying suitable rewriting tactics at the onset of the proof. Consequently, the proofs become shorter and are much easier to perform and understand, resulting in a substantial increase in the speed of proving. Without the inversion principle the proof took a few days (and we were often faced with goals that were more than 3 pages long!), while using the inversion principle it only took a couple of hours to complete the proof.

6   Conclusion

We have described the general structure of the Jakarta toolset, which provides a tool-independent front-end to specify and reason about the JavaCard platform. In particular, the toolset provides support to construct abstractions, in order to derive certified bytecode verifiers from the formalisation of the JavaCard virtual machine.

6.1   Related Work

Prototyping Environments and Proof Assistants The Jakarta Prover Interface provides a "shallow embedding" of JSL into proof assistants such as Coq and programming languages such as Caml—the embedding is called shallow because we do not formalise the syntax of JSL as datatypes in the target language, as a deep embedding would do. Several implementations relate such environments, including B, VDM, Z and Centaur, to proof assistants, see e.g. [1,11,26,34]. In contrast to Jakarta, these specification languages are extremely powerful, which makes it difficult to generate proof principles for the specifications automatically.

Abstractions The idea of deriving abstract functions from a concrete function and an abstraction function, which traces back to Cousot and Cousot's seminal paper [14], see also [12,13], has been exploited in a number of contexts, and in particular in the context of formal verification, see *e.g.* [4,8,17] for recent examples. Our work around JTK can be viewed as a simple application of abstract interpretation techniques to term-rewriting.

Applications to JavaCard Jakarta is tailored to the design of certified bytecode verifiers. There have been a number of related efforts, both to prove the standard bytecode verifier correct [7,27,33], and to suggest new bytecode verifiers based on more complex type systems [25]. Most of this work is tailored towards a particular security policy, to the exception of [27], where it is shown how to use a data flow analyser to construct a bytecode verifier from an abstract virtual machine. In contrast, our work is focused on deriving abstract virtual machines from defensive ones, and proving them correct. We are not aware of any similar effort, despite tremendous activity in the field—see *e.g.* [19] for a recent survey of ongoing work.

6.2 Future Work

The paper reports on preliminary results with the implementation and use of Jakarta. Clearly, much work remains to be done, *e.g.* extending JSL with modules, extending JPI to support other proof assistants, programming languages, and modifying JPI to translate JSL specifications as inductive relations... Below, we single out two important directions for future research.

JAK: Automating Correctness Proofs for Bytecode Verifiers We intend to combine the correctness proof of the data flow analyser of [27] with the correctness proofs for abstract virtual machines to achieve modular, highly automated proofs of correctness for a range of bytecode verifiers. As a first step in this direction, N. Baudru, S. Coupet-Grimal and D. Sanchez have ported Nipkow's development to Coq. Hence future work only needs to focus on automating the proof of correctness of abstract virtual machines. This involves automating the proof of

$$\forall \boldsymbol{x}.\ (\alpha\ (fx)) \in \underline{f}\ (\alpha\ \boldsymbol{x})$$

where α is the abstraction function, f is the function to be abstracted and $\underline{f}$ is the abstracted function—in some instances, the result only holds up to subtyping, see *e.g.* [3]. To this end, one needs to automate the proof of the inversion principle for f and to perform rewriting steps to conclude—in most cases, these two passes are sufficient; for instructions such as `invoke_virtual`, some further reasoning is required. In the latter case, we need to integrate rewriting techniques into Coq so that rewrite steps in the JSL execution model are translated into proof terms acceptable by Coq.

In order to apply our methodology, we are currently extracting an offensive virtual machine from our specification and building up appropriate defensive virtual machines that verify (1) initialisation and (2) information flow.

JTK: Support the Construction of Refined Virtual Machines Currently, JTK only supports abstractions. We are planning to extend it to support interactive refinements, *i.e.* tools to define a function $f' : \sigma' \to \sigma'$ from a previously defined function $f : \sigma \to \sigma$ and a refinement function $\alpha : \sigma' \to \sigma$; here it is assumed that σ' is more precise than σ, and that α forgets some of the information contained in σ'. In the context of reasoning about the JavaCard platform, refinement is useful *e.g.* to construct a JCVM with a more precise memory model—currently our formalisation does not treat transient objects.

References

1. S. Agerholm and J. Frost. Towards an integrated CASE and theorem proving tool for VDM-SL. In J. Fitzgerald, C. B. Jones, and P. Lucas, editors, *Proceedings of FME'97*, volume 1313 of *Lecture Notes in Computer Science,* pages 278-297. Springer-Verlag, 1997. 14
2. B. Barras, S. Boutin, C. Comes, J. Courant, Y. Coscoy, D. Delahaye, D. de Rauglaudre, J.-C. Filliâtre, E. Giménez, H. Herbelin, G. Huet, H. Laulhère, P. Loiseleur, C. Muñoz, C. Murthy, C. Parent-Vigouroux, C. Paulin-Mohring, A. Saïbi, and B. Werner. *The Coq Proof Assistant User's Guide. Version 6.3.1,* December 1999. 3
3. G. Barthe, G. Dufay, L. Jakubiec, B. Serpette, and S. Melo de Sousa. A Formal Executable Semantics of the JavaCard Platform. In D. Sands, editor, *Proceedings of ESOP'01,* volume 2028 of *Lecture Notes in Computer Science,* pages 302-319. Springer-Verlag, 2001. 2, 3, 15
4. S. Bensalem, V. Ganesh, Y. Lakhnech, C. Muñoz, S. Owre, H. Rueß, J. Rushby, V. Rusu, H. Saïdi, N. Shankar, E. Singerman, and A. Tiwari. An overview of SAL. In *Proceedings of NASA's Workshop on Formal Methods,* 2000. 15
5. J. Bergstra and J. W. Klop. Conditional rewrite rules: confluence and termination. *Journal of Computer and System Sciences,* 32:323-362, 1986. 7
6. P. Bertelsen. Semantics of Java Byte Code. Master's thesis, Department of Computer Science, Royal Veterinary and Agricultural University of Copenhagen, 1997. 2
7. Y. Bertot. Formalizing in Coq a type system for object initialization in the Java bytecode language. In G. Berry, H. Comon, and A. Finkel, editors, *Proceedings of CAV'01,* volume 2xxx of *Lecture Notes in Computer Science.* Springer-Verlag, 2001. 15
8. P. Bieber, J. Cazin, V. Wiels, G. Zanon, P. Girard, and J.-L. Lanet. Electronic purse applet certification: extended abstract. In S. Schneider and P. Ryan, editors, *Proceedings of the workshop on secure architectures and information flow,* volume 32 of *Electronic Notes in Theoretical Computer Science.* Elsevier Publishing, 2000. 15
9. E. Börger and W. Schulte. A Programmer Friendly Modular Definition of the Semantics of Java. In J. Alves-Foss, editor, *Formal Syntax and Semantics of Java,* volume 1523 of *Lecture Notes in Computer Science,* pages 353-404. Springer-Verlag, 1999. 2

10. P. Borras, D. Clément, Th. Despeyroux, J. Incerpi, G. Kahn, B. Lang, and V. Pascual. Centaur: the system. In *Proceedings of the ACM SIGSOFT/SIGPLAN Software Engineering Symposium on Practical Software Development Environments*, pages 14-24. ACM Press, 1988. 3

11. J. P. Bowen and M. J. C. Gordon. A shallow embedding of Z in HOL. *Information and Software Technology*, 37(5-6):269-276, 1995. 14

12. P. Cousot. Program analysis: The abstract interpretation perspective. *ACM Computing Surveys*, 28A(4es):165-es, December 1996. 15

13. P. Cousot. Types as abstract interpretations, invited paper. In *Proceedings of POPL'97*, pages 316-331. ACM Press, 1997. 15

14. P. Cousot and R. Cousot. Abstract interpretation: A unified lattice model for static analysis of programs by construction or approximation of fixpoints. In *Proceedings of POPL'77*, pages 238-252. ACM Press, 1977. 15

15. A. van Deursen, J. Heering, and P. Klint, editors. *Language Prototyping: an algebraic specification approach*. AMAST Series in Computing. World Scientific, 1996. 3

16. S. Drossopoulou and S. Eisenbach. Describing the semantics of Java and Proving Type Soundness. In J. Alves-Foss, editor, *Formal Syntax and Semantics of Java*, volume 1523 of *Lecture Notes in Computer Science,* pages 41-82. Springer-Verlag, 1999. 2

17. M. Dwyer, J. Hatcliff, R. Joehanes, S. Laubach, C. Pasareanu, Robby, W. Visser, and H. Zheng. Tool-supported program abstraction for finite-state verification. In *Proceedings of ICSE'01,* 2001. 15

18. P. Hartel. LETOS - a lightweight execution tool for operational semantics. *Software-practice and experience*, 29:1379-1416, September 1999. 3

19. P. Hartel and L. Moreau. Formalizing the Safety of Java, the Java Virtual Machine and Java Card. *ACM Computing Surveys*, 2001. To appear. 15

20. P. H. Hartel, M. J. Butler, and M. Levy. The Operational Semantics of a Java Secure Processor. In J. Alves-Foss, editor, *Formal Syntax and Semantics of Java*, volume 1523 of *Lecture Notes in Computer Science,* pages 313-352. Springer-Verlag, 1999. 2

21. B. Jacobs, J. van den Berg, M. Huisman, M. van Berkum, U. Hensel, and H. Tews. Reasoning about Java classes. *ACM SIGPLAN Notices*, 33(10):329-340, October 1998. 2

22. JavaCard Technology. http://java.sun.com/products/javacard 2

23. J. W. Klop. Term-rewriting systems. In S. Abramsky, D. Gabbay, and T. Maibaum, editors, *Handbook of Logic in Computer Science*, pages 1-116. Oxford Science Publications, 1992. Volume 2. 6

24. X. Leroy, D. Doligez, J. Garrigue, D. Rémy, and J. Vouillon. *The Objective Caml system, release 3.00*, 2000. 4

25. P. Müller and A. Poetzsch-Heffter. A type system for checking applet isolation in Java Card. In S. Drossopoulou, editor, *Formal Techniques for Java Programs*, 2001. To appear. 15

26. C. Muñoz. PBS: Support for the B-method in PVS. Technical Report SRI-CSL-99-01, SRI International, February 1999. 14

27. T. Nipkow. Verified Bytecode Verifiers. In F. Honsell and M. Miculan, editors, *Proceedings of FOSSACS'01*, volume 2030 of *Lecture Notes in Computer Science*, pages 347-363. Springer-Verlag, 2001. 2, 15

28. T. Nipkow and D. von Oheimb. Java/$_{light}$ is type-safe—definitely. In *Proceedings of POPL'98*, pages 161-170. ACM Press, 1998. 2

29. L. Paulson. *Isabelle: a generic theorem prover*, volume 828 of *Lecture Notes in Computer Science*. Springer-Verlag, 1994. 3

30. M. Petersson. *Compiling Natural Semantics*. PhD thesis, Linköping University, 1995. 3

31. C. Pusch. Proving the soundness of a Java bytecode verifier specification in Isabelle/HOL. In W. R. Cleaveland, editor, *Proceedings of TACAS'99*, volume 1579 of *Lecture Notes in Computer Science*, pages 89-103. Springer-Verlag, 1999. 2

32. N. Shankar, S. Owre, and J. M. Rushby. *The PVS Proof Checker: A Reference Manual*. Computer Science Laboratory, SRI International, February 1993. Supplemented with the PVS2 Quick Reference Manual, 1997. 3

33. R. Stata and M. Abadi. A type system for Java bytecode subroutines. *ACM Transactions on Programming Languages and Systems*, 21(1):90-137, January 1999. 15

34. D. Terrasse. *Vers un environnement d'aide au developpement de preuves en Semantique Naturelle*. PhD thesis, Ecole Nationale des Ponts et Chaussees, 1995. 14

Mechanising a Protocol for Smart Cards

Giampaolo Bella[1,2]

[1] Computer Laboratory, University of Cambridge
Pembroke Street, Cambridge CB2 3QG, UK
giampaolo.bella@cl.cam.ac.uk
[2] Dipartimento di Matematica e Informatica, Università di Catania
Viale A. Doria 6, I-95125 Catania, Italy
giamp@dmi.unict.it

Abstract. Paulson's Inductive Approach for verifying traditional cryptographic protocols is tailored to those where agents make use of smart cards. An intruder can actively exploit other agents' cards, which can be stolen or cloned. The approach is demonstrated on the Shoup-Rubin protocol, which is modelled and verified thoroughly. The protocol achieves strong goals of confidentiality, authentication and key distribution. However, our proofs highlight that a few messages require additional explicitness in order to guarantee those goals to the peers when the cards' data buses are unreliable.

Keywords: smart card protocols, Inductive Approach, confidentiality, authentication, key distribution.

1 Introduction

Smart card technology attempts to strengthen modern security protocols by offering essential computational power and data storage with high resistance to external tampering. Typically, all long-term secrets are stored into the cards, so each agent merely needs to remember the PIN to activate his own card. An increasing number of companies are considering the purchase of smart cards and related protocols at present. However, if on one side smart cards have become inexpensive, on the other side there still exists stringent demand for adequate guarantees that the new technology is worth buying. To our knowledge, the major attempt of satisfying that demand by mathematical proofs is due to Shoup and Rubin [14]. They take into account an existing session key distribution protocol due to Leighton and Micali [10], which does not use smart cards, and prove it secure using Bellare and Rogaway's notion of *provable security*. In short, this amounts to a complexity-theoretic study of confidentiality, which is conducted under the assumption that pseudo-random functions exist. Shoup and Rubin also design a new protocol for session key distribution in a three-agent setting where each agent is endowed with a smart card. Finally, they extend Bellare and Rogaway's approach to account for smart cards, and prove that the new

I. Attali and T. Jensen (Eds.): E-smart 2001, LNCS 2140, pp. 19–33, 2001.

protocol keeps the session keys confidential. Their proofs are conducted without mechanical tools. Shoup and Rubin's protocol was later implemented by Jerdonek et al. [9].

We have introduced a realistic treatment of smart cards into Paulson's Inductive Approach for verifying security protocols [12], which is mechanised by the interactive theorem prover Isabelle [11]. The protocol model is constructed by induction, so it allows an unbounded number of agents to interleave an unbounded number of protocol sessions. An intruder is modelled, *spy* below, who can exploit an unspecified set of *stolen* smart cards by preparing queries that conform to the cards' functional interface. The spy has reverse engineered another unspecified set of *cloned* cards and has discovered their internal secrets. The two sets are in no way related with each other so to model all possible conditions of the cards. The approach scales up, at the price of minor modifications, to all smart card protocols regardless of whether they assume secure or insecure means between agents and cards.

We demonstrate our extended approach on the Shoup-Rubin protocol, and verify its goals of confidentiality, authentication and key distribution. Our analysis supports the claim that the protocol achieves strong goals. However, if the data buses of the smart cards are corrupted so to produce outputs in an unspecified order, then two of the protocol messages necessitate extra explicitness to confirm the goals to the peers. The corresponding proofs suggest a simple fix.

The main results achieved by this paper are: (i) tailoring the Inductive Approach to the analysis of protocols based smart cards; (ii) the first full mechanisation (formal verification supported by a mechanised tool) of a provably secure protocol based on smart cards; (iii) the discovery that the protocol needs additional explicitness to achieve its goals of confidentiality, authentication and key distribution when the cards' buses are unreliable; (iv) a fix to that need of explicitness. The paper gives an abstract presentation of the Shoup-Rubin protocol (Sect. 2), and outlines our extensions to the Inductive Approach (Sect. 3). It goes on with the inductive modelling of the protocol (Sect. 4) and its verification (Sect. 5). Then, it analyses a version of the protocol with added explicitness (Sect. 6) and concludes (Sect. 7).

2   The Shoup-Rubin Protocol

This protocol presupposes that each agent P has a long-term key Kp that is stored into the agent's card C_p and is shared with the server. The card also stores its own long-term key K_{Cp}. All keys are symmetric. The concept of *pairkey* (due to Leighton and Micali [10]) is adopted to establish a long-term secret between the smart cards of a pair of agents. The pairkey is historically referred to the pair of agents: the one for agents A and B is $\Pi_{ab} = \{\!|A|\!\}_{Kb} \oplus \{\!|B|\!\}_{Ka}$, where $\oplus$ is the exclusive-or operator. While A's card can compute $\{\!|B|\!\}_{Ka}$ and then $\pi_{ab} = \{\!|A|\!\}_{Kb}$ from Π_{ab}, B's card can compute π_{ab} directly. Hence, the two cards share the long-term secret π_{ab}, which we call *pair-k* for A and B. The main goal

I :   1. $A \rightarrow S : A, B$
        2. $S \rightarrow A : \Pi_{ab}, \{\Pi_{ab}, B\}_{Ka}$

II :   3. $A \rightarrow C_a : A$
        4. $C_a \rightarrow A : Na, \{Na\}_{K_{Ca}}$

III :   5. $A \rightarrow B : A, Na$

IV :   6. $B \rightarrow C_b : A, Na$
        7. $C_b \rightarrow B : Nb, Kab, \{Na, Nb\}_{\pi_{ab}}, \{Nb\}_{\pi_{ab}}$

V :   8. $B \rightarrow A : Nb, \{Na, Nb\}_{\pi_{ab}}$

VI :   9. $A \rightarrow C_a : B, Na, Nb, \Pi_{ab},$
                          $\{\Pi_{ab}, B\}_{Ka}, \{Na, Nb\}_{\pi_{ab}}, \{Na\}_{K_{Ca}}$
        10. $C_a \rightarrow A : Kab, \{Nb\}_{\pi_{ab}}$

VII :   11. $A \rightarrow B : \{Nb\}_{\pi_{ab}}$

Fig. 1. The Shoup-Rubin protocol

of the protocol is distributing a session key, which is computed by the smart cards out of a pair-k and a nonce as explained below.

The full protocol (Fig.1) develops through seven phases. The odd ones take place over the network, while the even ones concern the communication between agents and smart cards.

Phase I. An initiator A tells the trusted server that she wants to initiate a session with a responder B, and receives in return the pairkey Π_{ab} and its certificate encrypted under her long-term key.

Phase II. A queries her card and receives a fresh nonce and its certificate encrypted under the card's long-term key. (The form of A's query is specified neither by the designers nor by the implementors, so our choice of message 3 is arbitrary).

Phase III. A contacts B sending her identity and her nonce Na.

Phase IV. B queries his card with the data received from A, and obtains a new nonce Nb, the session key Kab, a certificate for Na and Nb, and a certificate for Nb; Kab is constructed by a function of Nb and π_{ab}.

Phase V. B forwards his nonce Nb and the certificate for Na and Nb to A.

Phase VI. A feeds her card B's name, the two nonces (she has just received Nb), the pairkey and its certificate, the two certificates for the nonces; A's card computes π_{ab} from Π_{ab} and uses it with the nonce Nb to compute the session key Kab; the card outputs Kab and the certificate for Nb, which is encrypted under π_{ab}.

Phase VII. A forwards the certificate for Nb to B.

The protocol assumes secure means between agents and cards, so the spy cannot overhear the messages in transit between an agent and his card. The cards indeed output the session keys in clear. Although this assumption may seem unrealistic to make on a vast scale, in general it adds robustness to a protocol by reducing each agent's knowledge to the PIN to activate his card. The Shoup-Rubin protocol also works with cards that are not pin-operated, so agents know no long-term keys and can only identify the messages by the fact that they are compound or not. All encryption and decryption operations are performed by the smart cards. Should the spy steal a card, she would gain the card's computational power; should the spy also clone the card, she would also discover the card's stored secrets. In either case, the spy can discover a session key only by feeding the card the specific inputs that produce that key.

Also, certain features of the protocol design, such as both A and B's nonces sent in the clear (messages 5 and 8), may seem incautious, but an informal account for the consequences can be hardly given. In particular, B's nonce is used to compute the session key, but we formally verify that intercepting that nonce does not help the spy discover the session key as long as she cannot use A and B's cards.

3   Extending the Inductive Approach

Smart Cards. We associate a new type to the smart cards and define a function Card mapping the agents to their respective cards. Recall that agent is the Isabelle datatype for agents [12, Sect. 3.1] and includes: the trusted third party, Server (often abbreviated in S); a malicious eavesdropper, Spy; unlimited "friendly" agents, Friend i (i being a natural). The agents are associated to their keys shared with the server by the function shrK [12, Sect. 3.5], and likewise we associate the smart cards to their long-term keys by a function crdK. For example, crdK(Card A) denotes A's card's key. The cards' pins can be formalised in the same fashion. All these long-term secrets for a specific agent are are stored into the agent's smart card, as formalised below by the functions knows and initState.

We declare a set stolen of cards that can be used by the spy and not by their legal owners. Should the cards be pin-operated, the spy would also need to discover the pin to activate the stolen cards. She could do so either by monitoring the network or by colluding with the card's owner (the latter chance can be formally defined by trivial updates to the function initState, Sect. 4). Additionally, the spy may use modern techniques (such as *microprobing* [2]) to break the physical security of the card, access its EEPROM where the long-term secrets are stored and, in the worst case, reverse engineer the card's chip. At this stage, the spy would be able to build a clone of the card for her own use. Such cards are modelled by the set cloned.

The two sets are not related with each other, so that a card could even be temporarily stolen, then cloned, and finally returned to the owner, resulting in the set cloned but not in the set stolen. This seems impossible by current cloning techniques, which are *invasive* and therefore unrecoverably damage the original card, but in fact the spy could build two clones and return one to the unaware owner. The protocol model allows the spy to use her own card and those that are either stolen or cloned (Sect. 4.6). We assume that the cards' buses are unreliable as explained below.

Events. The existing approach includes a datatype event that formally allows three possible events: Says $A\,B\,X$, meaning that agent A sends agent B a message X; Notes $A\,X$, meaning that A notes down X [12]; Gets $B\,X$, meaning that B receives X [3]. We extend that datatype with two new events: Inputs $A\,C\,X$, meaning that agent A queries card C with message X; Outputs $C\,A\,X$, meaning that card C responds to agent A with message X. When an agent queries his card with a message, then the card certainly receives the message if the communication means is assumed to be secure, as with the Shoup-Rubin protocol. The same applies to a card's response in transit in the opposite direction. With protocols that assume insecure means between agents and cards, reception is not guaranteed because the spy can intercept any messages in transit, so two additional events modelling reception on both sides are needed.

A list of events, *trace* in the sequel, occurring when an (unbounded) population of agents run a protocol may be interpreted as a possible history of the network where the protocol is executed. The set of all possible traces is the formal model for the protocol [12]. Since the model is defined by induction, no event is forced to happen on a generic trace. This feature also formalises the failure mode of smart cards: the model cards can stop working at any time. Besides, events can take place in any order, so if a message X is sent in the network earlier than X', it could be received later than X'. Likewise, if X is input to a card earlier than X', the card could produce the output for X later than that for X'. This signifies that the cards' data buses are unreliable so to give outputs in an order that is not influenced by the order of the inputs. The more permissive is the model, the broader are the properties that can be investigated.

Agents' Knowledge. The knowledge that each agent derives from a trace of events is formalised by the function knows [4, Sect. 3], which takes as inputs an agent name and a trace, returning a set of messages. The function is defined inductively by the following six rules. We have added the last two to account for the events pertaining to the smart cards.

1. An agent knows his initial knowledge (which is defined in the next section).
2. An agent knows what he alone sends to anyone on a trace; in particular, the spy also knows all messages that anyone sends on it.
3. An agent knows what he alone notes on a trace; in particular, the spy also knows compromised agents' notes.
4. An agent, except the spy, knows what he alone receives on a trace.
5. An agent knows what he alone inputs to any card on a trace.
6. An agent knows what he alone is output from any card on a trace.

Case 4 states that the spy's knowledge must not be extended with any of the received messages because the formal protocol model (Sect. 4.1) only allows reception of those messages that were sent, so the spy already knows them by case 2. The last two cases also apply to the spy, so she only knows the inputs that she produces or the outputs that are addressed to her, for the means between agents and cards is secure.

4   Modelling Shoup-Rubin

The protocol never uses pairkeys to encrypt, so we model them as nonces, which are natural numbers. On the contrary, the pair-k's are used as proper keys. The session keys are computed out of nonces and pair-k's. The following functions construct these components.

- Pairkey : agent $*$ agent $\longrightarrow$ nat
- pairK : agent $*$ agent $\longrightarrow$ key
- sesK : nat $*$ key $\longrightarrow$ key

At the operational level, we are only interested in their abstract properties. For example, the function Pairkey cannot be assumed collision-free because it is implemented in terms of the exclusive-or operator, but we can assume that collision of keys is impossible.

We can now define the function initState for Shoup-Rubin, formalising the agents' initial knowledge. The server's comprises all long-term secrets.

$$\text{initState S} \triangleq \{\text{Key}\,(\text{crdK}\,C)\} \cup \{\text{Key}\,(\text{shrK}\,A)\} \cup$$
$$\{\text{Key}\,(\text{pairK}(A, B))\} \cup \{\text{Nonce}\,(\text{Pairkey}(A, B))\}$$

The friendly agents' initial knowledge is empty, so they cannot reveal secrets to the spy.

$$\text{initState}\,(\text{Friend}\,i) \triangleq \{\}$$

The spy's initial knowledge comprises all long-term secrets stored into cloned cards and those obtainable from them. From the definitions of pairkeys and pair-k's (Sect. 2), it follows that the spy can forge the pair-k for a pair of agents in case the card of the second agent is cloned, and a pairkey if both the corresponding cards are cloned.

$$\text{initState Spy} \triangleq \{\text{Key}\,(\text{crdK}\,C) \mid C \in \text{cloned}\} \cup$$
$$\{\text{Key}\,(\text{shrK}\,A) \mid (\text{Card}\;A) \in \text{cloned}\} \cup$$
$$\{\text{Key}\,(\text{pairK}(A, B)) \mid (\text{Card}\;B) \in \text{cloned}\} \cup$$
$$\{\text{Nonce}\,(\text{Pairkey}(A, B)) \mid (\text{Card}\;A) \in \text{cloned}\,\wedge$$
$$(\text{Card}\;B) \in \text{cloned}\}$$

We declare the constant shouprubin as a set of lists of events. It designates the formal protocol model and is defined in the rest of the section by means of inductive rules. The rules for phases III, V and VII are omitted here for space limitations.

4.1 Basics

The empty trace formalises the initial scenario, where no protocol session has begun. Rule *Base* settles the base of the induction stating that the empty trace is admissible in the protocol model. All other rules represent inductive steps, so they detail how to extend a given trace of the model. Rule *Reception* [3] allows messages sent in the network to be received by their respective intended recipients: once the trace evsR of the protocol model contains the event whereby A sends X to B, then evsR extended with the event whereby B receives X is still a trace of the model. All other rules have the same syntax.

> *Base*
> [] ∈ shouprubin
>
> *Reception*
> [| evsR ∈ shouprubin; Says A B X ∈ set evsR |]
> ⟹ Gets B X # evsR ∈ shouprubin

4.2 Phase I

Any agent except the server may initiate a protocol session at any time, hence the corresponding event may extend any trace of the model (*SR1*). Upon reception of a message quoting two agent names — initiator and responder of the session — the server computes the pairkey for them and sends it with a certificate to the initiator (*SR2*). The pairkey itself does not reveal its peers, but the certificate explicitly associates it to its peers.

> *SR1*
> [| evs1 ∈ shouprubin; A ≠ Server |]
> ⟹ Says A Server {|Agent A, Agent B|} # evs1 ∈ shouprubin
>
> *SR2*
> [| evs2 ∈ shouprubin; Gets Server {|Agent A, Agent B|} ∈ set evs2 |]
> ⟹ Says Server A {|Nonce (Pairkey(A,B)),
>   Crypt (shrK A) {|Nonce (Pairkey(A,B)), Agent B|}
> |} # evs2 ∈ shouprubin

4.3 Phase II

The initiator of a protocol session may query her own smart card provided that she received a message containing a nonce and a certificate (*SR3*). The initiator gets no assurance that the nonce is in fact the pairkey for her and the intended responder, or that the certificate is specific for the pairkey, because the message is compound. It would seem sensible that the agent forwarded the entire message to the smart card, which would be able to decrypt the certificate and verify the integrity and authenticity of the pairkey. However, the protocol specification does not state this, so we choose a simpler input message containing only the

initiator's name. Given the input, the card issues a fresh nonce and a certificate
for it (*SR4*). The card keeps no record of the nonce in order to conserve memory.
The certificate will subsequently show the card the authenticity of the nonce.
Both rules rest on a card that has not been stolen, so that it can be used by its
owner.

```
SR3
[| evs3 ∈ shouprubin; Card A ∉ stolen;
    Says A Server {|Agent A, Agent B|} ∈ set evs3;
    Gets A {|Nonce Pk, Cert|} ∈ set evs3 |]
⟹ Inputs A (Card A) (Agent A) # evs3 ∈ shouprubin


SR4
[| evs4 ∈ shouprubin; Card A ∉ stolen; Nonce Na ∉ used evs4;
    Inputs A (Card A) (Agent A) ∈ set evs4 |]
⟹ Outputs (Card A) A {|Nonce Na, Crypt (crdK (Card A)) (Nonce Na)|}
      # evs4 ∈ shouprubin
```

4.4 Phase IV

This phase sees the responder forward a compound message received from the
network to his smart card (*SR6*). The smart card issues a fresh nonce, computes
the pair-k for initiator and responder, and uses these components to produce a
session key. The nonce being fresh, the session key also results fresh. Finally, the
card outputs the nonce, the session key and two certificates (*SR7*). One certificate
establishes the association between the initiator's nonce and the responder's, and
will be inspected by the initiator's card in phase VI. The other certificate will
be retained by the responder, who will expect it again from the network in the
final phase.

```
SR6
[| evs6 ∈ shouprubin; Card B ∉ stolen;
    Gets B {|Agent A, Nonce Na|} ∈ set evs6 |]
⟹ Inputs B (Card B) {|Agent A, Nonce Na|} # evs6 ∈ shouprubin


SR7
[| evs7 ∈ shouprubin; Card B ∉ stolen;
    Nonce Nb ∉ used evs7; Key (sesK(Nb,pairK(A,B))) ∉ used evs7;
    Inputs B (Card B) {|Agent A, Nonce Na|} ∈ set evs7|]
⟹ Outputs (Card B) B {|Nonce Nb, Key (sesK(Nb,pairK(A,B))),
                        Crypt (pairK(A,B)) {|Nonce Na, Nonce Nb|},
                        Crypt (pairK(A,B)) (Nonce Nb)|}
      # evs7 ∈ shouprubin
```

4.5 Phase VI

The scenario returns upon the initiator. Before she queries her non-stolen card,
she verifies having taken hold of three messages, each containing a nonce and

a certificate. She takes on trust the nonce *Pk* as the pairkey and *Cert1* as its certificate, and recalls having obtained from her smart card a nonce *Na* and a certificate. Then, she treats *Nb* as the responder's nonce and *Cert3* as a certificate for *Na* and *Nb*. Finally, she feeds these components to her smart card (*SR9*). The card can verify that all the received components have the correct form and, if this is affirmative, computes the pair-k from the pairkey and then produces the session key and a certificate for the responder's nonce (*SR10*).

```
SR9
[| evs9 ∈ shouprubin; Card A ∉ stolen;
   Says A Server {|Agent A, Agent B|} ∈ set evs9;
   Gets A {|Nonce Pk, Cert1|} ∈ set evs9;
   Outputs (Card A) A {|Nonce Na, Cert2|} ∈ set evs9;
   Gets A {|Nonce Nb, Cert3|} ∈ set evs9 |]
⟹ Inputs A (Card A) {|Agent B, Nonce Na, Nonce Nb, Nonce Pk,
                      Cert1, Cert3, Cert2|}
      # evs9 ∈ shouprubin
```

```
SR10
[| evs10 ∈ shouprubin; Card A ∉ stolen;
   Inputs A (Card A) {|Agent B, Nonce Na, Nonce Nb,
                     Nonce (Pairkey(A,B)),
                 Crypt (shrK A) {|Nonce (Pairkey(A,B)), Agent B|},
                 Crypt (PairK (A,B)) {|Nonce Na, Nonce Nb|},
                 Crypt (crdK (Card A)) (Nonce Na)|}
      ∈ set evs10 |]
⟹ Outputs (Card A) A {|Key (sesK(Nb,pairK(A,B))),
                      Crypt (pairK(A,B)) (Nonce Nb)|}
      # evs10 ∈ shouprubin
```

4.6   Threats

Also the spy can act as a friendly agent and thus follow the rules given above. In addition, she may also act illegally. She observes the given trace, extracts all message components by the function analz, and builds all possible messages out of them by the function synth [12, Sect. 3.2]. She may send any of these fake messages in the network or input them to the cards that are either stolen or cloned. This is modelled by the following rule *Fake*.

```
Fake
[| evsF ∈ shouprubin; Card A ∈ stolen ∪ cloned;
   X ∈ synth (analz (knows Spy evsF)) |]
⟹ Says Spy B X # Inputs Spy (Card A) X # evsF ∈ shouprubin
```

We assume that the algorithm used by the cards to compute the session keys is publicly known. Therefore, if the spy obtains a nonce and a pair-k, she can compute the corresponding session key (*Forge*), thus acquiring knowledge of it. Since the pair-k's are never sent in the network, they can only be known initially (by definitions of initState and case 1 of knows).

Forge
```
[| evsFo ∈ shouprubin; Nonce Nb ∈ analz (knows Spy evsFo);
   Key (pairK(A,B)) ∈ knows Spy evsFo |]
⟹ Notes Spy (Key (sesK(Nb,pairK(A,B)))) # evsFo ∈ shouprubin
```

The model must be extended to allow the spy to obtain the outputs of the cards that are either stolen or cloned. Therefore, we must introduce a further rule per each card's output, formalising the fact that a card outputs towards the spy rather than its owner in case it lies in the spy's hands. Rule *SR4_Fake*, built from *SR4*, is presented below, while rules *SR7_Fake* and *SR10_Fake*, built in the same fashion from *SR7* and *SR10* respectively, are also needed but omitted here.

SR4_Fake
```
[| evs4F ∈ shouprubin; Card A ∈ stolen ∪ cloned;
   Nonce Na ∉ used evs4F;
   Inputs Spy (Card A) (Agent A) ∈ set evs4F |]
⟹ Outputs (Card A) Spy {|Nonce Na,
                         Crypt (crdK (Card A)) (Nonce Na)|}
      # evs4F ∈ shouprubin
```

4.7   Accidents

We complete the model by allowing accidents (or breaches of security) on session keys. This has been typically done by a single rule [8,12], or by two rules leaking two different kinds of session keys [7]. Shoup-Rubin requires both peers to handle the same session key, respectively in phases IV and VI. Therefore, the spy has a chance of learning the session key from both of them. In the worst case, she will also learn the nonce used to compute the key and the identity of its peers (*Oops1*, *Oops2*).

Oops1
```
[| evsO1 ∈ shouprubin;
   Outputs (Card B) B {|Nonce Nb, Key Sk, Cert,
                        Crypt (pairK(A,B)) (Nonce Nb)|}
      ∈ set evsO1 |]
⟹ Notes Spy {|Key Sk, Nonce Nb, Agent A, Agent B|}
      # evsO1 ∈ shouprubin
```

Oops2
```
[| evsO2 ∈ shouprubin;
   Outputs (Card A) A {|Key Sk, Crypt (pairK(A,B)) (Nonce Nb)|}
      ∈ set evsO2 |]
⟹ Notes Spy {|Key Sk, Nonce Nb, Agent A, Agent B|}
      # evsO2 ∈ shouprubin
```

The spy cannot learn any pair-k's by accident because no agent ever sees any.

5   Verifying Shoup-Rubin

While confidentiality is discussed in detail, authentication and key distribution are only introduced on an upgraded protocol (Sect. 6), due to space limitations.

5.1   Confidentiality

Given a trace *evs*, confidentiality of a message X on the trace is expressed as $X \notin$ analz(knows Spy *evs*), signifying that the spy cannot extract X from the analysis of the messages obtained from monitoring the trace *evs*.

The confidentiality argument for a protocol responder B who is not the spy concerns the session key. Message 7 delivers the session key to B. The event formalising that message, Outputs (Card B) B {|Nonce Nb, Key Sk, *Cert1*, *Cert2*|}, includes two certificates, *Cert1* and *Cert2*, that B cannot inspect because they are sealed by specific long-term keys (no agent knows any long-term keys).

We have attempted to prove Sk confidential on a trace *evs* that contains no oops event leaking Sk but does contain the mentioned event. In the attempt, B's card must be assumed not to be cloned otherwise the spy would know pairK(P, B) for any agent P and could forge the session key by rule *Forge*. The assumption that B is not the spy solves case *SR7*, and the freshness assumption on the session key solves case *SR7_Fake*. Cases *SR10* and *SR10_Fake* remain unsolved. The former shows that B's peer might be the spy, who could so obtain a copy of Sk from her own smart card and falsify the theorem. The latter subgoal shows that B's peer's card could be either stolen or cloned, so the spy would be able to use such card to compute Sk, regardless the identity of the card's owner. These situations are due to the fact that, while B's card issues a fresh session key in message 7, his peer's card in fact computes a copy of that key out of available components in message 10. Therefore, solving the corresponding subgoals requires assuming that B's peer is not the spy, and that B's peer's card cannot be used by the spy. But message 7 does not state the identity of such peer. This signifies that B gets no explicit information about the peer with which the session key is to be used, which violates a well-known explicitness principle due to Abadi and Needham [1, Principle 3]. If we inspect either one of the certificates, then the relevant assumptions can be stated and theorem 1 can be proved. Note that there is no need to assume B's card not to be stolen — were it stolen, it would compute a fresh key.

Theorem 1. *If A and B are not the spy, A's card is neither stolen nor cloned, B's card is not cloned, and evs contains*

Outputs (Card B) B {|Nonce Nb, Key Sk, *Cert*, Crypt(pairK(A, B))(Nonce Nb)|}

but does not contain Notes Spy {|Key Sk, Nonce Nb, Agent A, Agent B|}, *then*

Key $Sk \notin$ analz(knows Spy *evs*).

From B's viewpoint, trusting that his peer is not the spy and that his card cannot be used by the spy is indispensable. So is trusting that the key has not been leaked by accident. These assumptions, which are never verifiable, constitute the *minimal trust* [5,13]. However, B cannot even verify that the main event mentioned by the theorem ever occurs because he cannot inspect the encrypted certificate. Therefore, B certainly cannot apply the theorem, even under the minimal trust.

Analogous considerations apply to A's viewpoint. Message 10 delivers the session key to A, so we attempt to prove that key confidential on the assumption that the event formalising message 10, Outputs (Card A) A {Key Sk, $Cert$}, occurs. While the freshness assumption on the session key solves case $SR7$ as above, we need to assume that A's card is neither stolen nor cloned to solve case $SR10\_Fake$, otherwise the spy could exploit A's card to compute her copy of the session key. Cases $SR7$ and $SR10$ remain unsolved. The former highlights that A's peer could be the spy. The latter highlights that, even assuming that A is not the spy, A's card could be computing a session key already available to the spy who got it from A's peer's card. To solve these subgoals, we must assume that A's peer is not the spy, and that A's peer's card is neither stolen nor cloned. But message 10 fails to express A's peer. This theorem can be proved if the form of $Cert$ is explicit, resulting in a guarantee that cannot be applied by A even under the minimal trust. These weaknesses were not highlighted by the provable security analysis.

6   Verifying an Upgraded Shoup-Rubin

Our findings suggest to upgrade the protocol so that both messages 7 and 10 state explicitly the intended peer for the session key (Fig. 2). Quoting also the nonce in message 10 is not indispensable. It is straightforward to upgrade the protocol model accordingly.

$$7. \ C_b \rightarrow B : Nb, \underline{A}, Kab, \{\!|Na, Nb|\!\}_{\pi_{ab}}, \{\!|Nb|\!\}_{\pi_{ab}}$$
$$10. \ C_a \rightarrow A : \underline{Nb, B}, Kab, \{\!|Nb|\!\}_{\pi_{ab}}$$

Fig. 2. Adding explicitness to two messages of Shoup-Rubin

6.1   Confidentiality

In the upgraded protocol model, two significant confidentiality theorems (2 and 3) hold about the session key.

Theorem 2. *If A and B are not the spy, A's card is neither stolen nor cloned, B's card is not cloned, and evs contains*

Outputs (Card B) B {Nonce Nb, Agent A, Key Sk, $Cert1$, $Cert2$}

but does not contain Notes Spy {Key Sk, Nonce Nb, Agent A, Agent B}, *then*

Key $Sk \notin$ analz(knows Spy evs).

Theorem 3. *If A and B are not the spy, both A and B's cards are neither stolen nor cloned, and evs contains*

$$\text{Outputs}\,(\text{Card}\,A)\,A\,\{\!|\text{Nonce}\,Nb, \text{Agent}\,B, \text{Key}\,Sk, Cert|\!\}$$

but does not contain $\text{Notes}\,\text{Spy}\,\{\!|\text{Key}\,Sk, \text{Nonce}\,Nb, \text{Agent}\,A, \text{Agent}\,B|\!\}$, *then*

$$\text{Key}\,Sk \notin \text{analz}(\text{knows}\,\text{Spy}\,evs).$$

We prove these theorems following the reasoning developed in the previous section, which also motivates the assumptions about peers and cards. These theorems are applicable under the minimal trust by B and A respectively because the agents only need to verify the presence of the encrypted certificates without having to inspect them. If message 10 did not mention the nonce Nb, then theorem 3 would require a stronger assumption: the oops event universally quantified over the nonce it mentions.

6.2 Authentication

If B obtains the session key with the two certificates from his card and then receives the second of the certificates from the network, then theorem 4 states that A was alive and meant to communicate with him after he issued Nb.

Theorem 4. *If B is not the spy, both A and B's cards are neither stolen nor cloned, and evs contains*

$$\text{Outputs}\,(\text{Card}\,B)\,B\,\{\!|\text{Nonce}\,Nb, \text{Agent}\,A, \text{Key}\,Sk, Cert1, Cert2|\!\}\quad and$$
$$\text{Gets}\,B\,(Cert2)$$

then evs also contains

$$\text{Outputs}\,(\text{Card}\,A)\,A\,\{\!|\text{Nonce}\,Nb, \text{Agent}\,B, \text{Key}\,Sk, Cert2|\!\}.$$

The theorem certainly does not hold of the original protocol, where none of the two events verified by B expresses his peer A. The proof develops through the following steps. Since A is explicit in the first event, the complete form of $Cert2$ can be proved by induction. Because the means between agents and smart cards is secure, the second event (and not the first) implies that the certificate is known to the spy. Then, the authenticity argument for the certificate, omitted in this paper, derives that it originated with A in message 10 under the assumptions about peers and cards that theorem 4 reports.

Likewise, upon reception of message 10, theorem 5 informs A that B was alive and meant to communicate with her.

Theorem 5. *If B's card is neither stolen nor cloned, and evs contains*

$$\text{Outputs}\,(\text{Card}\,A)\,A\,\{\!|\text{Nonce}\,Nb, \text{Agent}\,B, \text{Key}\,Sk, Cert2|\!\}$$

then, for some Cert1, evs also contains

$$\text{Outputs}\,(\text{Card}\,B)\,B\,\{\!|\text{Nonce}\,Nb, \text{Agent}\,A, \text{Key}\,Sk, Cert1, Cert2|\!\}.$$

The theorem clearly does not hold of the original protocol, where A is not informed of her peer's identity. Once we prove by induction that the main assumption of the theorem implies that the certificate $\{Na, Nb\}_{\pi_{ab}}$ is known to the spy, the authenticity argument for the certificate, omitted here, completes the proof of theorem 5 at the price of the assumptions on B's card. Unlike B, A gets no assurances about how recently B was alive, because the event of the assumption contains no nonce invented by A [6].

Our theorems remark that the spy can impersonate any agent whose smart card is stolen or cloned: she just needs to intercept the relevant communication and to exploit that agent's card to acquire the necessary message components.

6.3 Key Distribution

Applying the definition of knows to the authentication theorems, we can prove formally that the upgraded protocol meets the goal of key distribution and confirms it to the peers. Theorem 6 formally assures agent A that the session key she receives is also available to her peer B. Theorem 7 provides the same guarantee to B. This goal cannot be proved formally of the original protocol because of the mentioned lack of explicitness.

Theorem 6. *If B is not the spy, both A and B's cards are neither stolen nor cloned, and evs contains*

> Outputs (Card B) B $\{$Nonce Nb, Agent A, Key Sk, $Cert1$, $Cert2\}$ *and*
> Gets B ($Cert2$)

then Key $Sk \in$ analz(knows A evs).

Theorem 7. *If B's card is neither stolen nor cloned, and evs contains*

> Outputs (Card A) A $\{$Nonce Nb, Agent B, Key Sk, $Cert2\}$

then Key $Sk \in$ analz(knows B evs).

7 Conclusions

Our work makes Paulson's Inductive Approach usable for analysing smart card protocols. We have mechanised the Shoup-Rubin protocol showing that it meets strong goals of confidentiality, authentication and key distribution. But two of the protocol messages must quote their intended recipients explicitly if the cards' buses can output in a random order. Our theorems show that verifying smart card protocols requires significant man-effort in understanding the roles played by the cards and in realising how the messages they compute may influence the protocol goals. However, none of the theorems discussed here executes in more than 10 seconds on a 600Mhz PentiumIII, so the computational resources necessary for the analysis are limited.

Acknowledgements

I am grateful to Peter Honeyman who kindly explained to me a few features of the Shoup-Rubin protocol. I am indebted to Larry Paulson and to Peter Ryan for their large comments on a draft of this paper. Thanks also to the anonymous referees for helping me improve the presentation. This work was funded by the EPSRC grant GR/R01156/01 *Verifying Electronic Commerce Protocols*.

References

1. M. Abadi and R. M. Needham. Prudent Engineering Practice for Cryptographic Protocols. *IEEE Transactions on Software Engineering*, 22(1):6–15, January 1996. 29
2. R. J. Anderson and M. J. Kuhn. Low Cost Attacks on Tamper Resistant Devices. In M. e. a. Lomas, editor, *Proc. of the 5th International Workshop on Security Protocols*, LNCS 1361, pages 125–136. Springer-Verlag, 1997. 22
3. G. Bella. Message Reception in the Inductive Approach. Research Report 460, University of Cambridge — Computer Laboratory, 1999. 23, 25
4. G. Bella. Modelling Agents' Knowledge Inductively. In *Proc. of the 7th International Workshop on Security Protocols*, LNCS 1796. Springer-Verlag, 1999. 23
5. G. Bella. *Inductive Verification of Cryptographic Protocols*. PhD thesis, University of Cambridge, Computer Laboratory, 2000. Research Report 493. 29
6. G. Bella and L. C. Paulson. Are Timestamps Worth the Effort? A Formal Treatment. Research Report 447, University of Cambridge — Computer Laboratory, 1998. 32
7. G. Bella and L. C. Paulson. Kerberos Version IV: Inductive Analysis of the Secrecy Goals. In J.-J. Quisquater, Y. Desware, C. Meadows, and D. Gollmann, editors, *Proc. of the 5th European Symposium on Research in Computer Security (ESORICS'98)*, LNCS 1485, pages 361–375. Springer-Verlag, 1998. 28
8. G. Bella and L. C. Paulson. Mechanising BAN Kerberos by the Inductive Method. In A. J. Hu and M. Y. Vardi, editors, *Proc. of the International Conference on Computer-Aided Verification (CAV'98)*, LNCS 1427, pages 416–427. Springer-Verlag, 1998. 28
9. R. Jerdonek, P. Honeyman, K. Coffman, J. Rees, and K. Wheeler. Implementation of a Provably Secure, Smartcard-based Key Distribution Protocol. In J.-J. Quisquater and B. Schneier, editors, *Proc. of the 3rd Smart Card Research and Advanced Application Conference (CARDIS'98)*, 1998. 20
10. T. Leighton and S. Micali. Secret-key Agreement without Public-key Cryptography. In D. R. Stinson, editor, *Proc. of Advances in Cryptography — CRYPTO'93*, LNCS 773, pages 456–479. Springer-Verlag, 1993. 19, 20
11. L. C. Paulson. *Isabelle: A Generic Theorem Prover*. LNCS 828. Springer-Verlag, 1994. 20
12. L. C. Paulson. The Inductive Approach to Verifying Cryptographic Protocols. *Journal of Computer Security*, 6:85–128, 1998. 20, 22, 23, 27, 28
13. P. Y. A. Ryan and S. A. Schneider. *The Modelling and Analysis of Security Protocols: the CSP Approach*. Addison-Wesley, 2000. 29
14. V. Shoup and A. Rubin. Session Key Distribution using Smart Cards. In U. Maurer, editor, *Advances in Cryptology — Eurocrypt'96*, LNCS 1070, pages 321–331. Springer-Verlag, 1996. 19

JCCM*: Flexible Certificates for smartcards with Java Card

Mª Celeste Campo, Andrés Marín, Arturo García, Ignacio Díaz,
Peter T. Breuer, Carlos Delgado, Carlos García

Universidad Carlos III de Madrid
Avd. Universidad 30 28911, Leganés
eticket@it.uc3m.es

Abstract. Smartcards and PKCS #11 are an appealing solution for combined storage and certificate management at the enduser level. Many applications use PKCS #11 primitives for security reasons: a popular browser, like Netscape Navigator contain a PKCS #11 cryptographic module that plays a critical role in secure web surfing and e-mail signing and encryption. Nevertheless, most market-ready solutions ([SMARTSIGN], [GPKPKCS#11], [SLBCBPKCS#11]) use non-programmable cards or else do not exploit the card's programmable capabilities. Instead they utilize cryptographic functions built into the card. This results in applications having the card manufacturer's semantics instead of PKCS #11 semantics.

In this article we present our work: Java Card Certificate Management (JCCM). **JCCM moves PKCS #11 middleware into the card** itself. This results in **greater flexibility and less implementation dependence** for applications. We have developed JCCM for two cards: the **GemXpresso RAD 211is** and the **Cyberflex for Linux Starter's Kit 2.1**. We have also developed the corresponding dynamic library for Netscape enabling our endusers to use JCCM in their daily.

1 Introduction

The number of users with Internet access keeps growing, and so do their security needs. The increasing number of sites offering sensitive information (like bank accounts) via HTTPS [HTTPS] protocol is an example. International e-mail, the "intelligence is in the net"-approach in network computing and e-business demand stronger security. Browsers do implement secure web surfing and digital signed and encrypted e-mail using digital certificates ([X.509]), but they lack corresponding secure certificate storage mechanisms.

Smartcards are tamper-proof devices, where tamper-resistance is a term with practical connotation that takes into account the cost/benefit relation of the attacks. Given unlimited funds we could break the security of a card. In [USENIX 99] some sophisticated chemical and physical attacks are described,

---

* This work has been partially supported by the project E-TICKET CYCYT N°2FD1997-1269-C02-01(TEL)

I. Attali and T. Jensen (Eds.): E-smart 2001, LNCS 2140, pp. 34–42, 2001.

together with effective and low-cost countermeasures. The article concludes that they see no really effective short-term protection against carefully planned invasive tampering (involving focused ion-beam tools). "Zeroization" mechanisms for erasing secrets when tampering is detected require a continuous power supply that the credit-card form factor does not allow. The attacker can thus safely disable the zeroization mechanism before powering up the processor.

2   The PKCS #11 Standard

RSA Laboratories has developed, in cooperation with representatives of industry, academia and government, a family of standards called Public-Key Cryptography Standards, or PKCS for short. These standards cover RSA encryption, Diffie-Hellman key exchange, password-based encryption, an extended-certificate syntax, cryptographic message syntax, private key syntax, and certification request syntax, as well as selected attributes.

Table 1. A significative set of Cryptoki functions

General purpose funtions	Slot and token management functions	Cryptographic functions
		C_EncryptInit
C_Initialize	C_GetSlotList	C_Encrypt
C_Finalize	C_GetSlotInfo	C_DecryptInit
C_GetInfo	C_GetTokenInfo	C_Decrypt
Objects management functions	C_GetMechanismList	C_SignInit
	C_SetPIN	C_Sign
C_CreateObject	**Session management functions**	C_VerifyInit
C_CopyObject		C_Verify
C_DestroyObject	C_OpenSession	C_DigestInit
C_GetAttributeValue	C_CloseSession	C_Digest
C_SetAttributeValue	C_CloseAllSessions	C_GenerateKey
C_FindObjectsInit	C_GetSessionInfo	C_GenerateKeyPair
C_FindObjects	C_Login	C_WrapKey
C_FindObjectsFinal	C_Logout	C_UnwrapKey

The PKCS #11 specifies an application programming interface (API) for cryptographic services, called Cryptoki, short for "cryptographic token interface". Cryptoki isolates an application from details of the cryptographic device, which is called "token'. Portable cryptographic tokens, such as smartcards, are inserted in "slots", which correspond to a physical reader or other device interface. A token stores objects and can perform cryptographic functions on it. Cryptoki defines three classes of object: data, certificates, and keys. A **data object** is defined by an application. A **certificate object** stores a certificate. A **key object** stores a cryptographic key and it further specialices in concrete types for the various cryptographic algorithms, such as RSA public and private key. Cryptographic operations are performed in the context of sessions, which represent and established communication path with a token present in a slot.

The Cryptoki API consists of a number of functions, encompassing slot and token management and object management, as well as cryptographic functions. Table 1 shows a significative set of these functions.

3   Netscape and PKCS #11

Netscape incorporates a security architecture that allows for web surfing and signed and encrypted e-mail. This security architecture, well-known as the "Netscape Security Library" (NSL), makes use of PKCS #11 cryptographic modules in order to offer the appropriate high level functionality. Netscape contains an internal module PKCS #11 that constitutes a fairly complete implementation of the standard: it includes mechanisms based on RSA as well as some symmetrical key mechanisms. The internal module offers a logical vision of the computer as a cryptographic device: it uses the file system for persistent storage of Cryptoki objects and the CPU for cryptographic processing. Thanks to this module, Netscape is able to offer the capabilities mentioned above, but it has a problem: the use of the file system to store certificates and keys breaks the premise of safe storage of sensitive data. The solution adopted by Netscape is password protecting data stored on disk and to allow the incorporation of external PKCS #11 modules, which then serve as specialized interfaces to cryptographic hardware, as in the case of our JCCM module. Another peculiarity of the NSL is that it allows the simultaneous presence of several PKCS #11 modules: our module can coexist with the internal module, and therefore it is not necessary to implement the mechanisms already supported; mechanisms oriented towards data encryption are not implemented (symmetric key) because the data transfer rate between the computer and the card makes it unsuitable for the encrypting arbitrary volumes of data.

A trace of all the calls to our library needed to sign a mail from Netscape is shown below. The trace has been simplified and includes only the exit trace line for each Cryptoki functions called.

- *Lines 1 to 10*: Library boot and initial data exchange. Lines 1 to 5, they are called when starting Netscape before we initiate any operation. Line 6, the token was present in the reader. Line 7, that obtains data about the token and its capabilities (lines 8 to 9). Finally, line 10, a session begins with the token.

```
 1 Mar  2 12:06:20: C_GetFunctionList Returns (CKR_OK) 0x0
 2 Mar  2 12:06:20: C_Initialize Returns (CKR_OK) 0x0
 3 Mar  2 12:06:20: C_GetInfo Returns (CKR_OK) 0x0
 4 Mar  2 12:06:20: C_GetSlotList Returns (CKR_OK) 0x0
 5 Mar  2 12:06:20: C_GetSlotList Returns (CKR_OK) 0x0
 6 Mar  2 12:06:21: C_GetSlotInfo Returns (CKR_OK) 0x0
 7 Mar  2 12:06:21: C_GetTokenInfo Returns (CKR_OK) 0x0
 8 Mar  2 12:06:21: C_GetMechanismList Returns (CKR_OK) 0x0
 9 Mar  2 12:06:21: C_GetMechanismList Returns (CKR_OK) 0x0
10 Mar  2 12:06:21: C_OpenSession Returns (CKR_OK) 0x0
```

- *Lines 11 to 14* : 32 seconds are spent from line 10 to 11; they correspond to the time spent in writing the e-mail. These lines correspond to the request for the PIN and the corresponding call to C_Login(). The elapsed time between lines 13 and 14 correspond to the manual introduction of the PIN.

```
11 Mar  2 12:06:53: C_GetSlotInfo Returns (CKR_OK) 0x0
12 Mar  2 12:06:53: C_GetSessionInfo Returns (CKR_OK) 0x0
13 Mar  2 12:06:53: C_GetSessionInfo Returns (CKR_OK) 0x0
14 Mar  2 12:06:57: C_Login Returns (CKR_OK) 0x0
```

- *Lines 15 to 66*: The rest of the trace corresponds to the calls made by Netscape in order to generate a digital signature for a e-mail. The two last lines correspond to the signature. The time used for this operation (lines 65 to 66) is only 2s, whereas the total time for the signature (lines 15 to 66) is 26s. Those extra 24s are used in certificate searches and data transfer from the token.

```
15 Mar  2 12:06:59: C_FindObjectsInit Returns (CKR_OK) 0x0

16 Mar  2 12:06:59: C_FindObjects Returns (CKR_OK) 0x0
17 Mar  2 12:06:59: C_FindObjectsFinal Returns (CKR_OK) 0x0
18 Mar  2 12:07:00: C_FindObjectsInit Returns (CKR_OK) 0x0
19 Mar  2 12:07:00: C_FindObjects Returns (CKR_OK) 0x0
20 Mar  2 12:07:00: C_FindObjectsFinal Returns (CKR_OK) 0x0
21 Mar  2 12:07:07: C_GetAttributeValue Returns (CKR_OK) 0x0
22 Mar  2 12:07:07: C_GetAttributeValue Returns (CKR_OK) 0x0
23 Mar  2 12:07:08: C_GetSessionInfo Returns (CKR_OK) 0x0
24 Mar  2 12:07:08: C_GetAttributeValue Returns (CKR_OK) 0x0
25 Mar  2 12:07:08: C_GetAttributeValue Returns (CKR_OK) 0x0
26 Mar  2 12:07:12: C_FindObjectsInit Returns (CKR_OK) 0x0
26 Mar  2 12:07:12: C_FindObjects Returns (CKR_OK) 0x0
27 Mar  2 12:07:12: C_FindObjectsFinal Returns (CKR_OK) 0x0
28 Mar  2 12:07:12: C_GetMechanismList Returns (CKR_OK) 0x0
29 Mar  2 12:07:12: C_GetMechanismList Returns (CKR_OK) 0x0
30 Mar  2 12:07:16: C_FindObjectsInit Returns (CKR_OK) 0x0
31 Mar  2 12:07:16: C_FindObjects Returns (CKR_OK) 0x0
32 Mar  2 12:07:16: C_FindObjectsFinal Returns (CKR_OK) 0x0
33 Mar  2 12:07:17: C_GetAttributeValue Returns (CKR_OK) 0x0
34 Mar  2 12:07:17: C_GetAttributeValue Returns (CKR_OK) 0x0
35 Mar  2 12:07:17: C_GetSessionInfo Returns (CKR_OK) 0x0
36 Mar  2 12:07:17: C_GetAttributeValue Returns (CKR_OK) 0x0
37 Mar  2 12:07:17: C_GetAttributeValue Returns (CKR_OK) 0x0
38 Mar  2 12:07:18: C_FindObjectsInit Returns (CKR_OK) 0x0
39 Mar  2 12:07:18: C_FindObjects Returns (CKR_OK) 0x0
40 Mar  2 12:07:18: C_FindObjectsFinal Returns (CKR_OK) 0x0
41 Mar  2 12:07:18: C_GetSlotInfo Returns (CKR_OK) 0x0
42 Mar  2 12:07:18: C_GetSessionInfo Returns (CKR_OK) 0x0
43 Mar  2 12:07:18: C_GetSessionInfo Returns (CKR_OK) 0x0
44 Mar  2 12:07:18: C_FindObjectsInit Returns (CKR_OK) 0x0
45 Mar  2 12:07:18: C_FindObjects Returns (CKR_OK) 0x0
46 Mar  2 12:07:18: C_FindObjectsFinal Returns (CKR_OK) 0x0
47 Mar  2 12:07:18: C_GetAttributeValue Returns (CKR_OK) 0x0
48 Mar  2 12:07:19: C_GetAttributeValue Returns (CKR_OK) 0x0
49 Mar  2 12:07:19: C_GetSessionInfo Returns (CKR_OK) 0x0
50 Mar  2 12:07:19: C_GetAttributeValue Returns (CKR_OK) 0x0
51 Mar  2 12:07:19: C_GetAttributeValue Returns (CKR_OK) 0x0
52 Mar  2 12:07:19: C_FindObjectsInit Returns (CKR_OK) 0x0
53 Mar  2 12:07:19: C_FindObjects Returns (CKR_OK) 0x0
```

```
54 Mar  2 12:07:19: C_FindObjectsFinal Returns (CKR_OK) 0x0
55 Mar  2 12:07:19: C_GetSessionInfo Returns (CKR_OK) 0x0
56 Mar  2 12:07:20: C_GetAttributeValue Returns (CKR_OK) 0x0
57 Mar  2 12:07:20: C_GetAttributeValue Returns (CKR_OK) 0x0
58 Mar  2 12:07:20: C_FindObjectsInit Returns (CKR_OK) 0x0
59 Mar  2 12:07:20: C_FindObjects Returns (CKR_OK) 0x0
60 Mar  2 12:07:20: C_FindObjectsFinal Returns (CKR_OK) 0x0
61 Mar  2 12:07:22: C_GetAttributeValue Returns (CKR_OK) 0x0
62 Mar  2 12:07:23: C_GetAttributeValue Returns (CKR_OK) 0x0
63 Mar  2 12:07:23: C_GetAttributeValue Returns (CKR_OK) 0x0
64 Mar  2 12:07:23: C_GetSessionInfo Returns (CKR_OK) 0x0
65 Mar  2 12:07:23: C_SignInit Returns (CKR_OK) 0x0
66 Mar  2 12:07:25: C_Sign Returns (CKR_OK) 0x0
```

It is necessary to point out that this penalty is only incurread the first time that the certificate and the associated private key is used; the generation of a digital signature for the next and subsequent messages takes only 6s.

4   Smartcards and Java Card

Smartcards, besides being practical tamper-proof devices have ever-increasing computation and storage capabilities. They can be integrated in a natural way with the users' applications, for instance a favourite browser, through the use of [PKCS#11].

Smartcards are present in a number of solutions on the market. Most of these solutions use the standard [PKCS#11] for certificate management, i.e., they provide the users with dynamic libraries that can be accessed by applications in order to handle security. The bad news is that these solutions ([SMARTSIGN], [GPKPKCS#11], [SLBCBPKCS#11]) tend to offer the applications a subset of PKCS #11 semantics, reduced to that provided by the smartcard manufacturer.

Java Card is a reduced version of Java. In particular the virtual machine is very restricted. There is no garbage collector, and every object is instantiated in persistent memory until the end of the life-cycle of the "cardlet" (Java application running in a card). With respect to language, Java Card restricts the available packages and datatypes. The programmer has to deal with a simplified Object class, no String class, and only 16 bit integers.

We have implemented our system in Java Card because this technology has several unique benefits:

- Platform independence: this allows us to run our cardlet Cryptoki on different vendors' cards.
- Uses the Java language: which enables high programmer productivity and all the advantages of object-oriented programming.
- Multi-application capable: multiple applications can run on a single card.
- Compatible with Existing Smart Card Standards, such as ISO7816.

5 JCCM: Java Card Certificate Management

We have designed and implemented a system named Java Card Certificate Management (JCCM). JCCM moves part of PKCS #11 code inside a Java Card. The JCCM *cardlet* is responsible for object management in conformance to Cryptoki, implementing the corresponding Cryptoki functions. This is one of the key issues in the JCCM design: the cardlet handles management layer in Cryptoki objects, implementing the full management functionality defined in Cryptoki, that is: creation, lookup, copy and deletion of objects, and cryptographic functions. The set of cardlet Cryptoki APDU's (Application Data Unit) is in Table 2.

Table 2. Set of cardlet Cryptoki APDU's

General purpose	Session management
Ident	DownLoadObj_Init
Object management	DownLoadObj_Attr
Login	DownLoadObj_Create
Logout	DownLoadObj_Copy
Cryptographic	DownLoadObj_SetAttr
Sign	DownLoadObj_Find
	GetAttr
	DeleteObj

Another key issue in our design is the dynamic memory management in smartcards. EEPROM memory is the place where persistent objects live. It is a very limited resource and must be handled carefully. Cryptoki object management functions need to allocate and free memory, and we have implemented a simple memory management layer for this reason. This layer defines a spool of memory blocks that are to be marked used or free. The first two bytes of a memory block contain a free/used bit and a 15-bit block length (2^{15} Bytes=32KB), sufficient to include full available EEPROM in the current Java Cards. These implementation details are hidden from the calling functions. Memory management also merges small blocks into larger ones to avoid fragmentation.

PKCS #11 represents objects as arrays of attributes. Attributes are fixed-size structures formed by three fields: attribute type, value pointer and the length of the value. A JCCM cardlet uses a similar scheme. An object structure is formed by three fields:

- The "next object" pointer, 2 bytes. All the objects that are created in the card are maintained in a linked list.
- Number of attributes of the object, 1 byte. This field can be deduced based on the size of the block in dynamic memory, but it has been chosen to include it: typically the card will store solely two objects, a certificate and a associated private key.

– A variable number of structures of attributes, so many as number of attributes has the object.

An attribute object has the following fields:

– Type of attribute, 4 bytes. It is the binary value defined in the standard.
– An attribute pointer, 2 bytes. The value is stored in its own block of dynamic memory. The length of this field is obtained from the head of the block of dynamic memory in which it is stored.

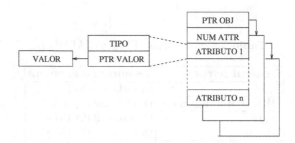

Fig. 1. Objects structure

A Java class encapsulates each of these structures; the class `ObjPatr` for the objects and the class `AttrPatr` for the attributes. These classes cannot be instantiated due to the lack of garbage collection mentioned in the Section 4, they have only static methods and members. They are used to map the array of dynamic memory to the corresponding object structure: they also have methods to set/get the value of each field and to release the associated dynamic memory. These two classes extend the class `Patr`, that supplies basic access to fields of type multibyte. Before using one of these classes to access a structure stored in dynamic memory it is necessary to establish the address of the structure by means of a call of `setAddr(short addr)`, which sets the reference address used by all the methods that access the members of the structure (`get...()`,`set...()`).

6   JCCM Implementation

We have developed the corresponding dynamic library for Netscape that enables our final users to use JCCM in their security operations. The implementation has been done in Linux, using PC/SC Muscle and Netscape. We are porting now to Netscape for Microsoft Windows.

To demonstrate device independence, we have ported JCCM to cards from two different manufacturers: Gemplus **GemXpresso RAD 211is** and Schlumberger **Cyberflex for Linux Starter's Kit 2.1**. The differences we found are twofold: the cryptographic capabilities are not standard in Java Card 2.0 (there were no Java Card 2.1 kits on the market when we begun to develop JCCM), so we are forced to use proprietary hooks, and the way to load software differs between the cards.

- **GemXpresso RAD 211is** [GemXpresso RAD 211 UG] uses Visa Open Platform for cardlet uploading. DES and 3DES are available, but not RSA. We need to transfer the private key to the computer to perform digital signing with RSA.
- **Cyberflex for Linux Starter's Kit 2.1**, [Cyberflex SDK] uses a proprietary application (based on TCL/TK) for software loading. RSA via Schlumberger's extension `javacardx.crypto`.

With respect to the cardlet itself, there are some differences; for example, the maximum size of the responses. The source code contains some compilation directives which adapt the code to the cards and it has to be precompiled to obtain java code that is then optimized for the card in question. A comparison of both cards is in Table 3. The size of the cardlet in the GemXpresso is much larger than in the Cyberflex, but in both cards there is room enough for storing up to 4 certificates (each certificate takes 1KB). GemXpresso is significantly faster storing and retrieving certificates (almost twice as fast as Cyberflex), perhaps because of better efficiency of the virtual machine implementation.

Table 3. Cardlet comparison

Card	Size of Cardlet (Bytes)	Storage (ms)			Retrieval (ms)
		Private key	Public key	Certificate	Certificate
GemXpresso	6437	20312	12998	16228	8934
Cyberflex	3992	38122	28180	34036	16155

References

[ISO/IEC 7816-4] "ISO/IEC 7816-4: Integrated circuit(s) cards with contacts. Part 4: Interindustry commands for interchange", ISO/IEC, 1995.

[ISO/IEC 7816-3] "ISO/IEC 7816-3: Integrated circuit(s) cards with contacts. Part 3: Electronic signals and transmission protocols", ISO/IEC, 1997.

[JCADG 2.1] "Java Card Applet Developer's Guide. Java Card Version 2.0", SUN Microsystems, Agosto de 1998.

[JCADG 2.0] 'Java Card Applet Developer's Guide. Java Card Version 2.1", SUN Microsystems, Agosto de 1999.

[GemXpresso RAD 211 UG] "GemXpresso RAD 211 User Guide Version 1.0", Gemplus, Octubre 1999

[GemXpresso RAD 211 CRM] "GemXpresso RAD 211 Card Reference Manual Version 1.0", Gemplus, Octubre 1999

[Cyberflex PG] "Cyberflex Access Developer's Series. Programmer's Guide", Schlumberger, Septiembre 1999.

[Cyberflex SDK] "Cyberflex Access Software Developer's Kit 2 - Release Notes", Schlumberger, Noviembre 1999.

[HTTPS] "HTTP Over TLS", Rescorla, E., IETF RFC 2818, Mayo 2000.

[X.509] "Internet X.509 Public Key Infrastructure Operational Protocols: FTP and HTTP". R. Housley, P. Hoffman. IETF RFC 2585, Mayo 1999.

[USENIX 99] "Design Principles for Tamper-Resistant Smartcard Processors" by Oliver Kömmerling, Markus Kuhn, Workshop on Smartcard Technology Proceedings, Chicago, Illinois, USA, Mayo 10-11, 1999

[SC SDK] 'Smart Card Developer's Kit", Scott B. Guthery, Timothy M. Jurgensen. Macmillan Technical Publishg. 1998.ISBN 1-57870-027-2.

[SC APP. DEV. JAVA] 'Smart Card. Application Developement Using Java", Uwe Hansmann, Martin S. Nicklous, Thomas Schack y Frank Seliger, Springer, 2000. ISBN 3-540-65829-7.

[PKCS#11] "PKCS #11 v2.10: Cryptographic Token Interface Standard", RSA Laboratories Inc., Diciembre 1999 (003-903052-210-000-000).

[PKCS#1] "PKCS #1 v2.1: RSA Cryptography Standard", RSA Laboratories Inc.

[PKCS#5] "PKCS #5 v2.0: Password-Based Cryptography Standard", RSA Laboratories Inc.

[PKCS#8] "PKCS #8 v1.2: Private-Key Information Syntax Standard", RSA Laboratories Inc.

[STALL99] 'Cryptography and Network Security: Principles and Practices", Stallings, W., 2ed, Prentice-Hall Inc., 1999

[SMARTSIGN] "Smart Sign", Tommaso Cucinotta,
http://sourceforge.net/projects/smartsign

[GPKPKCS#11] "GemSAFE Products", Gemplus,
http://www.gemplus.com/products/software/gemsafe/index.html

[SLBCBPKCS#11] "Cyberflex Access SDK", Schlumberger,
http://www.cyberflex.com/Products

Context Inference for Static Analysis of Java Card Object Sharing

Denis Caromel, Ludovic Henrio, and Bernard Serpette

INRIA Sophia Antipolis, CNRS - I3S - Univ. Nice Sophia Antipolis,
BP 93, 06902 Sophia Antipolis Cedex - France
First.Last@inria.fr

Abstract. This article presents an analysis to statically check the Java
Card sharing policy. From the program text, both the violation and the
guaranty of correctness can be detected in certain cases avoiding Run-
time exception.
Using type inference techniques, a specific inference algorithm is proposed in order to achieve such result. The current implementation is
outlined, and experimental results are given on a benchmark program.

Keywords: Java Card, security, type inference, static analysis, objects

1   Introduction

Within the framework of increasing need for secured software, many systems
are using sophisticated policies to ensure some level of security. Most of them
involve dynamic checks, with de facto presence of dynamic errors and exceptions.
In order to avoid the occurrence of such runtime errors, static analysis has to
be used – to figure out, for instance, information on the calling graph, the heap
structure, or alias information. Those forms of analysis require sophisticated and
time consuming algorithms, which can make them rather ineffective on actual
size programs.

In this paper, we propose to use for the same purpose a rather simpler technique: type inference-like algorithms for security checks. We experienced that
idea on the Java Card security system.

Java Card security policy is based on a firewall and a marker interface
(`Shareable`). The firewall separates objects in different contexts: there is one
context per package. Two objects belonging to two different contexts cannot ac-
cess each other directly: the firewall in that case throws a dedicated exception
(`SecurityException`). Method calls can only occur between contexts through
Shareable interface.

Our aim is to statically detect which accesses to objects may throw a *SecurityException* in order to help the applet developer to improve his sharing
mechanism and avoid such exceptions. The applet developer needs to provide
the byte code of the set of applets he wants to analyse. Our context inference
analysis will return the set of instructions which may throw a security exception.

I. Attali and T. Jensen (Eds.): E-smart 2001, LNCS 2140, pp. 43–57, 2001.

Then, the developer will know which parts of his program have to be improved in order to avoid this kind of exceptions.

This paper presents a context inference method to analyse the sharing of objects. The basic idea is to define an abstract context as the set of all possible creation contexts of an object. Then we apply a type-inference like and a type-checking like mechanism, considering abstract context as a type. For example, a call statement o.foo (...) is guaranteed to be correct only if type of o is a sub-interface of Shareable or if the potential context of o is unique and identical to the context of execution.

The current inference system is defined on a large and representative subset of the Java Card Bytecode. With minor modifications, the system could as well be directly specified and implemented on the Java Card source code.

Section 2 presents the JavaCard security policy and related work on static analysis and type inference. Section 3 presents the object sharing analysis. In section 4, we briefly describe an implementation of the analysis, and experimental results on a benchmark program.

2   Context and Related Work

2.1   Java Card, Sharing, and Security

The Java Card language is a restriction of the Java language described in [1], [13] and [16]. In this section we present the Java Card security policy and a reduced set of bytcodes on which the analysis will be described.

Java Card application are called Applets. The Java Card Runtime Environment (JCRE) is the operating system of the card ([14]).

Java Card Security   The Java Card firewall is described in the section 6 of [14]. Some Java Card security limitations and how to improve it are presented in [5], [6] and [8]. The main principles of Java Card firewall are described below.

The Java Card firewall partition the set of existing objects into contexts. A context is associated to each applet when it is installed. There is one context per package so two applets declared in the same package won't be separated by the firewall. The JCRE belongs to its own context. At any point, there is a currently active context. Each object belongs to a context which is the context which was active when the object has been created. A context switch occurs when executing certain method invocations. When a bytecode accesses an object (field access, cast or method invocation), a runtime check is performed and if the access is refused then a SecurityException is thrown.

An access to an object is allowed if the current execution context is the same as the object context, that is to say an object can only be accessed by its owning context except in the cases below.

Static fields and methods do not belong to any context and can be accessed from any context.

The JCRE can access to objects in every context. The JCRE can specify objects as entry points, their methods are accessible from any context. In the same way, fields of global arrays are accessible from any context.

In order to allow the dialog between two applets, Shareable interfaces have been defined. An interface is Shareable if it extends the interface `Shareable`. A method can be invoked through a Shareable interface even if the object context is different from the current context.

When a non-static method is invoked, and the call is authorised, the VM performs a context switch if necessary that is to say the current context is switched to the context of the object of the invoked method.

Bytecode Subset We present a subset of Java Card bytecode that is sufficient for understanding and designing the analysis. The whole bytecodes are described in [15]

aload i pushes the ith local variable on the operand stack;

astore i pops an element of the stack and writes it in the ith local variable;

getfield f pushes on the operand stack the field f of an object popped from the stack;

putfield f pops a value and an object from the stack and writes the value in the field f of the object;

new A allocates a new instance of the class A and puts the new reference on the stack;

invokeVirtual M calls method M. M is a reference to the method corresponding to the static type of the object accessed;

invokeStatic M calls the static method M;

invokeShareable M calls method M on a shareable interface;

return returns the top of the stack from a method.

invokeShareable does not correspond to any Java Card bytecode but we can statically classify `invokeInterface` commands into the `invokeShareable` instructions and the others which can be considered as `invokeVirtual` for our analysis. Indeed, we determine statically if an `invokeInterface` command concerns a `Shareable` interface or not.

Our analysis is based on bytecode because ambiguities (name resolution) are removed during compilation. Moreover, since the JVM is the target of several languages (see [17] for a complete list of such languages), our analysis may be applied independently of the source language.

If we wanted to apply our analysis on Java Card language, we would have to resolve all these ambiguities and most of the analysis would be redundant with the compilation phase. In fact the context analysis would be translated easily but we would need to extend our analysis with aspects that are independent from Java Card sharing mechanism.

2.2 Static Analysis Techniques

The firewall characteristics brought us to think about static analysis techniques because firewall analysis could be rewritten in terms of aliasing between contexts which could be analysed like [2,3,4,10,11]. But such analysis are very difficult to implement especially because we need a precise interprocedural analysis (cf. [12]) and both may and must-aliasing properties must be computed if we want to give precise results to the developer.

Our analysis infers a set of possible creation contexts for each object. The context inference is similar to set constraints [7] but constraints solving is much simpler because abstract contexts does not contain function symbols. Indeed function symbols are used in [7] to introduce more complex constraints and are not necessary in our analysis.

2.3 Java Card Exceptions

The LOOP project (see for example [9]) developed a tool to specify pre- and post-conditions for Java methods. It provides static verification that a program will not throw certain kind of exception. Our aim is to provide a mechanism dedicated to object sharing and to ensure that a program will not throw a security exceptions with a static analysis. Moreover, an important contribution of our analysis is to provide context inference for Java Card programs. In our case, the developer do not have any information to specify nor source code annotation to write.

3 Sharing Analysis

3.1 Aim and Principles of the Analysis

The aim of the analysis is to determine if an access to an object may throw a security exception or not. So, we have to compare, for each access to an object (field access, field update or method invocation), the creation context of this object and the execution context of the instruction we are analysing. Statically, we infer a set of possible creation contexts (abstract context) for every location containing objects. We suppose that the analysed bytecode is correct that is to say, a program that would be rejected by the type checker can not be analysed.

3.2 Overview of the Analysis

In order to make context inference, we extract from the bytecode of the program a set of *inequations*. These inequations represent the dependencies between Abstract Contexts (AC) and are obtained from data dependencies by adding relations between contexts, for example between current method context and the context of an allocated object upon a new instruction,

We need to define temporary variables named *ACVariable* to denote locations before an AC has been inferred.

$M \in Methods$

$T \in ACVariable ::= M.Local[i] \mid M.Return \mid label \mid ACVariable.field$

Where $M.Local[i]$ is the *ACVariable* denoting the abstract contexts of the ith local variable of method M. $M.Return$ is an *ACVariable* corresponding to the object returned by method M. *label* is a variable corresponding to an object allocation bytecode (we write $(new\ A)^{label}$). There should be a unique label for each **new** instruction. $ACVariable.field$ denotes the AC of the field *field* of the objects corresponding to *ACVariable*.

The analysis determines an AC for every *ACVariable* which has been created. Then, for each object access bytecode, we compare object's AC set with the set of possible execution contexts to find instructions which may throw a security exception.

The analysis consists of five steps:

1. Establish dataflow information from the bytecode. Here we obtain a partial dataflow graph which does not take into account possible aliases between objects.
2. Add dataflow dependencies due to possible aliases. After this step, we must obtain a relation $x \rightarrow_F y$ which can be read as "every value stored in x can be stored in y".
3. Create context flow graph from the dependence graph. This step consists in adding to dataflow some context dependencies specific to Java Card security policy (e.g. the context of an object is the context of the method which instantiates it).
4. Infer an abstract context for each location representing an object. That means find the smallest solution of constraints expressed by the context flow graph.
5. Abstractly execute the bytecode to determine which object accesses may throw a security exception or not.

Alike a control flow insensitive algorithm, the context inference presented here does not take into account the order of instructions. In fact order of instructions are only useful to determine the abstract execution stack. This could be improved by other techniques like aliasing [2] or shape analysis [11] which would generally be more complicated and slower. Our analysis is based on type inference like algorithm. The dataflow information obtained here is sufficient in order to make type inference (they could be seen as some kind of type constraints). Then, the abstract context obtained could be considered as a type.

3.3   Abstract Stack

In table 1, we describe the action of each bytecode instruction on the abstract stack. The stack is represented by a list of *ACVariables*. In the following, CM is the method currently analysed.

Table 1. Abstract execution of bytecode

$$aload\ i \vdash S \rightarrow CM.Local[i] :: S \quad (1)$$

$$astore\ i \vdash T :: S \rightarrow S \quad (2)$$

$$getfield\ f \vdash T :: S \rightarrow T.f :: S \quad (3)$$

$$putfield\ f \vdash T_v :: T :: S \rightarrow S \quad (4)$$

$$(new\ A)^T \vdash S \rightarrow T :: S \quad (5)$$

$$invokeVirtual\ M_0 \vdash T_k :: .. :: T_0 :: S \rightarrow M_0.Return :: S \quad (6)$$

$$invokeStatic\ M_0 \vdash T_k :: .. :: T_0 :: S \rightarrow M_0.Return :: S \quad (7)$$

$$invokeShareable\ M_0 \vdash T_k :: .. :: T_0 :: S \rightarrow M_0.Return :: S \quad (8)$$

$$Return \vdash T :: S \rightarrow S \quad (9)$$

The signature of the abstract stack definition rules is :
$Instruction \vdash ACVariable^* \rightarrow ACVariable^*$
For instance $ins \vdash s_1 \rightarrow s_2$ means that the abstract execution of ins on the abstract stack s_1 produces the abstract stack s_2.

3.4 Dataflow Analysis

In order to make a sharing analysis, we first need dataflow information to be able to infer an AC. We compute a dataflow graph from source bytecode. $\rightarrow_F$ is the dataflow dependence relation. It is a transitive relation on *ACVariable*. $x \rightarrow_F y$ must be read as every value stored in x can be stored in y.

The rules presented in table 2 describe how a set of dependence constraints can be extracted from the program source. Every affectation (explicit or implicit) is interpreted as a dataflow constraint.

In order to take into account the dynamic binding without analysing the possible types of each variable, we added a relation $M \leq M'$ defined in rules 17 and 18 which is the reflexive extension of the overloading relationship. Then every invocation of a method M' can dynamically invoke the method M. This implies the data flow dependencies expressed in the rules 12, 14 and 15.

3.5 Aliasing

The relation we have obtained with the rules above does not really correspond to a complete dataflow dependence relation. Indeed, some aliases between references may cause additional dataflow edges. If two locations may reference the same object then any object modifications on one location may act on the other. That is why we define the alias relation $\leftrightarrow_A$ on *ACVariable*.

Table 2. Data flow rules

Rules related to affectations:

$$\frac{astore\ i \vdash T :: S \to S}{T \to_F CM.Local[i]} \quad (10)$$

$$\frac{putfield\ f \vdash T_v :: T :: S \to S}{T_v \to_F T.f} \quad (11)$$

$$\frac{invokeVirtual\ M \vdash T_k :: .. :: T_0 :: S \to S' \quad \wedge \quad M_0 \leq M}{\forall i \in 0 \ldots k, T_i \to_F M_0.Local[i]} \quad (12)$$

$$\frac{invokeStatic\ M \vdash T_k :: .. :: T_0 :: S \to S'}{\forall i \in 0 \ldots k, T_i \to_F M.Local[i]} \quad (13)$$

$$\frac{invokeShareable\ M \vdash T_k :: .. :: T_0 :: S \to S' \quad \wedge \quad M_0 \leq M}{\forall i \in 0 \ldots k, T_i \to_F M_0.Local[i]} \quad (14)$$

$$\frac{Return \vdash T :: S \to S' \quad \wedge \quad CM \leq M}{T \to_F M.Return} \quad (15)$$

Transitivity:

$$\frac{T \to_F T' \quad \wedge \quad T' \to_F T''}{T \to_F T''} \quad (16)$$

Method overloading:

$$\frac{Method2\ \text{redefines}\ Method1}{Method2 \leq Method1} \quad (17)$$

$$M \leq M \quad (18)$$

The table 3 defines an alias relation $\leftrightarrow_A$ and the influence of aliasing on dataflow graph. $\leftrightarrow_A$ is a reflexive relation. It determines whether two *ACVariable* may represent references which may be aliased. The rules 19 and 20 corresponds to this definition of aliasing. Moreover field access expressions of aliased variables are aliased (21). The last rule (22) correspond to effects of aliases on dataflow: if two objects are aliased then a field update on one object may update the other one.

Table 3. Aliasing

$$\frac{T\to_F T' \quad \wedge \quad T\to_F T''}{T'\leftrightarrow_A T''} \quad (19)$$

data flow $\Rightarrow$ aliasing

$$\frac{T\to_F T'}{T\leftrightarrow_A T'} \quad (20)$$

alias $\Rightarrow$ fields alias

$$\frac{T\leftrightarrow_A T'}{T.x\leftrightarrow_A T'.x} \quad (21)$$

Alias acts upon field update:

$$\frac{T\leftrightarrow_A T' \quad \wedge \quad T''\to_F T.x}{T''\to_F T'.x} \quad (22)$$

3.6   Context Flow

Given a dataflow graph, we need to add context information to infer abstract contexts. We define Context Variables

$V \in ContextVariable ::= T \mid M.CC \mid (T \cap M.CC) \mid Package$

Where $M.CC$ represent the execution context (current context) of method M. Dynamically, the current context can be included in the current frame properties. A new frame is created when a method is invoked. As we decided to have one AC for each variable of the program, we only need to have an abstract current context by method.

The table 4 presents the specification of context additional properties. Context flow($\sqsubset_c$) is obtained from data flow by adding creation context and context switch information. In our simplified bytecode, context switch can occur only if a shareable interface method is called. Then, we obtain a context flow graph which express constraints between $ACVariable$ due to dataflow or context dependencies. $\sqsubset_c$ is a transitive relation between ContextVariables. $x \sqsubset_c y$ must be read as abstract context of x is included in abstract context of y.

Table 4. Context flow

---

dataflow $\Rightarrow$ context inclusion

$$\frac{T \to_F T'}{T \sqsubseteq_c T'} \quad (23)$$

Object creation context:

$$\frac{(newC)^T \vdash S \to T :: S}{CM.CC \sqsubseteq_c T} \quad (24)$$

Applet context:

$$\frac{\begin{array}{c} \text{applet A is defined in package } Package \quad \wedge \\ \text{M corresponds to install, process, (de)select or} \\ \text{getShareableInterfaceObject} \end{array}}{Package \sqsubseteq_c M.CC} \quad (25)$$

Current context propagation for method invocation:

$$\frac{invokeVirtual\ M_0 \vdash T_k :: .. :: T_0 :: S \to M_0.Return :: S}{(T_0 \cap CM.CC) \sqsubseteq_c M_0.CC} \quad (26)$$

$$\frac{invokeStatic\ M_0 \vdash T_k :: .. :: T_0 :: S \to M_0.Return :: S}{CM.CC \sqsubseteq_c M_0.CC} \quad (27)$$

$$\frac{invokeShareable\ M_0int \vdash T_k :: .. :: T_0 :: S \to M_0.Return :: S}{T_0 \sqsubseteq_c M_0.CC} \quad (28)$$

Transitivity:

$$\frac{V_1 \sqsubseteq_c V_2 \quad \wedge \quad V_2 \sqsubseteq_c V_3}{V_1 \sqsubseteq_c V_3} \quad (29)$$

Context intersection :

$$\frac{P \sqsubseteq_c V_1 \quad \wedge \quad P \sqsubseteq_c V_2}{P \sqsubseteq_c (V_1 \cap V_2)} \quad (30)$$

The rule 25 initialises the context of applet specific methods with their definition package. This corresponds to the fact that the JCRE instantiates and activates an applet in a context corresponding to the package of applet definition.

The rule 26 could be simplified by only requiring $CM.CC \sqsubseteq_c M_0.CC$ or $T_0 \sqsubseteq_c M_0.CC$ which would be correct but less precise. It is the role of the type checker to verify that $T_0 = CM.CC$. Thus requiring $(T_0 \cap CM.CC) \sqsubseteq_c M_0.CC$ is only useful when the sharing checking can not determine whether an exception could be raised by the *invokeVirtual* statement or not. In this case, we consider in the rest of the analysis that no exception has been raised by this method invocation.

3.7   Context Inference

Context inference consists in determining an AC for each *ContextVariable*. From the context flow graph, the AC of a *ContextVariable* V is given by the set of all packages P such that $P \sqsubseteq_c V$. Leaves of context flow graph should be packages. We can not infer contexts from other kind of leaves which would correspond for example to instructions which would never be executed. An AC is a set of type Packages.

$$AC ::= Package^*$$
$$C \; : \; ContextVariable \rightarrow AC$$
$$C(Package) \; = \; \{Package\}$$
$$C(V) \; = \; \bigcup_{P \sqsubseteq_c V} P$$

$C(V)$ is the AC inferred for the *ContextVariable* V. It gives the smallest set verifying the constraints expressed in the context flow graph.

3.8   Sharing Checking

This step looks like a type checking phase. It classifies the accesses to the object in three categories:

- The instructions that will never throw a security exception. This case occurs when:
  - both execution and object accessed contexts are identical singletons.
  - the instruction is a method invocation on a shareable interface or a JCRE entry point.
- The instructions that may throw a security exception: intersection of execution and object accessed contexts is non empty.
- The instructions that will always throw a security exception: intersection of execution and object accessed contexts is empty.

This step consists of an abstract execution of each instruction of the programs. It behaves like a classical type checker but returns a classification of the instructions accessing to objects (`getfield`, `putfield`, `invokeVirtual`) in accordance with the categories defined above and the security policy of the Java Card firewall.

3.9 Sharing Analysis of Java Card Programs

In order to analyse real Java Card programs within our implementation, the most important characteristics that have been added to the analysis formally presented above are the following.

Manipulations of simple data do not generate constraints but we need to have an *ACVariable* to represent them in the stack. One *ACVariable* for every simple type constant and variables is sufficient.

As for Arrays, they are abstracted by a unique variable. That is sufficient when all elements belong to the same context.

For conditional branches we need to make a union of abstract stacks at each junction point. In order to do this, we only replace abstract stack at this point by an abstract stack composed of new *ACVariable* and add new dataflow relations between abstract values before the junction and *ACVariable* at the junction.

Exceptions have not been implemented at all in our analysis. As our analysis is insensitive to control flow, analysing exception would be simple. Indeed the point where the exception can be thrown is not important for our analysis.

4 Implementation, Performance, and Results

4.1 The Cap Tool Framework

The Cap Tool (figure 1) is a tool taking cap files (Java Card bytecode) and returning a structured and linked program. It provides visualisation of the byte-code of each method and a bytecode interpreter. We use this linked version of bytecode to implement our analysis. We have implemented a simple sharing analysis on the bytecode language except exception handling. The results of the analysis are integrated to the bytecode as comments. Every instruction accessing to object is annotated with OK if it is sure, ??? if an exception may be thrown or ERROR if the access will always throw a security exception.

4.2 Examples of Results

Figure 2 gives an example to illustrate the sharing analysis mechanism. It defines two applets, a class A and its shareable interface. These applets have been analysed by our type inference mechanism. The results of the analysis have been inserted in the code comments. Figure 1 shows the results of the analysis of method applet0.process.

In figure 2, there are 4 instructions accessing to objects. In instruction **1**, an object can be instantiated in two different contexts and the result is control flow dependant. It is impossible to determine whether an exception will be thrown or not. In instruction **2**, our analysis can not infer that aa is always instantiated in the calling context. A more precise version of our analysis, for example control flow dependant analysis or an analysis which would analyse a method twice if it is executed in two different contexts could improve this result.

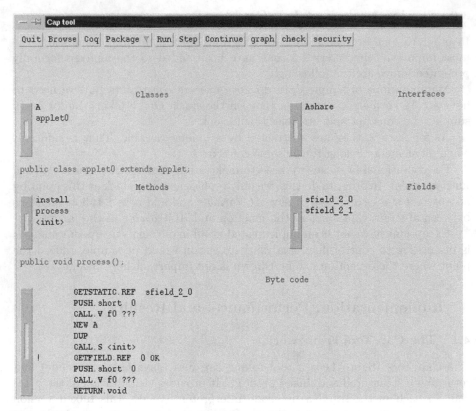

Fig. 1. The Cap Tool and partial results of the analysis
The Bytecode is a part of the method *process* of class *Applet0* of figure 2

In instruction **3** the object is accessed in his creation context. And in instruction **4** it is accessed through a `shareable` interface. In these two cases our analysis verify that no security exception will be thrown.

This example shows some interesting cases and limitations of our analysis. A lot of cases where our analysis can not determine whether a security exception can be raised or not could only be improved by taking into account the control flow corresponding to the program. For example we could greatly improve our analysis by duplicating the bytecode of some functions and analysing it twice depending on the execution context. Such a solution is in fact a mean of improving the interprocedural analysis.

```
package applet0;
import javacard.framework.*;

public interface Ashare
    extends Shareable{

  public void f0(byte e);
}
```

(a) AShare.java

```
package applet0;

public class A implements Ashare{
    public A aa;
    public A() {
        aa=this;
    }
    public void f0(byte e){
    }
}
```

(b) A.java

```
package applet0;
import javacard.framework.*;

public class applet0
    extends Applet {

  public static A a;
  public static Ashare shareA;

  public static void install(A a0) {
    a=new A();
    shareA=new A();
  }

  public void process()    {
    a.f0((byte)0); // **1**
      // a  may be instantiated
      // by applet1 -> ???
    (new A()).aa.f0((byte)0);//**2**
      // aa can be modified in
      // constructor A which can be
      // called from applet1 -> ???
    }
}
```

(c) Applet0.java.

```
package applet1;
import javacard.framework.*;
import applet0.*;

public class applet1
    extends Applet {

  public static void install() {
    A b=new A();
      // b is instantiated in
      // the context of applet1
    b.aa=applet0.a; //**3**
      // acces to b in the
      // context of applet1 -> OK
    (new applet1()).process();
  }

  public void process()    {
    applet0.a=new A();
      // can change the
      // context of field a
      // of applet0
    applet0.shareA.f0((byte)3);//**4**
      // access to shareable
      //interface -> OK
    }
}
```

(d) Applet1.java

Fig. 2. Example of analysed code

5   Conclusion

We have presented a sharing analysis for Java Card language. It is based on a type inference like analysis. Indeed contexts could be considered as some kind of types and a security exception as an incompatibility between such types. Our analysis abstracts the dynamic context by a set of possible contexts. It is based on the Java Card bytecode but could be implemented on Java Card language as well.

Our objective is to help the developer to design complex sharing mechanisms. We provide him the list of instructions that may throw a security exception. The developer will only have to focus on these instructions in order to determine whether they may really throw a security exception or not. Moreover, we give him the set of possible creation contexts for each variable and the set of possible execution contexts for each method of the analysed applets.

In order to improve our analysis, we can duplicate some method. For example, we could create an instance of a method for each possible execution context. This would make us analyse more functions but could greatly improve the precision of our analysis on some crucial locations.

References

1. Zhiqun Chen. How to write a java card applet: A developer's guide. http://www.javaworld.com/javaworld/jw-07-1999/jw-07-javacard_p.html. 44
2. A. Deutsch. Interprocedural may-alias analysis for pointers: Beyond k-limiting. In *SIGPLAN'94 Conf. on Programming Language Design and Implementation*, pages 230–241, Orlando (Florida, USA), June 1994. ACM. SIGPLAN Notices, 29(6). 46, 47
3. Alain Deutsch. A storeless model of aliasing and its abstractions using finite representations of right-regular equivalence relations. In *Proceedings of the IEEE 1992 International Conference on Computer Languages*, pages 2–13, San Francisco, April 1992. IEEE Press. 46
4. Alain Deutsch. Semantic models and abstract interpretation techniques for inductive data structures and pointers. In *Proceedings of the ACM SIGPLAN Symposium on Partial Evaluation and Semantics-Based Program Manipulation*, pages 226–229, La Jolla, California, June 21–23, 1995. 46
5. Anup K. Ghosh. Security risks of java cards. In *Proceedings of the Twelfth IFIP WG 11.3 Working Conference on Database Security*, Greece, 1999. 44
6. Pierre Girard. Which security policy for multiapplication smart cards. In *Proceedings of the USENIX Workshop on Smartcard Technology (SMARTCARD-99)*, pages 21–28, Berkeley, CA, May 10–11 1999. USENIX Association. 44
7. Nevin Heintze. Set constraints in program analysis. Technical report, Carnegie-Mellon University, July 1993. 46
8. Michael Montgomery and Ksheerabdhi Krishna. Secure object sharing in java card. In *Proceedings of the USENIX Workshop on Smartcard Technology (SMARTCARD-99)*, pages 119–128, Berkeley, CA, May 10–11 1999. USENIX Association. 44
9. Erik Poll, Joachim van den Berg, and Bart Jacobs. Specification of the JavaCard API in JML. In *Fourth Smart Card Research and Advanced Application Conference (IFIP Cardis)*. Kluwer Academic Publishers, 2000. 46
10. M. Sagiv, T. Reps, and S. Horwitz. Precise interprocedural dataflow analysis with applications to constant propagation. *Lecture Notes in Computer Science*, 915:651–??, 1995. 46
11. Mooly Sagiv, Thomas Reps, and Reinhard Wilhelm. Parametric shape analysis via 3-valued logic. Technical Report CS-TR-1998-1383, University of Wisconsin, Madison, August 1998. 46, 47
12. M. Sharir and A. Pnueli. Two approaches to interprocedural data flow analysis. 1981. 46
13. SUN microsystems. Java card 2.1 platform api specification. http://java.sun.com/products/javacard/htmldoc/index.html. 44
14. SUN microsystems. Java card 2.1 runtime environment (jcre) specification. http://java.sun.com/products/javacard/JCRESpec.pdf. 44

15. SUN microsystems. Java card 2.1 virtual machine specification.
    http://java.sun.com/products/javacard/javacard21.html.   45
16. SUN microsystems. Java card applet developper's guide.
    http://java.sun.com/products/javacard/AppletDevelopersGuide.html. 44
17. Robert Tolksdorf. Programming languages for the java virtual machine.
    http://grunge.cs.tu-berlin.de/ tolk/vmlanguages.html.   45

Automated Test and Oracle Generation
for Smart-Card Applications*

Duncan Clarke, Thierry Jéron, Vlad Rusu and Elena Zinovieva
{dclarke|jeron|rusu|lenaz}@irisa.fr

IRISA/INRIA Rennes, Campus de Beaulieu, Rennes, France

Abstract. We present work we are engaged in to develop symbolic test
generation techniques and apply those techniques to testing of smart
card applications. Beginning with (1) a system specification and (2) a
test purpose expressed as symbolic labelled-transition-systems, we automatically derive tests to check conformance of an implementation to the
behaviors of the specification selected by the test purpose. We present
an example taken from a case-study we are developing based on the
application of these techniques to the CEPS e-purse specifications.

1   Introduction

After decades of research into techniques for formal system specification,
test generation, notions of test coverage, and methods for automating the
evaluation of test results, the practice of software testing remains largely
unchanged for most software developers. A developer familiar with the
informal requirements for an application designs test cases in an ad-hoc
fashion, runs those tests against an implementation, and compares the
outputs of the implementation to his or her intuition regarding what the
requirements dictate for the associated test case. Human-centric testing
methodologies like this (1) are prone to error, (2) make poor use of existing
formal specifications, and (3) make poor use of human resources.

Indeed, researchers and developers working in some specific problem
domains have noted these facts, and taken steps to establish development methods with a sound formal basis that are open to automation.
One of the most successful such efforts to date is in specification and
conformance testing of protocols [ISO92]. In protocol specification and
conformance testing a formal model of the protocol is created using a well-
defined formalism with a sound mathematical basis such as SDL [IT94]

---

* Supported in part by DYADE action FormalCard, a joint project of INRIA and
Bull/CP-8.

I. Attali and T. Jensen (Eds.): E-smart 2001, LNCS 2140, pp. 58-70, 2001.

or LOTOS [ISO88], a conformance criterion [Tre94] is defined to establish exactly what it means for an implementation to conform to its specification, and a set of tests can be generated that have the ability to check conformance by driving a system under test through a desired sequence of states and comparing replies received to expected values. These techniques are developed to the point that several tools for the automatic creation of such test suites are available, including TorX [BFdV⁺99], TGV [JM99] and TestComposer [KJG99].

Our work is an attempt to leverage the ideas underlying protocol conformance testing and high-efficiency test generation as embodied in the TGV tool, to automate the generation of tests for a more general class of applications. TGV, like most existing formal analysis tools, performs its analysis by enumerating the specification's state space. This leads to two significant problems when generating tests for large-scale systems: (1) state space explosion, as the variables in the specification are instantiated with all of their possible values, and (2) tests that are not readily understandable by humans when represented by a large network of states and transitions in a pure labelled transition system. To avoid these problems we are applying symbolic techniques to perform our analysis.

In [RdBJ00] the authors presented a method for the generation of symbolic test cases from system specifications and test purposes expressed in the Input/Output Symbolic Transition System (IOSTS) formalism. The models used are symbolic in the sense that items represented by variables over data domains in the control and computation steps of the specification remain variables in the generated tests. At no point in the analysis is it necessary to enumerate the state space of the specifications, test purposes or generated tests.

In addition to the elimination of the need for state space enumeration, the principal benefits of this approach are four-fold: (1) The derivation of tests *and* oracles from formal, operational specifications can be fully automated; (2) The tests are symbolic in the variables and parameters of the specification, so a single test can be generated and applied to implementations based on different specification parameter values; (3) The resulting tests are concrete, in the sense that once parameters are instantiated the tests can be translated easily to a test language and applied directly to real implementations (provided the model and the system under test are compatible at the interface level); and (4) the theory underlying the derivation of tests guarantees certain desirable properties, such as correctness and completeness of verdicts relative to the given test purpose.

Recent work by Martin and du Bousquet shares our goal of automation of test generation for smart-card applications. In [MdB00] they describe a testing methodology for smart card applications based on UML specifications, the use of TGV for on-the-fly test generation, and translation of TGV-generated tests to Java code for the creation of executable tests. There are three important points of contrast between their approach and ours: (1) They present their work using high-level UML specification models; at present our methods are based on the low-level IOSTS formalism, which will ultimately be used as an intermediate representation format. (2) The use of TGV for test generation introduces a risk of state space explosion if there are large data domains for inputs of the tester; the technique we describe is all symbolic, so there is no risk of state space explosion. And (3), TGV requires parameter values to be bound to individual values before test generation; the technique we describe allows system parameters to be bound to values as late as test execution time.

The remainder of this paper is structured as follows: Section 2 briefly describes the IOSTS formalism and an overview of symbolic test generation. Section 3 presents a brief example demonstrating the application of symbolic test generation to one feature described in the CEPS [CEP00] e-purse specifications. Section 4 describes the tool we are developing to automate symbolic test generation from formal specifications down to executable C++ test code. Section 5 closes the paper with summary remarks.

2   Symbolic Test Generation

Test generation is a program-synthesis problem: starting from the formal specification of a system under test and from a test purpose describing a set of behaviors to be tested, compute a reactive program that observes an implementation of the system to detect non-conformant behavior, while trying to control the implementation towards satisfying the test purpose. In this section we briefly describe our approach [RdBJ00] for generating symbolic test cases in the form of extended input-output automata.

The model. IOSTS (Input-Output Symbolic Transition Systems) are a model for reactive programs with symbolic processing of variables, parameters, and inter-process value passing. Several examples of IOSTS are given in the figures of Section 3. The syntax and semantics are formally defined in [RdBJ00]. We use IOSTS for describing specifications, test purposes, and test cases, and assume nothing about the black-box implementation other than that it is interface-compatible with the specification. Furthermore, we restrict our attention here to specifications and implementations that are *command-response*, meaning that an input, or sequence of inputs, may only be followed by at most one output (*i.e.*, a command is followed by at most one response), and there are no infinite loops of internal actions.

The IOSTS notation is rather low-level and is mainly convenient for processing by machine as done in symbolic test generation. For specifying systems at the user level, we plan to use a higher-level language which translates automatically to IOSTS (cf. Figure 1). The part of the diagram within the dashed box corresponds to the current status of the test generation tool. We also plan to incorporate mechanisms to automatically compute test purposes from, e.g., coverage criteria [RW85].

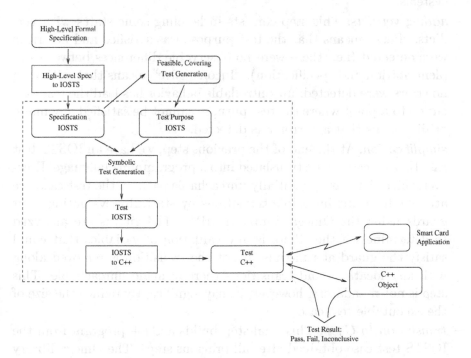

Fig. 1. Symbolic Test Generation Process.

The process. Symbolic test generation consists in computing, from specification and test purpose, a test case that covers all the behaviors of the intersection of these two elements. Then, the test case is translated into executable code to be run on the black-box implementation. Test generation consists of the following steps.

- *product* between test purpose and specification. This allows the selection of a subgraph of the specification that formally leads to the satisfaction of the test purpose. That is, only the subgraph leading to accepting states of the test purpose is kept. Here "formally" refers to the fact that symbolic variables and parameters are not interpreted, thus, actual reachability of the accepting states is not guaranteed. This problem is addressed in the simplification step.

- *closure* and *determinization* of the product. This operation attempts, through a set of heuristics, to produce a trace-equivalent system that has no (or fewer) internal actions and is deterministic. The heuristics will successfully terminate when applied to command-response systems.

- *adding verdicts.* This step consists in labeling some states with verdicts. "Pass" means that the test purpose was satisfied and no errors were detected (i.e., there were no observable differences between implementation and specification). "Inconclusive" means that, although no errors were detected, uncontrollable behavior has lead the test execution to a point where the test purpose cannot be satisfied any more. "Fail" means that an error was detected.

- *simplification.* At the end of the previous step, we have an IOSTS test case that is ready to be translated into a programming language. However, since there are potentially unreachable parts in the test case, we attempt to prune infeasible transitions by statically evaluating their guards using the Omega library [KMP+]. The guards are analyzed to determine whether there is any valuation of variables that could satisfy the guard at run-time. If not the transition is removed along with any locations and transitions thereby made unreachable. This step is not mandatory, however, it may significantly reduce the size of the executable test case.

- *translation to C++.* This final step builds a C++ program from the IOSTS test case obtained after all previous steps. The Omega library [KMP+] is called whenever there is a need to compute values to instantiate a symbolic output. The program is then ready to be compiled and linked with the implementation for test case execution.

Correctness of test cases. In [RdBJ00] we prove that the generated IOSTS test cases have, by construction, a set of correctness properties, meaning essentially that they do not produce false "Pass", "Fail" and "Inconclusive" verdicts. Furthermore, every test case generated from a given specification and test purpose has a *relative completeness* property, meaning that a "Fail" verdict will be produced in every circumstance where the implementation exhibits a non-conformance with the specification in a behavior targeted by the test purpose.

3   Example

In this section we present a brief example of symbolic test generation based on a feature of the CEPS e-purse specifications. CEPS (Common Electronic Purse Specifications) is a standard for creating inter-operable multi-currency smart card e-purse systems. The feature that we will generate tests for is the "CEP Inquiry - Slot Information" specified in Section 8.7.1 of the CEPS technical specifications[CEP00]. This feature provides a means for iterating through the slots, where each slot corresponds to one currency and its respective balance. The number of currency slots in the purse is implementation dependent, and the number of slots actually loaded with currency can vary during use, so a generic iteration scheme is provided for viewing each slot in turn. The specification requires that each currency be returned exactly once followed by an end-of-data marker. The order in which currencies are returned is unspecified and implementation dependent.

As described in Section 2, the process of test generation consists of (1) creating an IOSTS specification, (2) creating an IOSTS test purpose, and (3) generating an IOSTS test. We begin with the specification.

The specifications. Figure 2 presents the part of the IOSTS model of the CEPS specifications that describes iterative extraction of slot information from the card's point of view. The IOSTS is made up of locations and transitions. Transitions are decorated with their guard expressions, their input or output action (preceded by a "sync" keyword), and their assignments (using the ":=" notation for assignment). A transition is firable when its guard is satisfied and a complementary action is offered by the environment for synchronization. Transitions labelled with action "tau" are internal actions that can fire without synchronizing with the environment.

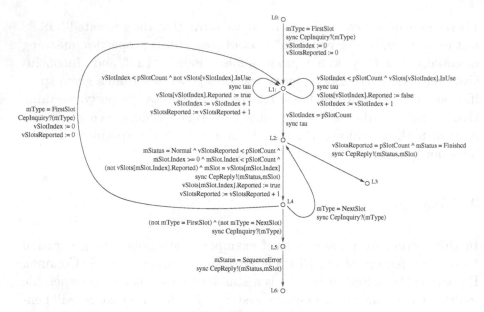

Fig. 2. Specification

The terminal to card interface for CEPS is based on command/response pairs, so the interaction between terminal and card begins with a CepInquiry command with a parameter mType equal to FirstSlot (*i.e.*, the transition from L0 to L1). After receiving this command the application performs internal computations to initialize the array of slot information (vSlots), marking slots that are in use as ready for reporting (*i.e.*, vSlots[...].Reported := false). This array has parametric size specified as pSlotCount. The initialization is in essence a "for" loop on variable vSlotIndex from zero to pSlotCount minus one at location L1.

When vSlotIndex reaches pSlotCount, an internal action is executed, taking the application to location L2 where it is ready to send its first reply and, if applicable, accept commands requesting subsequent slots. If the card has zero slots to report (*i.e.*, there are no currencies stored in the card), a reply with status "Finished" is sent (transition from location L2 to location L3) and the feature has completed its processing. If the card has one or more currencies to report, the transition from location L2 to location L4 is taken, returning the balance of one slot to the requester and marking that slot as having been reported.

At location L4 the application waits for the next balance request command, returning to location L2 when it is received. Receiving a "FirstSlot" command at this point will re-initialize the iteration (transition L4

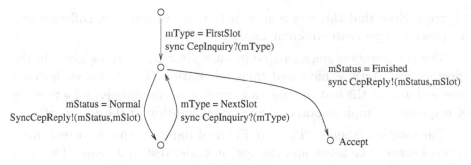

Fig. 3. Test Purpose

to L1). If a command other than "FirstSlot" or "NextSlot" is received a sequence error is generated (transition L4 to L5 to L6).

The test purpose. A test purpose is used to select the behaviors from the specification that are to be exercised by the derived test. Figure 3 illustrates a test purpose that selects from the CEPS slot inquiry feature a test that exercises a single iteration through all the slots of the card, uninterrupted by sequence errors or re-starting of the iteration.

The test purpose is also an IOSTS, with locations and transitions. The generation of tests takes place through the computation of a product between the specification IOSTS and the test purpose IOSTS. Thus, locations in the test are pairs made up of a location from the specification and a location from the test purpose, and transitions between these locations are added when (1) a specification transition action has the same label as a test purpose action (resulting in a guard that is the intersection of the specification and test purpose transition guards), or (2) the specification is capable of advancing on an internal action (with the guard taken directly from the specification edge). The location "Accept" in the test purpose indicates locations in the test IOSTS that should be interpreted as final, indicating successful execution of the test.

The test purpose of Figure 3 was constructed to select behaviors that (1) begin with a "FirstSlot" command, (2) loop as many times as necessary to process all slots, and (3) accept behaviors that conclude with a "Finished" reply. When there are no slots loaded with currency in the purse "Finished" may correctly be generated without any "Normal" replies being generated.

The test. Finally, Figure 4 shows the IOSTS that results from symbolic test generation using the specification of Figure 2 and test purpose of

Figure 3. Note that this test is specific to this test purpose. Different test purposes will generate different tests.

The computation steps carried out are identical to those given in the specification. Actions have had their orientation (*i.e.*, input vs. output) reversed so that the test becomes a generator of commands and a receiver of responses, complementary to an implementation of the specifications.

The location labelled "Pass" in Figure 4 indicates that a correct interaction between the tester and the system under test took place. The symbolic test generation method also generates transitions from every location to a new location "Fail" that absorb incorrect responses from the system under test and lead to the "Fail" state, indicating non-conformance of the implementation. For the sake of clarity of presentation, only one of these transitions is shown in detail in the figure. In fact each possible erroneous input action the tester could receive generates a transition to "Fail" from each location of the graph.

Note that the test shown in Figure 4, like all tests generated by this method, incorporates its own oracle. All of the computation steps necessary to verify the correctness of numeric results are extracted from the specification and used by the tester to verify arguments as they are received. This is in contrast to test generation techniques that simply produce a sequence of inputs to drive the implementation through a specific path.

4   Test Automation

A goal of our work is to produce a fully automated process for symbolic test generation and execution, from high-level specifications down to executable test programs. Our present work is focused on test generation from IOSTS (a formal model intended as an intermediate representation) down to C++ test objects. In this section we present a summary of tool support for test generation, and outline the test execution phase

Tool Support. The test derivation technique described in Section 3 is implemented in a tool called "Symbolic Test Generator," or simply STG. This tool currently implements the functions outlined by a dashed box in Figure 1. This includes (1) reading and parsing IOSTS specifications expressed in a dialect of IF [BFG+99], (2) computing an IOSTS test case from an IOSTS specification and IOSTS test purpose according to the theory of [RdBJ00], and (3) translation of the IOSTS test case to C++,

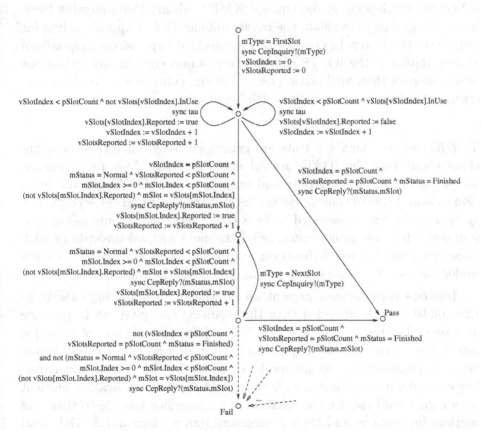

Fig. 4. Test

ready to be compiled, linked to an interface-compatible implementation, and executed.

The inputs of the tool, (1) the IOSTS specification and (2) the IOSTS test purpose(s), are constructed manually by the system engineer using a text editor. Ultimately our goal is to create these inputs automatically based on a pre-existing formal high-level specification model, and higher level descriptions of test objectives such as coverage criteria.

For translation of test cases to executable code the guard expressions of system inputs are limited to formulas in Presburger arithmetic. This is because we depend on the Omega [KMP$^+$] library (for analyzing Presburger formulas) to evaluate the constraints and select specific values for outputs of the tester. In practice this means that expressions on guards of system inputs in the IOSTS specification cannot contain any operations more complex than arithmetic (*I.e.,* addition, subtraction, relational operators, boolean operators) or multiplication by constant factors.

Test Execution The C++ tests are generated based on various assumptions about how the IOSTS model maps into the C++ programming language. For example, inputs and outputs of the IOSTS become function calls and return values, respectively, in the generated C++ code. The system under test is assumed to be a C++ class, and inputs to the system under test are implemented as synchronous method invocations with messages passed through function arguments. The reply of the system under test is the received return value of the method invocation.

Implementations that present an interface corresponding exactly to this model can be compiled with the resulting test program to produce an executable test. Other systems will require the creation of a simple intermediate module that implements the interface described and translates communication into the model expected by the system under test. For example, in the smart card domain, testing of an application resident on a card would require the creation of an interface module to translate method invocations and their parameters into a command APDU, send the APDU to the card over the terminal-to-card interface, wait for the reply APDU, interpret the reply APDU and return the reply value(s) to the method's caller.

Once a test and interface-compatible system are compiled together into executable code, the actual execution of the test consists of (1) supplying any parameter values that are required by the model, and (2) observing the final verdict of the test: "pass," "inconclusive" or "fail."

5 Summary

This paper has presented a symbolic test generation technique which has been successfully applied to test generation for smart card applications. The symbolic generation technique (1) automatically derives test cases in order to check conformance of an implementation with respect to the behavior of a specification selected by the test purposes; (2) automatically determines whether the results of the test execution are correct with respect to the specification. It performs test derivation as a symbolic process, up to and including the generation of test program source code. The reason to use symbolic techniques instead of enumerative is that symbolic test generation allows us to produce (1) more general test cases with parameters and variables which should be instantiated only before the test cases execution, and (2) test cases that are more readable by humans. We presented an example based on the application of these techniques to a feature of the CEPS e-purse specifications.

We are currently using the IOSTS language and STG to develop a large-scale case study based on the CEPS specifications. The IOSTS graphs presented in Section 3 are a small part of the current model, which will ultimately include all of the command processing functions of the CEPS specifications. During the development of this model, STG is being used to incrementally test a prototype implementation of the specifications.

Other directions for our future work include, firstly, the use a higher-level language (*e.g.*, LOTOS, SDL, etc.) for specifying systems at the user level. Second, we plan to work on the implementation of a mechanism to automatically compute test purposes from the system specification using, for example, coverage criteria instead of test purposes written by hand. Third, we continue to work on simplification of test cases, as we want to reduce the size of test cases, which would result in reduced execution time, improved readability, elimination of paths leading to "Inconclusive" verdicts, etc. There are two directions to solve the problem: (1) the test cases could be simplified using automated static analysis and proof strategies; or (2) the test cases could be derived from an abstraction of the system specification instead of the concrete specification.

References

[BFdV+99] A. Belinfante, J. Feenstra, R. de Vries, J. Tretmans, N. Goga, L. Feijs, and S. Mauw. Formal test automation: a simple experiment. In *International*

Workshop on the Testing of Communication Systems (IWTCS'99), pages 179–196, 1999.

[BFG⁺99]   M. Bozga, J.-C. Fernandez, L. Ghirvu, S. Graf, J.P. Krimm, and L. Mounier. If: An intermediate representation and validation environment for timed asynchronous systems. In *Proceedings of World Conference on Formal Methods, FM'99*, volume 1708 of *LNCS*, pages 307–327, Toulouse, France, September 1999. Springer-Verlag.

[CEP00]   CEPSCO. Common Electronic Purse Specifications, Technical Specification (http://www.cepsco.org), May 2000.

[ISO88]   ISO/IEC. LOTOS - a formal description technique based on the temporal ordering of observational behaviour. Technical Report 8807, International Organization for Standards - Information Processing Systems - Open Systems Interconnection, 1988.

[ISO92]   ISO/IEC. International Standard 9646-1/2/3, OSI-Open Systems Interconnection, Information Technology - Open Systems Interconnection Conformance Testing Methodology and Framework, 1992.

[IT94]   ITU-T. Recommendation Z-100. Specification and Description Language (SDL), 1994.

[JM99]   T. Jéron and P. Morel. Test generation derived from model-checking. In *Computer Aided Verification (CAV '99)*, volume 1633 of *LNCS*, pages 108–122, 1999.

[KJG99]   A. Kerbrat, T. Jéron, and R. Groz. Automated test genration from S-DL specifications. In *Proceedings of SDL Forum*. Elsevier Science (North Holland), 1999.

[KMP⁺]   W. Kelly, V. Maslov, W. Pugh, E. Rosser, T. Shpiesman, and D. Wonnacott. The Omega library interface guide. Available at http://www.cs.umd.edu/projects/omega.

[MdB00]   H. Martin and L. du Bousquet. Automatic test generation for java-card applets. In *Proceedings of the Java-Card Workshop*, Cannes, September 2000.

[RdBJ00]   Vlad Rusu, Lydie du Bousquet, and Thierry Jéron. An approach to symbolic test generation. In *International Conference on Integrating Formal Methods*, volume 1945 of *Lecture Notes in Computer Science*, pages 338–357, Dagstuhl, Germany, November 2000. Springer-Verlag.

[RW85]   Sandra Rapps and Elaine J. Weyuker. Selecting software test data using data flow information. *IEEE Transactions on Software Engineering*, SE-11(4):367–375, April 1985.

[Tre94]   J. Tretmans. A formal approach to conformance testing. In *The 6th International Workshop on Protocol Test Systems*, number C-19 in IFIP Transactions, pages 257–276, 1994.

An Internet Authorization Scheme
Using Smart-Card-Based Security Kernels

Yves Deswarte, Noreddine Abghour, Vincent Nicomette, and David Powell

LAAS-CNRS,
7 avenue du Colonel Roche, 31077 Toulouse Cedex 4, France
{Yves.Deswarte,Noreddine.Abghour,Vincent.Nicomette,David.Powell}@laas.fr

Abstract. This paper presents an authorization scheme for applications distributed on the Internet with two levels of access control: a global level, implemented through a fault- and intrusion-tolerant authorization server, and a local level implemented as a security kernel located on both the local host Java Virtual Machine (JVM) and on a Java Card connected to this host.

1   Introduction

Today, most Internet applications are based on the client-server model. In this model, typically, the server distrusts clients, and grants each client access rights according to the client's identity. This enables the server to record a lot of personal information about clients: identity, usual IP address, postal address, credit card number, purchase habits, etc. Such a model is thus necessarily privacy intrusive.

Moreover, the client-server model is not rich enough to cope with complex transactions involving more than two participants. For example, an electronic commerce transaction requires usually the cooperation of a customer, a merchant, a credit card company, a bank, a delivery company, etc. Each of these participants has different interests, and thus distrusts the other participants.

Within the MAFTIA[1] project, we are developing authorization schemes that can grant to each participant fair rights, while distributing to each one only the information strictly needed to execute its own task, i.e., a proof that the task has to be executed and the parameters needed for this execution, without unnecessary information such as participant identities. These schemes are based on two levels of protection:

- An *authorization server* is in charge of granting or denying rights for high-level operations involving several participants; if a high-level operation is authorized, the authorization server distributes capabilities for all the elementary operations that are needed to carry it out.

---

[1] MAFTIA (Malicious- and Accidental-Fault Tolerance for Internet Applications) is a European project of the IST Program. MAFTIA partners are University of Newcastle upon Tyne (GB), prime contractor, DERA(GB), IBM Zurich Research Lab. (CH), LAAS-CNRS (F), University of Lisbon (P) and University of Saarland (D). See http://www.maftia.org/.

I. Attali and T. Jensen (Eds.): E-smart 2001, LNCS 2140, pp. 71-82, 2001.
© Springer-Verlag Berlin Heidelberg 2001

- On each participating host, a *security kernel* is responsible for fine-grain authorization, i.e., for controlling the access to all local resources and objects according to the capabilities that accompany each request. To enforce hack-proofing of such security kernels on off-the-shelf computers connected to the Internet, critical parts of the security kernel will be implemented on a Java Card.

In the following sections, the general authorization architecture and the security kernel are described, and an illustrative example is presented. Finally, our approach is compared to related work.

2   General Authorization Architecture

In [Nicomette & Deswarte 1997], we proposed a generic authorization scheme for distributed object systems. In this scheme, an application can be viewed at two levels of abstraction: high-level operations and method executions. A high-level operation corresponds to the coordinated execution of several object methods towards a common goal. For instance, printing file F3 on printer P4 is a high-level operation involving the execution of a *printfile* method of the spooler object attached to P4, which itself has to request the execution of the *readfile* method of the file server object managing F3, etc.

A request to run a high-level operation is authorized or denied by an authorization server, according to *symbolic rights* stored in an access control matrix managed by the authorization server. More details on how the authorization server checks if a high-level operation is to be granted or denied are given in [Nicomette & Deswarte 1996] and [Abghour *et al.* 2001]. If the request is authorized, capabilities are created by the authorization server for all the method executions needed to realize the high-level operation. These capabilities are simple method capabilities if they are used directly by the object requesting the execution of the high-level operation, i.e., used by this object to directly call another object's methods. Alternatively, the capabilities may be indirect capabilities or *vouchers*, if they cannot be used by the calling object but must be delegated to another object that, itself, will invoke other object methods to participate in the high-level operation. In fact, the notion of high-level operation is recursive, and a voucher can contain either a method capability or the right to execute a high-level operation.

This delegation scheme is more flexible than the usual "*proxy*" scheme, by which an object transmits to another object some of its access rights for this delegated object to execute operations on behalf of the delegating object. Our scheme is also closer to the "*least privilege principle*", since it helps to reduce the privileges needed for performing delegated operations. For instance, if an object O is authorized to print a file, it has to delegate a *read-right* to the spooler object, for the spooler to read the file to be printed. To delegate this read-right, with the proxy scheme, O must possess this read-right; so O could misuse this right by making copies of the file and distributing them. In this case, the read-right is a privilege much higher than a simple print-right. In our scheme, if O is authorized to print a file, O will receive a *voucher* for the spooler to read the file, and a capability to call the spooler. The voucher, by itself, cannot be used by O. With the capability, O can invoke the spooler and transmit the voucher to the spooler. The spooler can then use the voucher as a capability to read the file.

Since only high-level operations are managed by the authorization server, it is relatively easy to manage: the users and the security administrators have just to assign the rights to execute high-level operations, they do not have to consider all the elementary rights to invoke object methods. Moreover, since only one request has to be checked for each high-level operation, the communication overhead can be reduced.

The authorization server is a trusted-third-party (TTP), which could be a single-point-of-failure, both in case of accidental failure, or in case of successful intrusion (including by a malicious administrator). To prevent this, with the MAFTIA authorization architecture [Abghour *et al.* 2001], the authorization server will be made fault- and intrusion-tolerant: an authorization server is made of diverse security sites, operated by independent persons, so that any single fault or intrusion can be tolerated without degrading the service. The global architecture is given by Figure 1.

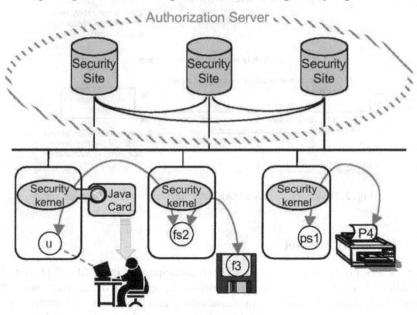

Fig. 1. Authorization architecture

The dialogue between a MAFTIA object and the authorization server may typically be the following one:

Object O asks the authorization server for the authorization to carry out an operation in the system. This operation may be the simple invocation of a particular method of a particular object or may be a "high-level operation" that requires the collaboration between several objects in the system.

In the first case, if object O is authorized to carry out the operation, it receives a capability. This capability will be presented and checked by the security kernel located on the site of the invoked object.

In the second case, the user may receive capabilities and vouchers. Capabilities are directly used by object O to invoke particular methods of particular objects. Vouchers are not used by object O but are delivered to object O for objects that are involved in the realization of the high-level operation (e.g., a capability for 0' to invoke a method m of object O", as a part of the high-level operation). These vouchers will thus be transferred by object O to other objects, which will then realize their part of the high-level operation thanks to these vouchers. A voucher may be a capability or the right to realize another high-level operation.

The following figure summarizes this protocol:

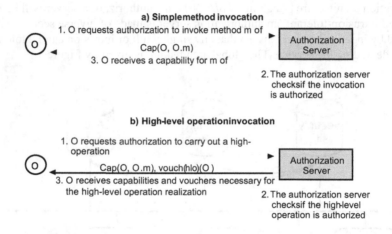

Fig. 2. Protocol between a MAFTIA object and the authorization server

3   Security Kernel

There is a security kernel on each host participating in a MAFTIA-compliant application. The security kernel is responsible for granting or denying local object method invocations, according to capabilities and vouchers distributed by the authorization server. In the context of wide-area networks (such as the Internet), the implementation of such a security kernel is complicated since, due to the heterogeneity of connected hosts, it would be necessary to develop one version of the security kernel for each kind of host. Moreover, since the hosts are not under the control of a global authority, there is no way to ensure that each host is running a genuine security kernel, or the same version thereof. This is why we have chosen to implement them by using Java Cards.

3.1   Implementation

A security kernel in the context of a MAFTIA site is composed of a local Java Virtual Machine (JVM), a Java Card and a Dispatcher. The Dispatcher is a local object that always runs on each MAFTIA site and that is in charge of dispatching remote requests to the local objects (a more precise description is given in the next section). There is no specific requirement for the local JVM, it may be the JVM of a browser such as Netscape or Internet Explorer for instance. This JVM must simply be compliant with JDK1.2 and thus able to check a signature (for a signed class).

The Java Card has the responsibility of deciding whether or not to authorize the invocation of particular methods on particular objects on the local host by checking that the corresponding capabilities are presented. These checks represent the central part of the authorization scheme, and thus have to be protected as strongly as possible. We have chosen to implement them on a Java Card, which we consider as sufficiently tamperproof. In particular, any software, even that within an operating system or a JVM, can be copied and modified by a malicious user who possesses all privileges on a local host. In particular, on Internet, any hacker can easily have these privileges on his own computer! With capability checks run on the Java Card, we can be sure that any remote request to execute a MAFTIA-application is genuine (if the capability is correct), and that a genuine MAFTIA request can only be executed on the host for which the capability is valid. The hacker's privileges on his host gives him no privilege outside that host.

The capability checks carried out by the Java Card are based on strong cryptographic functions. Several cryptographic keys must be included in the Java Card:

- The MAFTIA public key, that we note PKm (this key is associated to the MAFTIA private key SKm, which is not stored in the Java Card);
- A private/public key pair specific to the Java Card, that we note SKj, PKj;
- The authorization server public key, PKas (this key is associated to the private key of the authorization server, SK_{as}).

The role of these cryptographic keys is explained in Section 3.3.

3.2   Programming Paradigm

Each MAFTIA application is implemented by means of a set of Java classes. Each MAFTIA object is thus a Java object loaded by a local JVM. The interaction between objects is realized through Java RMIs (Remote Method Invocations). All parameters (including capabilities, vouchers and returned values) are thus exchanged between objects by passing messages corresponding to these Java RMIs.

Each dispatcher is known by the authorization server and all requests to objects on a site must be intercepted by the local dispatcher. Then, each capability or voucher created by the authorization server and returned to an object requesting to carry out an operation in the system, is accompanied by the reference of the corresponding dispatcher. The object that receives this capability or voucher must invoke the dispatcher and present it the capability it has received from the authorization server. The capabilities are checked using the cryptographic functions included in the Java card, as explained in the next section.

3.3   Protocol

A distributed MAFTIA application is executed by means of method invocations between MAFTIA objects located on MAFTIA-compliant hosts. The objects are signed off-line by the global MAFTIA private key SK_m, and this signature is checked by the local JVM of the host (since version 1.2, the Java Development Kit includes software that allows classes to be signed and the signatures to be checked at load time).

As explained in the previous section, invocations are conveyed between objects by message passing. When an object is authorized to invoke a particular method of a particular object, it invokes the dispatcher of the corresponding site and gives it the capabilities received from the authorization server that authorize this access (see Step 1 of Figure 3).

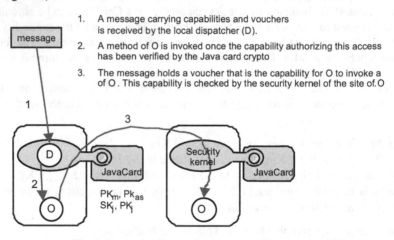

1. A message carrying capabilities and vouchers is received by the local dispatcher (D).

2. A method of O is invoked once the capability authorizing this access has been verified by the Java card crypto

3. The message holds a voucher that is the capability for O to invoke a of O. This capability is checked by the security kernel of the site of.O

Fig. 3. Example of a voucher corresponding to a capability

Capabilities are ciphered by the public key PK_j of the local Java Card and signed by the private key SK_{sa} of the authorization server. The capability signature must first be verified using the authorization server's public key, and then deciphered by the cryptographic functions of the Java Card using the private key SK_j, which is stored only in the Java Card. Each access to a method of an object on a MAFTIA site is thus controlled by its local Java Card. This verification corresponds to step 2 of Figure 3.

The invocation message may contain vouchers. As explained before, a voucher may be a capability or the authorization to carry out a high-level operation in the system. A voucher is not used by the object requesting the operation but is delegated to another object involved in the realization of the current operation.

If the voucher is a capability, this capability is thus ciphered by the public key of the corresponding Java Card and thus, will be checked by the corresponding security kernel. Step 3 of Figure 3 presents an example of such a voucher.

If the voucher is the authorization to realize a high-level operation, it is transmitted to another object, which uses this voucher in the following way: the voucher is presented to the authorization server as a proof that the object is authorized to realize a particular operation (step 3 of Figure 4). The authorization server simply checks the validity of this voucher and then delivers to the object the corresponding capability and vouchers.

1. A message carrying capabilities and vouchers is received by the local dispatcher (D).

2. A method of O is invoked once the capability authorizing this access has been verified by the Java card crypto functions.

3. The message holds a voucher that is the right for O to carry out a high-level operation. This voucher is presented to the authorization server in order to obtain the corresponding capabilities and vouchers.

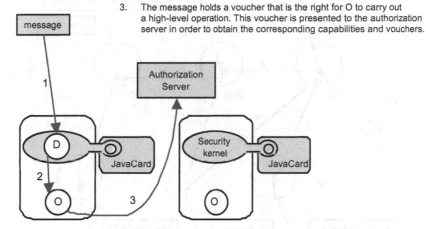

Fig. 4. Example of a voucher corresponding to a high-level operation right

4 A Healthcare Example

In the following example, we consider that a doctor wants to transfer a copy of a patient medical file to another healthcare professional. The set of objects that take part in the execution of this high-level operation are presented in Figure 5. In this figure, U is a doctor, V is another healthcare professional (with role HCP)[2], DBS (of class $DATABASESERVER$) is a database server, Pmf (of class $PATIENTMEDICALFILE$) is the medical file of a patient of Doctor U. $MTA1$ and $MTA2$ are mail transport agents, which are given the responsibility to transmit electronic mail. The class of these objects is MTA. Finally, tf is a transient file located on the site of DBS.

Using delegation of rights through vouchers, a sufficient access control matrix is given in the following table:

Table 1. Access control matrix

	...	HCP Role	{Pmf(U)}
U		TPmf({Pmf(U)}, this)	read, write, TPmf (this, HCP Role)
DBS	...		
...			

---

[2] We also use the notations U and V to designate the objects representing these persons in the information system.

The scenario that enables U to transfer a copy of a patient medical file to another healthcare professional is described here. We indicate in this scenario the functions of the authorization server and the security kernels with respect to capability distribution and verification.

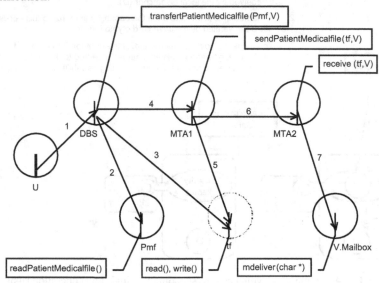

Fig. 5. Example of a high-level operation

User U wants to transfer a patient medical file to a user V. The user U asks the authorization server for the authorization to execute the high-level operation *transferPatientMedicalfile (Pmf, V)*. The authorization server checks that in the access matrix, U's row holds sufficient symbolic rights to grant the authorization of this operation (see footnote 2). In this case, U has the symbolic right *TPmf* for any user with the role *HCP* (HealthCare Professional), and for the *Pmf* of all U's patients[3]. Since V is a healthcare professional, *TPmf (Pmf, Role (V))* and *TPmf (PatientMedicalFile, V)* are both authorized and the high-level operation authorization has to be granted.

Consequently, the authorization server transfers the following privileges to user U[4]:

{   *Cap (U, DBS.transferPatientMedicalfile (Pmf, V)),*
        [Cap (DBS, Pmf.readPatientMedicalfile ())],
        [Cap (DBS, MTA1.sendPatientMedicalfile (char *, V)],
        [R (deliverPatientMedicalfile)(MTA1, char *, V)]   }

---

[3]   *{Pmf(U)}* represents the set of the medical files of all patients of Doctor U. In this access control matrix, U also possesses the rights to invoke methods *read* and *write* of any object in the set *{Pmf(U)}*.

[4]   *Cap(O, O'.m())* denotes the capability for object O to invoke method m of object O'. *[Cap(O', O''.m())]* represents a voucher containing the capability for O' to invoke method m of object O''. *[R(hlo)(O', <parameters>)]* represents a voucher containing the right for O' to realize the high-level operation *hlo*. This voucher notation *[X]* is equivalent to the notation vouch(*X*) in Figure 2.

- *Cap (U, DBS.transferPatient*Medicalfile (Pmf, V)) is the capability for U to invoke DBS's method transferPatientMedicalfile with parameters corresponding to the specific patient medical file Pmf and to the heathcare professional V.
- The voucher [Cap (DBS, Pmf.readPatientMedicalfile ())] represents the capability for the database server DBS to read the patient medical file.
- The voucher [Cap (DBS, MTA1.sendPatientMedicalfile (char *, V)] represents the capability for the database server DBS to send a patient medical file to V.
- The voucher [R (deliverPatientMedicalfile)(MTA1, char *, V)] represents the right for the mail transport agent *MTA1* to perform a high-level operation *deliverPatientMedicalfile (char *, V)*. This voucher is accompanied by the capability to invoke *transferpatientmedicalfile* and returned to the object authorized to carry out the action *transferPatientMedicalfile (Pmf, V)*. This object will transfer the voucher to *DBS*, which will transmit it to *MTA1* when it wants to carry out a high-level operation *deliverPatientMedicalfile (char *, V)*.

U invokes method *transferPatientMedicalfile* of *DBS*. This invocation carries the capability *Cap (O, DBS. transferPatientMedicalfile (Pmf, V))* and the 3 vouchers (message 1). The invocation authorization is checked by the security kernel located on the site of *DBS*, which verifies that the capability is valid.
DBS then invokes method *readPatientMedicalfile* to read the patient medical file *Pmf* and presents the voucher received previously from U (message 2). The security kernel located on *Pmf*'s site checks the validity of the capability
Cap (DBS, Pmf.readPatientMedicalfile ()).
DBS receives data from the patient medical file and creates a temporary file *tf* to be used by *MTA1*. When creating *tf*, *DBS* receives the owner capability on this file from its local security kernel. Then *DBS* copies *Pmf* into *tf* by the way of message 3 (the write access to *tf* is authorized because *DBS* presents the owner capability to the security kernel).
DBS asks the security kernel to create capabilities for *MTA1* to access *tf* methods *read* and *delete* (by presenting the owner capability to the security kernel). Using the voucher [*Cap (DBS, MTA1.sendPatientMedicalfile)(char *, V))*] received from U, *DBS* invokes method *sendPatientMedicalfile* of *MTA1* and transfers *tf read* and *delete* capabilities and the voucher [*R (deliverPatientMedicalfile)(MTA1, char *, V)*] to *MTA1* for it to perform the high-level operation *deliverPatientMedicalfile (tf, V)* (message 4). The security kernel located on the site of *MTA1* controls the invocation by checking the capability *Cap (DBS, MTA1.sendPatientMedicalfile)(char *, V))*.
MTA1 asks the authorization server for the authorization to execute the high-level operation *deliverPatientMedicalefile (tf, V)* and presents the voucher received from *DBS*.
The authorization server checks that the voucher presented by *MTA1* is valid (i.e., is a right for *MTA1* created by the authorization server). Then the authorization server identifies *MTA2* as the mail transport agent for *V*, and finally gives *MTA1* the privileges corresponding to the action *deliverPatientMedicalfile (tf, V)*, which are { *Cap (MTA1, MTA2.receive (char *, V.))*, [*R (deliver)(MTA2, char *, V)*] }.
[*R (deliver)(MTA2, char *, V))*] is a voucher that has to be delegated to *MTA2* to perform the high-level operation *deliver.*

MTA1 calls method *read* of *tf* (message 5). This invocation is controlled by *tf*'s local security kernel, which checks that *MTA1* holds the capability for method *read* of *tf*. Then *MTA1* invokes method *receive(<content of tf>, V)* of *MTA2* (message 6). Once this method has been invoked, *MTA1* sends a request to delete *tf*. The security kernel located on the site of *MTA2* checks the validity of the capability
*Cap (MTA1, MTA2.receive (char *, V.))*.

MTA2 asks the authorization server for the authorization to execute the operation *deliver* on *V*'s mailbox and presents the voucher [*R (deliver)(MTA2, char *, V))*] received from *MTA1*.

The authorization server first checks that the voucher is valid, and gives *MTA2* the capability *Cap (MTA2, VMailbox.mdeliver(char *))*, enabling it to invoke the method *mdeliver* of the object *Vmailbox* corresponding to *V*'s mailbox (message 7).

5   Related Work

The basic authorization scheme was developed in [Nicomette 1996]. This work was the first attempt to introduce the voucher delegation scheme, and to demonstrate its ability to implement closely the least privilege principle.

Other schemes have been recently introduced to provide more flexibility and more efficiency than the client-server model. In particular, [Ao *et al.* 2001] proposes to carry out access control in a distributed system by means of "communal laws". This paper addresses also the problem of revocation, which is not directly addressed in our scheme, even if an expiry time can be included in our capability and vouchers. However it seems that the scheme presented in [Ao *et al.* 2001] may be difficult to implement.

The notion of "authorization server" is now relatively common when consistent access control has to be implemented in distributed systems. Even some public key infrastructure (PKI) implementations, such as SPKI [Ellison 1999], can be seen as a kind of authorization service. In the same way, Kerberos V5 Ticket Granting Server [Neuman & Tso 1994] and SESAME Privilege Attribute Services [Parker 1991], manage some authorization, but only at a coarse-grain level, for client-server interactions. Delta-4 [Blain & Deswarte 1990] proposed also an authorization service, which has been implemented to control access to a persistent file storage service. Delta-4 was also the first attempt to implement fault- and intrusion-tolerant security services. Other recent authorization server implementations are the HP Praesidium [HP 1998] and Adage [Zurko *et al.* 1999].

Concerning the use of smart cards for authorization, let us cite [Au *et al.* 2000] which proposes to use smart cards as portable, tamperproof storage for authorization tokens delivered by an authorization server and checked by an "authorization manager" (the equivalent of our security kernel) on each application server. In their approach, the smart card is not used to implement the authorization manager of the application server, it is just used to store the authorization token. JCCap [Hagimont & Vandewalle 2000] proposed the use of capabilities to manage access controls between applications located on Java Cards, but their capabilities are defined statically by means of "views" during program development, rather than created dynamically by an authorization server. We consider that our approach is more flexible and closer to the least privilege principle.

6   Conclusion

The authorization scheme presented in this paper is flexible, easily managed (at the coarse-grain level of "high-level operations"), and efficient (fine grain access control at the object method invocation level, tamperproof security kernels implemented with Java Cards). Moreover, it is not privacy intrusive, since personal information is disclosed to participants only on a "need-to-know" basis.

Since the implementation has just begun, no performance measurements are currently available. But since the authorization server is accessed only once for each high-level operation, we hope that the induced overhead will be acceptable with respect to the gained security and privacy.

Acknowledgement

This study is partially supported by the MAFTIA project of the European IST Programme (RTD Research Project IST-1999-11583). For more information, visit http://www.maftia.org/.

References

[Abghour et al. 2001] N. Abghour, Y. Deswarte, V. Nicomette and D. Powell, *Specification of Authorisation Services*, MAFTIA Project IST-1999-11583 Contract Report, LAAS-CNRS, N°01.001, Jan. 2001, <http://www.maftia.org/deliverables/D27V13.pdf>.

[Ao et al. 2001] X. Ao, N. H. Minsky and V. Ungureanu, "Formal Treatment of Certificate Revocation Under Communal Access Control", in *IEEE Symposium on Security and Privacy,* (Oakland, CA), pp.116-127, IEEE Computer Society Press, 2001.

[Au et al. 2000] R. Au, M. Looi and P. Ashley, "Cross-Domain One-Shot Authorization using Smart Cards", in *7th ACM Conference on Computer and Communications Security (CCS-2000),* (S. Jajodia and P. Samarati, Eds.), (Athens, Greece), pp.220-226, ACM Press, 2000.

[Blain & Deswarte 1990] L. Blain and Y. Deswarte, "Intrusion-Tolerant Security Server for Delta-4", in *ESPRIT 90 Conference,* (CEC-DG-XIII, Ed.), (Brussels (Belgium)), pp.355-370, Kluwer Academic Publishers, 1990.

[Ellison 1999] C. Ellison, *SPKI Requirements,* IETF, RFC 2692, September 1999, pp.

[Hagimont & Vandewalle 2000] D. Hagimont and J.-J. Vandewalle, "JCCap: Capability-Based Access Control for Java Card", in *4th IFIP WG8.8 Working Conference on Smart Card Research and Advanced Applications (CARDIS-2000),* (J. Domingo-Ferrer, D. Chan and A. Watson, Eds.), (Bristol, UK), pp.365-388, Kluwer Academic Publishers, 2000.

[HP 1998] HP, *HP Praesidium Authorization Server 3.1: Increasing Security Requirements in the Extended Enterprise,* November 2, 1998, accessible at the following URL:
<http://www.hp.com/security/products/authorization_server/papers/whitepaper/>.

[Neuman & Tso 1994] B. C. Neuman and T. Tso, *"Kerberos: an Authentication Service for Computer Networks"*, IEEE Communications, 32 (9), 1994.

[Nicomette 1996] V. Nicomette, *La protection dans les systèmes à objets répartis,* Thèse de Doctorat de l'Institut National Polytechnique de Toulouse, LAAS Report 96496, 1996, (in French).

[Nicomette & Deswarte 1996] V. Nicomette and Y. Deswarte, "Symbolic Rights and Vouchers for Access Control in Distributed Object Systems", in *Proc. 2nd Asian Computing Science Conference (ASIAN'96),* (Singapour), LNCS n°1179, pp.193-203, Springer-Verlag, 1996.

[Nicomette & Deswarte 1997] V. Nicomette and Y. Deswarte, "An Authorization Scheme for Distributed Object Systems", in *Proc. Int. Symposium on Security and Privacy,* (Oakland, CA, USA), pp.21-30, IEEE Computer Society Press, 1997.

[Parker 1991] T. Parker, "A Secure European System for Applications in a Multi-vendor Environment (The SESAME project)", in *14th National Computer Security Conference,* (Washington (DC, USA)), pp.505-513, NCSC and NIST, 1991.

[Zurko *et al.* 1999] M.-E. Zurko, R. Simon and T. Sanfilipo, "A User-Centered, Modular Authorization Service Built on an RBAC Foundation", in *IEEE Symposium on Security and Privacy,* (Berkeley (CA, USA)), pp.57-71, 1999.

Turning Multi-applications Smart Cards Services Available from Anywhere at Anytime: A SOAP/MOM Approach in the Context of Java Cards

Didier Donsez[1], Sébastien Jean[2], Sylvain Lecomte[1], and Olivier Thomas[1]

[1] University of Valenciennes, LAMIH/ROI
Le Mont Houy, BP 311, 59313 Valenciennes Cedex 9, France
{didier.donsez,sylvain.lecomte}@univ-valenciennes.fr
[2] University of Lille, LIFL/RD2P
Bat. M3/111, 59655 Villeneuve d'Ascq Cedex, France
sebastien.jean@lifl.fr

Abstract. This paper presents a way to improve smart card integration in distributed information systems. Multi-application smart cards are able to offer a lot of services, but at the same time they are mainly disconnected. Our main goals are to ease the use of such services and to increase their availability. In order to reach them, we propose a JMS-SOAP based platform that enables remote clients both to discover what services a smart card provides and to request any service either synchronously and asynchronously.

1 Introduction

Four years ago, Java Cards induced a revolution in smart cards world. With Java Cards, smart card application design is no more a specialist job. Although smart card application *Time-to-Market* was before about 6 months long, every programmer familiar with the Java language and technology is now able to write and ship his first smart card application in few days. Consequently, open smart cards boosted smart card use.

Even if Java Cards are mostly involved in simple client-servers applications, one of the most promising role for open smart cards in distributed informations systems is to act as mobile agents or application servers. Emerging technologies consider World Wide Web as a universal medium for interoperable services deployment, discovery and use. We think that open smart cards, and particularly Java Cards, can smartly take a place in such a model. Nevertheless, smart cards are disconnected most of their lifetime, even if SIM[1] cards (in mobile phones) are exceptions. This feature of smart cards has to be taken into account. In this paper, we present how multi-applications smart cards, and distributed applications in which they are involved, can take benefits of middlewares that provide interoperability and asynchronous messaging.

---

[1] Subscriber Identification Module

I. Attali and T. Jensen (Eds.): E-smart 2001, LNCS 2140, pp. 83–94, 2001.
© Springer-Verlag Berlin Heidelberg 2001

Next Section briefly presents SOAP and related technologies as well as Message Oriented Middlewares (MOM). After this overview, Section 3 takes a look at five years of Java Cards application model evolution. Then, Section 4 explains why and how to involve Java Cards in heterogeneous information systems where exchanges are synchronous or not, and gives implementation issues. Finally, Section 5 concludes and presents future work.

2   MOMs and Services over the Web

In this Section, we discuss technologies and concepts involved in our proposal. We briefly overview MOM technology and present emerging standards for deploying and using services aver the Web.

2.1   Message Oriented Middlewares

Message Oriented Middlewares (MOM) [1] are based on asynchronous messages as the single structure for communication, coordination and synchronization, thus allowing desynchronized execution of components. Reliable communication is guaranteed by message queuing techniques or specific communication protocols that can be added independently from the programming of software components. Asynchronous communication property decouples producers of information from consumers. They do not need to be both ready for execution at the same time. MOM's goal is also to maximize the portability of the transmission of messages between several applications.

JMS [2] is a specification of a MOM based on Java Technology. It defines a set of interfaces for messages queuing. JMS provides the application designers with two messaging models, as presented on Figure 1. The first is *Point-To-Point*, where a producer and one ore more consumers are highly coupled[2]. The other is *Publish-Subscribe*, where a producer delivers messages related to an existing topic and where consumers have just to subscribe in order to receive next messages of the subscribed topic. JMS is just a standard *de facto*, it is not a product by itself. However, there are a lot of commercial implementations compliant with this specification and a lot of open-source projects (as the example of JORAM[3]).

2.2   SOAP, UDDI and WDSL: Deploying Services over WWW

The World Wide Web was originally created to enable information exchange in a simple and portable way across the Internet. It resides in a combination of four elements:

1. HyperText Transport Protocol (HTTP), a client-server protocol on top of TCP-IP.
2. Uniform Resource Locator (URL), a universal binding system.

---

[2] However JMS, as a MOM, guarantees that a message is delivered only once even if several consumers are connected to the producer's queue

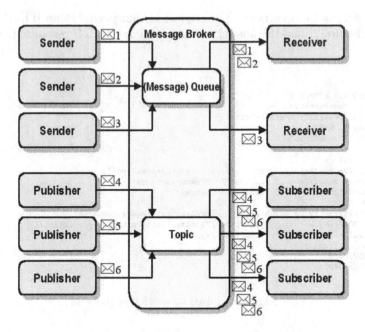

Fig. 1. Messaging models in JMS

3. HyperText Markup Language (HTML).
4. Web browsers.

From sharing information between scientists, WWW moved to mass market. Server-side Scripting technologies, like CGI (Common Gateway Interface), turned the Web as a universal medium for client-server applications. These technologies have however some drawbacks, like the hardness to manage sessions and the lack of interoperability. So, Client server programming over the web had to evolve to reach the goal of interoperability, simplicity and portability: the answer was SOAP.

SOAP [4] is a lightweight protocol for exchange of information in a decentralized, distributed environment. It is an XML based protocol that consists of three parts:

1. An envelope that defines a framework for describing what is in a message and how to process it.
2. A set of encoding rules for expressing instances of application-defined data types.
3. Conventions for representing remote procedure calls, responses and errors.

SOAP can potentially be used in combination with a variety of other protocols. However, the bindings defined for the moment describe how to use SOAP in combination with HTTP, and how to wrap RPC on SMTP and HTTP. An example of SOAP messages (transported with HTTP) is presented below, in the context of a quotation service. The request is transported in an HTTP's POST request (Figure 2) and the answer comes back in an HTTP response (Figure 3).

```
POST /StockQuote HTTP/1.1
Host: www.stockquoteserver.com
Content-Type: text/xml; charset="utf-8"
Content-Length: 478
SOAPAction: "/StockQuote"

<SOAP-ENV:Envelope
    xmlns:SOAP-ENV="http://schemas.xmlsoap.org/soap/envelope/"
    xmlns:xsi="http://www.w3.org/1999/XMLSchema-instance"
    xmlns:xsd="http://www.w3.org/1999/XMLSchema">
  <SOAP-ENV:Body>
    <m:GetLastTradePrice xmlns:m="http://www.stockquoteserver.com/ns"
          SOAP-ENV:encodingStyle="http://schemas.xmlsoap.org/soap/encoding/">
      <symbol xsi:type="xsd:string">DIS</symbol>
    </m:GetLastTradePrice>
  </SOAP-ENV:Body>
</SOAP-ENV:Envelope>
```

Fig. 2. Quotation service request

```
HTTP/1.1 200 OK
Content-Type: text/xml; charset="utf-8"
Content-Length: 490

<SOAP-ENV:Envelope
    xmlns:SOAP-ENV="http://schemas.xmlsoap.org/soap/envelope/"
    xmlns:xsi="http://www.w3.org/1999/XMLSchema-instance"
    xmlns:xsd="http://www.w3.org/1999/XMLSchema">
  <SOAP-ENV:Body>
    <m:GetLastTradePriceResponse xmlns:m="http://www.stockquoteserver.com/ns"
          SOAP-ENV:encodingStyle="http://schemas.xmlsoap.org/soap/encoding/">
      <Price xsi:type="xsd:float">34.5</Price>
    </m:GetLastTradePriceResponse>
  </SOAP-ENV:Body>
</SOAP-ENV:Envelope>
```

Fig. 3. Quotation service response

A service request using SOAP/HTTP is completed according to the followings steps:

1. the client builds the SOAP message, according to the service description
2. The SOAP message is encapsulated in an HTTP POST request and transported to the Web server hosting the service
3. The Web server forwards the SOAP message to an *RPC router* server-side script or servlet

4. The RPC router:
    (a) parses the SOAP message,
    (b) realizes the invocation,
    (c) gets the response,
    (d) sends back and HTTP response containing the SOAP response (normal or error)
5. The SOAP response is sent back to the client
6. The client parses the SOAP response and processes it

SOAP is an easy and extensible way to request services across the Web. It is independent from operating systems, programming languages and transport protocols. SOAP is not an object-oriented distributed system, there is no garbage collection neither object activation (parameters are not object references but values).

However, having a simple and interoperable way to request services is not useful if there is no way to know what a service looks like. UDDI and WSDL are recent standards that address this feature. The Universal Description, Discovery and Integration (UDDI) specification [5] describes a conceptual cloud of Web services and a programmatic interface that define a simple framework for describing any kind of Web service. The specification consists of several related documents and an XML schema that defines a SOAP-based programming protocol for registering and discovering Web services. WSDL [6] is an XML format for describing network services as a set of endpoints operating on messages containing either document-oriented or procedure-oriented information. The operations and messages are described abstractly, and then bound to a concrete network protocol and message format to define an endpoint. Related concrete endpoints are combined into abstract endpoints (services). WSDL is extensible to allow description of endpoints and their messages regardless of what message formats or network protocols are used to communicate, however, the only bindings described in WSDL documents describe how to use it in conjunction with SOAP 1.1, HTTP GET/POST, and MIME.

3   JavaCard and Its Integration in Information Systems

The arrival of Java Card [7], and others open smart cards like Smart Card for Windows (SCW) and Multos was a kind of revolution in the smart cards world. Java Card technology allows applets written in the Java language to be executed on a smart card, within the Java Card Runtime Environment (JCRE), and provides a wide API to help developers to create applets. Both JCRE and APIs are modeled after the smart card ISO 7816 specification [8]. Java Card offers code sharing between applets, isolation with a sandboxing mechanism called *applet firewall*, and comes with a cryptographic API. Java Card is the most widely accepted open smart card. This is firstly due to its symbiosis with an increasing Java computing world. The integration of Java Card Technology into mobile phone technology [9] is another key of its success.

As Scott Guthery titled in [10], Java Card was initially thought as a mobile platform for Internet Computing. Sometimes, like the example Java language originally dedicated to washing machines, technologies are not firstly used for what they have been though. Java Card is in this case, and four years after the first Java Card announcement it is not yet widely used for Internet purposes. The first applications of Java Cards were maybe loyalty ones. The application model was a client-server one, were the client is usually on the terminal where the card was plugged. Designing applications involving smart cards was originally not an easy task because the most part of the code was used to manage the communication between the card and the client parts of the application through the card reader. Hopefully, nowadays this task is much more easier using frameworks like OCF [11].

Even if Java Cards can offer helpful services in an off-line mode, their use takes another dimension if plugged over a wired or wireless network. Java card can then be seen as a mobile *physical* agent serving its owner and representing him over distributed information systems. Open smart card is a young technology, and for the it does not yet play this role. However, as what Weiser called *ubiquitous computing* becomes a reality, mobile services provider is the most promising future for Multi-application smart cards.

Interaction with Java Cards has been widely studied. All the mechanisms provided are however very similar because they consider the smart card as a server. Some researches have successfully turned the Java Card as a mobile Web server [12]. Close to the problematics of the WebSim project, The WebCard [13] is a Java Card applet implementing a lightweight IP/HTTP stack. WebCard is promising because it shows that a smart card can be seen as a traditional internet platform speaking IP. Morever, Schlumberger/Bull CP8 recently announces the commercialization of an HTTP based card named *iSimplify*. The two previous examples consider Java Cards like data servers, but another approaches try to integrate Java Cards as parts of distributed applications. A first example is the JC-RMI [14] technique that gives a Remote object view of embedded applets. It goes further in easing smart card application design, enabling for Java Cards the well known RMI tools used to build *classical* Java distributed applications. Here, applets as seen as Java remote objects. JC-RMI tools alleviate the burden of application designer by automatically generating stubs and skeletons. These proxies transparently manages the communication protocol and just let distributed object access to applets. One step more is Java Card and JINI enclosure. Some work, done [15] or still in progress [14], intends to turn Java Card applets into JINI-based services. In such an approach, when a Java Card is plugged somewhere, its services are automatically registered and become available for distributed applications that are able to discover them through JINI's lookup service. Once discovered, the services can be used as far as the smart card offering these services grant their access. Each step in open smart card integration in distributed information systems lets the card plays a smarter role. In the future, we argue that smart cards should be much more interactive and not only passive servers [16].

4 Toward a Generic, Dynamic, Asynchronous Access to Smart Card Services

4.1 Motivations

As the Java Card is becoming a more and more *common* computing platform, a simple and interoperable mechanism of interaction is needed in order to turn the embedded services available from any platform. Frameworks such as OCF [17] address such problem but reduce the platform range (here to Java-powered ones). Moreover, it might be interesting to assume service discovery and induced dynamic operation invocation. For example, when a smart card becomes plugged in a CAD that is part of the user's Personal Area Network (PAN), a daemon discovers what it is and what it can do. After this discovery time, the smart card authentication and privacy service is used to ensure trust in the user's PAN.

Aiming to ease integration of Java cards in a synchronous way is obvious. But, since smart cards are disconnected 99.9 percent of their lifetime, one has to consider this fact while using smart card in distributed applications. Some smart cards applications may be dedicated to work in an off-line mode. We give here two examples of such applications where the smart cards does not need to be permanently slotted. It can firstly be useful for a requester (which can be an application provider, a card issuer,...) to be able to alert the card or make updates when needed (i.e. not only when the smart card is connected). Card Management Systems (CMS) and Application Management Systems (AMS) now take an important place in smart card world because controlling and managing a fleet and thousands issued smart card that embed several evolving applications is not an easy task. Ideally, an AMS should not wait for smart card insertion to decide for application update. A better way should be to asynchronously notify smart cards that a later version of a given application has been issued and to automatically upgrade it if necessary. As a smart card is not able for the moment to emit request to a reference server in order to poll for updates, using an asynchronous messaging platform should be the easiest way to update applet version or personalization info for thousand cards at the same time. Another example is agenda management. Such an application does not need strong synchronization. The differents partners who want to meet do not need to wait each other to request an appointment. In this case, a software agent (representing the card) takes into account appointment requests when the card is disconnected. When the card slots again, waiting appointments are transmitted to the card service that confirms or cancels them.

4.2 Architecture and Prototype

In order to turn embedded services available to remote hosts, some requirements have to be fulfilled. We have to separate the transport part on the gateway from services requests on slotted cards. We have designed the architecture presented on Figure 4 to plug several transport layers on one side and several layers called SPI (Service Provider Interface) on the other side. SPIs introspect and invoke applications installed on slotted cards while transport layers exchange SOAP messages between clients and the gateways. The SOAP messages encapsulate the services requests and the belonging responses (that can be error messages in case of request mismatch) into XML messages transported from point to point (i.e. from remote host to a reference host for the smart card). In the case of synchronous requests, the transport protocol is mainly HTTP.

In the case of asynchronous requests, the SOAP messages are transported by SMTP/POP3 protocols or by a Message Broker that is JMS-compliant in the prototype. The *by-MOM* request requires message queues : one permanent queue per card and one temporary queue per client. The client firstly sends a SOAP message to the card queue. Next time the card is slotted, the gateway reads queued messages and invokes corresponding applets in the card. Responses are sent back to the client's temporary queue. In a similar manner, the SMTP/POP3 invocation requires one mailbox per card and one temporary mailbox for the client. The client firstly sends a SOAP message to the card mailbox through SMTP. Next time the card is slotted, the gateway downloads all received messages and invokes corresponding applets in the card. Responses are sent back to the client's temporary mailbox.

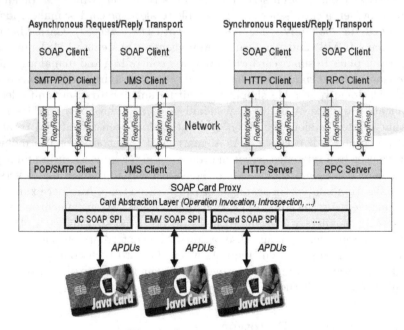

Fig. 4. Gateway Architecture

The second part of the gateway provides a generic mechanism to enable smart card services discovery as well as to invoke operations. We separate the concept of service from the one of card applet. A service offered by an open smart card can involve one or several applets (for example, a gambling service can be provided using a dedicated applet using a banking one for payment issues). The two previous generic functions are done by a Service Provider. The Service Provider is dependent of the card type and fits SOAP messages according to the card profile. The SPI is loaded as the card is slotted. The first task of SPIs is to manage card introspection and services descriptions. Turning services requests dynamic means that the embedded services interfaces must be known or discovered at invocation time. So, in other words, service introspection has to be provided.

We propose two different ways to get introspection. The first way is to store services descriptions on smart cards or on remote repositories (see Figure 5, left). Due to interoperability issues, descriptions are represented according to an XML DTD grammar that is closed to WSDL and UDDI. When the card is slotted, the SPI gather AIDs (Application IDentifiers) of installed applications. These AIDs are used by the SPI to retrieve services descriptions from a remote repository. Descriptions are used to transform SOAP messages from/to APDU commands (parameters marshalling, . . .). In this approach, services descriptions can be registered and replicated on several servers over the Web. Descriptions can be also cached locally by the gateway on which a card is slotted.

The second way consists to store services descriptions on the card itself (see Figure 5, right). This requires to add introspection facilities to the card. In the case of the Java Card, we propose to install a *repository* application that stores services descriptions. This application also stores the address and associated credentials of the card mailbox and queue. The gateway uses this information to get SOAP invocation messages and to invoke operations on the card. The *repository* is updated by the application installer when applications are installed or removed. This *repository* function should be one of function of the next generation smart card operating systems. This second approach is better in an off-line context since it avoids to get descriptions from the network.

A prototype been developed for testing purpose is based on the use of a GemXPresso 211 Java Card from Gemplus. The services invocations and responses are transported either synchronously with HTTP or asynchronously with a JMS-compliant MOM. The HTTP prototype is based on a subset of classes from Apache/SOAP package and Jakarta/Tomcat for servlet execution platform. The MOM prototype is based on JORAM [3], an open source implementation of JMS specification. This prototype has validated the previously presented architecture.

As described on Figure 5, a card-side SOAP proxy (implemented by a servlet) provides introspection and invocation facility. It relies on the use of OCF to manage readers and cards access. The discovery mechanism is implemented inside the card by the way of the Introspection applet that manages XML-based descriptions. The test application consists of a distributed client based on a Web interface that connects to a targeted Java Card, dynamically discovers inside applications (here, an agenda and a loyalty application) and invokes operations on them.

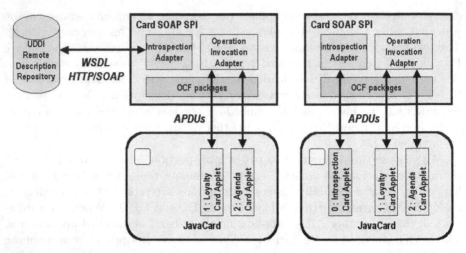

Fig. 5. Providers for Java Card using *on-the-web* application description (a) and *in-card* application description

5   Conclusion and Further Work

The objective presented in this paper is relevant with regard to necessities in communications. More and more services are available on the Internet as well as on mobile telephony. Smart cards take a more and more important place in services offering over these networks. To seamlessly integrate multi-application smart cards in order to turn them in common object-oriented execution platforms (regarding to client applications), interoperable operation invocations must be provided. As smart cards are not so frequently connected, the use of asynchronous messages can open new perspectives. In this paper, we have presented how to enable interoperability and asynchronism for distributed applications that involve multi-applications smart cards. To achieve this goal, we take benefits of SOAP and MOMs technologies. A software architecture has been defined in order to enable SOAP-based operation invocations for smart cards. A SOAP proxy provides introspection facilities that, combined with an on-card introspection mechanism, makes able distributed clients to dynamically discover and use the embedded services offered. We also define a MOM layer which, placed on top of SOAP, enables asynchronous invocations. Although we focus on the Java Card case, the approach and platform we describe can be easily generalized to others multi-applications smart cards such as the Smart Card for Windows [18] or Multos [19].

Appendix: SOAP/HTTP Envelopes for a Smart Card Loyalty Application

Invocation

```
POST card:gcr410_com1:loyalty/invoke HTTP/1.1
Content-Type: text/xml; charset="utf-8"
Content-Length: 478
SOAPAction: "card123456789:loyalty/invoke"

<SOAP-ENV:Envelope xmlns:SOAP-ENV="http://schemas.xmlsoap.org/soap/envelope/"
    xmlns:xsi="http://www.w3.org/1999/XMLSchema-instance"
    xmlns:xsd="http://www.w3.org/1999/XMLSchema">
  <SOAP-ENV:Body>
    <loy:GetBonus xmlns:loy="http://schemas.loyaltycard.org/"
          SOAP-ENV:encodingStyle="http://schemas.xmlsoap.org/soap/encoding/">
        <service xsi:type="xsd:string">ACME</service>
    </loy:GetBonus>
  </SOAP-ENV:Body>
</SOAP-ENV:Envelope>
```

Response

```
HTTP/1.1 200 OK
Content-Type: text/xml; charset="utf-8"
Content-Length: 484

<SOAP-ENV:Envelope xmlns:SOAP-ENV="http://schemas.xmlsoap.org/soap/envelope/"
    xmlns:xsi="http://www.w3.org/1999/XMLSchema-instance"
    xmlns:xsd="http://www.w3.org/1999/XMLSchema">
  <SOAP-ENV:Body>
    <loy:GetBonusResponse xmlns:loy="http://schemas.loyaltycard.org/"
          SOAP-ENV:encodingStyle="http://schemas.xmlsoap.org/soap/encoding/">
        <bonus xsi:type="xsd:int">1900</bonus>
    </loy:GetBonusResponse>
  </SOAP-ENV:Body>
</SOAP-ENV:Envelope>
```

References

1. Bernstein, P. A., Newcomer, E.: Principles of Transaction Processing for the Systems Professional. Morgan Kaufmann (Eds), 1997. ISBN 1-55860-415-4. 84
2. Sun Microsystems : Java Message Service API Specification, v. 1.0.2. 1999, http://java.sun.com/products/jms. 84
3. ObjectWeb : JORAM homepage. http://www.objectweb.org/joram/joramHomePage.htm. 84, 91
4. Scribner, K., Stiver, M. C., Scribner, K.: Understanding SOAP: The Authoritative Solution. In: Sams (eds), Jan 2000. ISBN: 0-672-31922-5. 85
5. UDDI homepage. http://www.uddi.org. 87
6. Ariba, International Business Machines Corporation, Microsoft: Web Services Description Language (WSDL) Specification v 1.0 . 2000. http://msdn.microsoft.com/xml/general/wsdl.asp 87
7. Java Card Forum : http://www.javacardforum.org. 87
8. International Standard Organisation (ISO): Information Technology - Identification cards - Integrated circuit(s) cards with contacts. ISO/IEC 7816-1,2,3,4,5,6,7,8. 1987-1999. 87

 9. European Telecommunications Standards Institute (ETSI): Digital cellular telecommunications system (Phase 2+); Subscriber Identity Module Application Programming Interface (SIM API); SIM API for Java Card; Stage 2 (GSM 03.19 version 7.1.0 Release 1998). May 2000. 87

10. Guthery, S. B.: Java Card: Internet Computing on a Smart Card. IEEE Internet Computing, 1 (1997). 88

11. Hansmann, U., Nicklous, M. S., Schäck, T., Seliger, F.: Smart Card Application Development Using Java. In: Springer-Verlag (eds), 2000. ISBN 3-540-65829-7. 88

12. Guthery, S. B., Kehr, R., Posegga, J.: How to turn a GSM SIM into a Web Server. In: Domingo-Ferrer, J., Chan, D., Watson, A. (eds.): Fourth IFIP TC8/WG8.8 Working Conference on Smart Card Research and Advanced Applications (CARDIS'2000), sept 2000, Bristol, United Kingdom. Kluwer Academic Publishers (2000) 209–222, ISBN 0-7923-7953-5. 88

13. Rees, J., Honeyman, P.: Webcard : a Java Card Web Server. In: Domingo-Ferrer, J., Chan, D., Watson, A. (eds.): Fourth IFIP TC8/WG8.8 Working Conference on Smart Card Research and Advanced Applications (CARDIS'2000), sept 2000, Bristol, United Kingdom. Kluwer Academic Publishers (2000) 197–207, ISBN 0-7923-7953-5. 88

14. Vetillard, E.: Tools for Integrating the Java Card API into Jini Connection Technology. In: Sun's Worldwide Java Developer Conference (JavaOne 2000), 2000. 88

15. Kehr, R., Rohs, M., Vogt, H.: Mobile Code as an Enabling Technology for Service-oriented Smartcard Middleware. In : Proceedings of the 2nd International Symposium on Distributed Objects and Applications(DOA'2000), Antwerp, Belgium, september 2000. IEEE Computer Society (eds), pp. 119-130. 88

16. Jean, S., Donsez, D., Lecomte, S. : Smart Card Integration in Distributed Information Systems: The Interactive Execution Model. In: Proceedings of IEEE 1st International Symposium on Advanced Distributed Systems, (Guadalajara, Mexico), March 2000. 88

17. Opencard Framework : http://www.opencard.org. 89

18. Talvard, L.: The API services provided by the SCW. In: Proceedings of 1st Gemplus Developper Conference (GDC '99), Paris, France, 1999. 92

19. Maosco Ltd: Multos homepage. http://www.multos.com. 92

An Operational Semantics
of the Java Card Firewall

Marc Éluard[1], Thomas Jensen[1], and Ewen Denne[2]

[1] IRISA, Campus de Beaulieu
35042 Rennes Cedex, France
{eluard,jensen}@irisa.fr
[2] Division of Informatics, University of Edinburgh
Edinburgh, Scotland
ewd@dai.ed.ac.uk

Abstract. This paper presents an operational semantics for a subset
of Java Card bytecode, focussing on aspects of the Java Card firewall,
method invocation, field access, variable access, shareable objects and
contexts. The goal is to provide a precise description of the Java Card firewall using standard tools from operational semantics. Such a description
is necessary for formally arguing the correctness of tools for validating
the security of Java Card applications.

1   Introduction

Java Card is being promoted as a high-level language for programming of multi-
application smart cards. The high-level nature of the language should ease the
programming and the reasoning about such applications. Java Card keeps the
essence of Java, like inheritance, virtual methods, overloading, etc, but leaves
out features such as large primitive data types (long, double and float), characters and strings, multidimensional arrays, garbage collection, object cloning,
the security manager, etc. (see the specification [1] and also [8]). Furthermore,
given the security-critical application areas of Java Card, the language has been
endowed with an elaborate security architecture.

Central to this architecture is the Java Card firewall. Applets installed on
the card are separated by a firewall that prevents one applet from accessing
objects owned by another applet. Shareable objects and interfaces are used to
provide communication between otherwise separated applets. A limited form of
stack inspection allows a server applet to know the identity of the client that
requested a particular service. These mechanisms (that will be further detailed
in section 2) facilitate the design of secure applications but do not in themselves
guarantee security. They do, however, offer the possibility of formal verification
of the security of an application using tools from semantics and static program
analysis. The purpose of this paper is to give a formal semantic description of
the Java Card firewall. The interest of such a description lies in its use as a
foundation for designing and proving static analysis methods for verifying the

I. Attali and T. Jensen (Eds.): E-smart 2001, LNCS 2140, pp. 95–110, 2001.
© Springer-Verlag Berlin Heidelberg 2001

security of a multi-application Java Card, but for lack of space we do not detail this here.

The paper is organised as follows. In section 2 we give a description of the central security features of Java Card 2.1.1. This is followed by the definition of semantics domains in section 3 and the operational semantic of selected byte-code in section 4. In section 5, we discuss related work.

2   The Java Card Firewall

The Java Card platform is a multi-application environment in which an applet's sensitive data must be protected against malicious access. In Java, this protection is achieved by using class loaders and security managers to create private name spaces for applets. In Java Card, class loaders and security managers have been replaced with the Java Card firewall. The separation that is enforced by the firewall is based on the package structure of Java Card (which is the same as that of Java) and the notion of *contexts.*

When an applet is created, the JCRE gives it a unique applet identifier (AID) from which it is possible to retrieve the name of the package in which it is defined. If two applets are instances of classes coming from the same Java Card package, they are said to belong to the same context (which we identify by the package name). In addition to the contexts defined by the applets executing on the card, there is a special "system" context, called the JCRE context. Applets belonging to this context can access objects from any other context on the card. Thus, the set *Contexts* of contexts can be defined by:

$$Contexts = \{JCRE\} \cup \{pckg : pckg \text{ is a legal package name}\}$$

Every object is assigned a unique *owner context viz.*, the context of the applet that created the object. A method of an object is said to execute in the owner context of the object[1]. It is this context that decides whether an access to another object will succeed. The firewall isolates the contexts in the sense that a method executing in one context cannot access any fields or methods of objects belonging to another context.

There are two ways in which the firewall can be circumvented: via JCRE entry points and via shareable objects. JCRE entry points are objects owned by the JCRE that have been designated specifically as objects that can be accessed from any context. The most prominent example is the APDU buffer in which commands sent to the card are stored. This object is managed by the JCRE and in order to allow applets to access this object, it is designated as an entry point. Other examples include the elements of the table containing the AIDs of the applets installed on the card. Entry points can be marked as *temporary*. References to temporary entry points cannot be stored in objects (this is enforced by the firewall).

---

[1] In the case of static call, the execution is in the caller's context.

Two applets in different contexts may want to share some information. For that, Java Card offers a sharing mechanism, called *shareable objects*, that gives limited access to objects across contexts. An applet can allow access to an object's methods from outside its context (it is impossible to share fields) by using a shareable interface that is, an interface which extends javacard.framework.-Shareable. In this interface, the applet gives the list of the method's signatures that it wants to share. The class of the object to be shared must implement this interface. The "server" applet must define a method, getShareableInterface-Object. This method is called when an applet is asked to provide a shared object. It is passed as parameter the AID of the "client" applet which requested the shared object. This allows different objects to be shared with client applets.

In the following section, we give a small example to illustrate these sharing mechanisms.

2.1   A Simple Scenario

We have 3 applets: Alice, Bob and Charlie, each belonging to a different context. Alice implements a shareable interface MSI and she is prepared to share an object MSIO with Bob (MSIO is an instance of a class that implements MSI). When Alice receives a request for sharing (using the method getShareableInterfaceObject, she verifies that the caller is Bob. If it is Bob, she returns the MSIO, otherwise she returns null (see also section 4).

```
public class Alice extends Applet implements MSI {
    public Shareable getShareableInterfaceObject (AID client, byte param){
        if (client.equals (BobAID, (short)0, (byte)BobAID.length) == false)
            return null;
        return (this); } }
```

Using the method JCSystem.getAppletShareableInterfaceObject, Bob asks for a shareable object from Alice. Assume now that Bob (inadvertantly) leaks a reference to MSIO to the third applet Charlie[2]. With it, Charlie can access the same methods as Bob.

```
public class Bob extends Applet {
  public static MSI AliceObject;
  AliceObject =
    (MSI)JCSystem.getAppletShareableInterfaceObject(AliceAID,(byte)0);}
```

```
public class Charlie extends Applet {
  private static MSI AliceObject;
  AliceObject = Bob.AliceObject;
  // The method void foo () exists in MSI
  AliceObject.foo (); }
```

Alice has some doubts about Bob so she decides to verify, at each access to one of her shared methods, the identity of the caller. In this case Charlie can't access MSIO anymore.

---

[2] for example, by storing the reference into a public static field (there are other more subtle ways in which this can happen)

```
public class Alice extends Applet implements MSI {
  public void foo () {
    // The caller is Bob?
    AID client = JCSystem.getPreviousContextAID ();
    if (client.equals (BobAID, (short)0, (byte)BobAID.length) == false)
       ISOException.ThrowIt (SW_UNAUTHORIZED_CLIENT);
    ... // OK, the caller was Bob } }
```

2.2   Limitations of the Firewall

As illustrated by this example, Java Card has a limited form of the stack in-spection mechanism that underlies the Java 2 security architecture. The Java 2 checkPermission instruction verifies whether all callers on the call stack have a specific permission (e.g. to write a file in a given directory). Java Card contains a mechanism for knowing from which context a method was called but there is no mechasnism for obtaining the identity of all the callers. More precisely, an applet can get a description of the last *context switch* that took place, by calling the method getPreviousContextAID. (Notice that this context switch could have happened several levels down in the call stack.) In the example, Alice does not know whether the call made by Bob is in turn a result of Bob being called by some other applet. Neither can she know what Bob will do with the result of the call. This is problematic since an object is only marked as shared, not with whom it is supposed to be shared. Thus, while the firewall can serve to prevent direct information flow, further program analysis is required in order to verify that all information flow of the application respects a given security policy.

3   Semantic Description of the Java Card Firewall

In the following we describe the semantic domains of a modified version of Java Card bytecode. Rather than a stack-oriented bytecode we shall be working with a "three-address" bytecode where arguments and results of a bytecode instruction are fetched and stored in local variables instead of being popped and pushed from a stack. This format is similar to the intermediate language used in the Java tool Jimple [17]. Furthermore, we assume that the constant pool has been expanded *i.e.* that indices into the constant pool have been replaced by the corresponding constant. For example, the bytecode instruction invokevirtual takes as parameter the signature of the method called, rather than an index into the constant pool. The transformation of code into this format is standard and straightforward.

3.1   Notation

The term $\mathcal{P}(X)$ denotes the power set of X: $\mathcal{P}(X) \equiv \{S \mid S \subseteq X\}$. A product type $X = A \times B \times C$ is sometimes treated as a labelled record: with an element x of type X we can access its field with the names of its constituent types ($x.A$,

$x.B$ or $x.C$). A list can be given by enumeration of its elements: $x_1 :: \cdots :: x_n$. Given a list v we can access one of its element by its position in the list ($v(i)$ for the ith element). And finally, we can concatenate two lists: $(x_1 :: \cdots :: x_n) ::: (x_m :: \cdots :: x_p) = x_1 :: \cdots :: x_n :: x_m :: \cdots :: x_p$. We denote, by X^*, the type of finite lists, whose elements are of type X. We use the symbol $\rightarrow$ to form the type of partial functions: $X \rightarrow Y$. We can update a function f with a new value v for an argument x: $g := f[x \mapsto v]$. We (ab)use the same notation for objects: the object obtained from object o by modifying field f to have value v is written $o[f \mapsto v]$.

3.2 Semantic Types

Our semantic domains follow the same structure as the domains defined by Bertelsen [5,6].

Before introducing the representation of the different elements, we define some basic types. Id_p, Id_c, Id_i, Id_f and Id_m are the types of qualified name of a package, a class, an interface, a field and a method, respectively[3]. When we want to talk about a class or an interface name, we can use the set Id_{ci} ($Id_{ci} = Id_c \cup Id_i$). Id_v is the type of (unqualified) names of variables. We assume furthermore a set Pc of program counters. A program counter identifies an instruction within the whole class hierarchy (i.e. it is relative to a class hierarchy and not just a method). We assume a set $Label$ which represents the different labels used with a jump instructions.

General Types We use types to stand for abstract primitive values. For example, `byte` instead of 12. A type can be an array type (type between square brackets), or a simple type where a simple type is a *Primitive* or the name of a class or of an interface (Id_{ci}).

$$Primitive = \{\ \text{boolean, short, byte, int}\ \}$$
$$Type = \text{'['}SType\text{']'} \cup Stype$$
$$SType = Primitive \cup Id_{ci}$$

Classes A class or an interface descriptor consists of the set of the associated access modifiers ($\mathcal{P}(Mod_{ci})$[4]), the name of the class or interface (Id_{ci}), the name of the direct superclass or the names of direct superinterfaces (Ext), the name of the interfaces that the class implements (Imp), the name of its package (Id_p), field declarations (Fld), method declarations and implementations (Mtd). A class must have a superclass, the default being `java.lang.Object`, but an interface can

---

[3] The qualified name of an entity is the complete name. For a class, it is $p.c$ where p is the name of the package and c the (unqualified) name of the class. For a method ($c.m$) or a field ($c.f$), it is the qualified name of the class and the (unqualified) name of the method or field.

[4] The access modifier `Interface` is used to specify that the declaration is for an interface.

have zero, one or more superinterfaces. Only a class can implement an interface, so for an interface this field is the empty set.

The fields of a class are described by a map from field names (Id_f) to a set of access modifiers ($\mathcal{P}(Mod_f)$) together with a type descriptor ($Type$). The type descriptor defines what type of values can be stored in the field.

$$
\begin{aligned}
Desc_{ci} &= \mathcal{P}(Mod_{ci}) \times Id_{ci} \times Ext \times Imp \times Id_p \times Fld \times Mtd \\
Mod_{ci} &= \{\ \texttt{Public, Package, Final, Abstract, Shareable, Interface}\ \} \\
Ext &= Id_c \cup \mathcal{P}(Id_i) \\
Imp &= \mathcal{P}(Id_i) \\
Fld &= Id_f \rightarrow Desc_f \\
Desc_f &= \mathcal{P}(Mod_f) \times Type \\
Mod_f &= \{\ \texttt{Public, Package, Private, Protected, Final, Static}\ \}\ \mathit{3}
\end{aligned}
$$

Methods The methods are described by a map that to a method signature (Sig) associates a method descriptor ($Desc_m$). This structure consists of the set of the associated access modifiers ($\mathcal{P}(Mod_m)$), the code of the method ($Code$), a description of the formal parameters ($Param$) and the local variables of the method ($Varl$). A signature is the name of the method (Id_m) and the list of type descriptors for its parameters ($Type^*$). Code is a list whose elements consist of a program counter value (Pc) and the instruction at this address ($Bytecode$). The set of local variables is the list of all variable names (Id_v) with their type descriptor ($Type$).

$$
\begin{aligned}
Mtd &= Sig \rightarrow Desc_m \\
Sig &= Id_m \times Type^* \\
Desc_m &= \mathcal{P}(Mod_m) \times Code \times Param \times Varl \\
Mod_m &= \{\ \texttt{Public, Package, Private, Protected, Static}\ \} \\
Code &= Inst^* \\
Inst &= Pc \times Bytecode \mid Pc \times Bytecode \times Label \\
Varl &= (Id_v \times Type)^* \\
Param &= (Id_v \times Type)^*
\end{aligned}
$$

For this paper we consider a small set of bytecodes that is sufficient for illustrating the different features of the semantics. In the following, NT and T range over local variables. The `invokevirtual` instruction takes as argument a fully qualified method name, indicating the point of declaration of the method. The explainations of these intructions are given in section 4.2.

$$
\begin{aligned}
Bytecode = \ &NT := \texttt{getstatic}\ C.f \\
\mid\ &\texttt{putfield}\ C.f\ T_1\ T_2 \\
\mid\ &NT := \texttt{invokevirtual}\ C.m\ T_0\ T_1\ \cdots\ T_n\ S_1{::}\cdots{::}S_n \\
\mid\ &\texttt{goto}\ label \\
\mid\ &NT := \texttt{new}\ C \\
\mid\ &NT := \texttt{invokestatic}\ getAID \\
\mid\ &NT := \texttt{invokestatic}\ getPrevCtx \\
\mid\ &NT := \texttt{invokestatic}\ getASIO\ T_1\ T_2
\end{aligned}
$$

3.3   The Run-Time State

This section defines the run-time values used in the semantics. We are primarily interested in modelling the object structure and ownership so we abstract primitive values such as booleans and integers to their type. In addition to the values already introduced we have a set, *Ref*, of references for modelling the heap of objects. A particular element $Null \in Ref$ denotes the undefined reference. We introduce two kinds of reference, Ref_i (respectively Ref_a) can point to class instances Obj_i (respectively array instances Obj_a) and the union of them with $Null$ is *Ref*.

Ownership   The notion of ownership in Java Card is very clear, an object is owned by the active applet at the moment of its creation. We extend the definition of an owner with the context (package) of its creation. We model this notion with a pair *(Package, Applet)*.

$$Owner = Id_p \times Ref_i$$

The owner of an applet is the applet itself.

Values

$$Value = Ref \cup Primitive$$
$$RValue = Object \cup Primitive$$
$$Object = Obj_i \cup Obj_a$$
$$Obj_i = Id_{ci} \times Owner \times JCREep \times tJCREep \times Fldv$$
$$Fldv = Id_f \to Value$$
$$Obj_a = \text{'['} \: SType \: \text{']'} \times Owner \times JCREep \times tJCREep \times global \times Elt$$
$$Elt = \mathcal{P}(Value)$$

We have three kinds of values: class instances, arrays and primitive values (such as bytes and booleans). A class instance contains the name of the class, the owner of this instance, boolean flags indicating whether or not it is a JCRE entry point and a temporary JCRE entry point (*cf.* section 2) and the set of fields. The set of fields maps a field name to a value.

   An array instance is described by the type of its elements, the owner, the information about being an entry point or not, a flag indicating whether the array is global or not and finally the set of its elements.

The State   With these types, we can define the state used in the semantics. A state consists of a call stack of frames, the memory and the class hierarchy. The latter is part of the run-time state because it is used to store the values of static fields. We write the call stack as a sequence of frames such that the currently active frame appears as the first element of the sequence.

$$State = Frame^* \times Mem \times E_{ci}$$
$$Frame = Inst \times Ref \times Locals$$
$$Locals = Id_v \rightarrow Value$$
$$Mem = Value \rightarrow RValue$$
$$E_{ci} = Id_{ci} \rightarrow Desc_{ci} \times FldS$$
$$FldS = Id_f \rightarrow Value$$

The current frame contains the current instruction and a reference to the object on which the method currently executing has been invoked. This object represents the currently active context. An element of the set *Locals* maps a local variable to its value. The memory (also called the heap of objects) is modelled by a map from references to values. The class hierarchy is represented as a map that to a class or an interface name associates its descriptor and its static fields.

AIDs and the Table of Installed Applets The JCRE keeps a table recording the applets installed on the card. These applets are identified by an applet identifier, an *AID*. An AID is an object of class AID containing a byte array with a number that identifies the applet together with a method for testing whether two AIDs represent the same number. With a reference to an AID, we can find a reference to the corresponding applet instance through the table *Applet_tbl* of installed applets:

$$Applet\_tbl : Ref \rightarrow Ref.$$

Were we to model the dynamic installation of applets this table would have to be made part of the state but we do not consider this here.

3.4   Auxiliary Functions

We follow Bertelsen [5,6] and define a number of functions that abstract the syntactic structure of a list of bytecodes.

$$Succ : Inst \rightarrow \mathcal{P}(Inst)$$
$$Find : Label \rightarrow Inst$$
$$First : Desc_m \rightarrow Inst$$

The flow of control inside a method is modelled by the function *Succ* that for each instruction yields the set of instructions that can follow in the execution. The need for returning a set of instructions is due to the fact that we have abstracted away all primitive values; in particular, the semantics will not be able to evaluate the value of the condition in a branching statement. The function *Find* permits us to find an instruction with a given label. Finally, the function *First* takes a method descriptor and returns the first instruction of this method.

The function *Lookup* models the dynamic resolution of virtual method calls. It takes as arguments the signature of a method, the dynamic class of the object on which the method is invoked, the class in which the method is declared and the class hierarchy. It returns the method descriptor of the implementation of the method designated by the signature.[5]

$$Lookup : Sig \times Id_{ci} \times Id_{ci} \times E_{ci} \rightarrow Desc_m.$$

The function *Imp_Shareable?* determines if the class of an object implements a *Shareable* interface. This function is recursive on the field *Imp* of the class.

$$Imp\_Shareable? : \mathcal{P}(Id_i) \rightarrow boolean.$$

The function *Ext_Shareable?* determines if an interface extends the interface Shareable. This function is recursive on the field *Ext* of the interface.

$$Ext\_Shareable? : Id_i \rightarrow boolean.$$

Initialisation The function *Init_Var* constructs a function that maps the local variables of a method to their initial values.

$$Init\_Var : Param \times Value^* \times Varl \rightarrow Locals.$$

It takes the name and the descriptor of the formal parameters, the value of the actual parameters and the name of local variables of the frame to be constructed. The result is a function that maps the formal parameters to the value of the corresponding arguments and is default on local variables. The default value for a object and an array is *Null*. For a primitive, the default value is type of the primitive value.

Similarly, when creating a new object instance, we use a function *Init_Fields* to prepare the set of instance fields for a specified class and all of its superclasses:

$$Init\_Fields : Id_{ci} \rightarrow Fldv.$$

It takes the name of the class and returns a function in which a field name maps the default value for its type (the default value is the same as defined for *Init_Var*).

4   Operational Semantics for Instructions with the Firewall

In this section we give an operational semantics for a small subset of Java Card instructions. The main feature that distinguishes this semantics from a Java bytecode semantics is the modelling of the Java Card firewall. The rules for instructions that can violate the firewall include an extra hypothesis that formalises when the instruction can be executed without raising a security exception.

---

[5] In this paper we do not describe any further the details of dynamic method lookup in Java(see [11, section 15.12] and [9]).

4.1   Firewall Checks

The checks made by the firewall are formalised through a collection of predicates. Covering all bytecode instructions requires eight different predicates. We give the exact formula only for the two predicates used in this paper.

CheckVirtual? This check is performed during a call to a virtual method.
$$CheckVirtual? : Object \times Object \to boolean.$$
For $(o_1, o_2) \in Object \times Object$, the access is authorized if and only if the context represented by o_1 is the context of the JCRE ($o_1.Owner.Id_p = JCRE$) or if the contexts of o_1 and o_2 are the same ($o_1.Owner.Id_p = o_2.Owner.Id_p$) or if the object o_2 is global ($o_2.global$) or if the object o_2 is a JCRE entry point ($o_2.JCREep$).
CheckVirtual? $(o_1, o_2) =$
$(o_1.Owner.Id_p = JCRE) \vee (o_1.Owner.Id_p = o_2.Owner.Id_p) \vee (o_2.global) \vee$
  $(o_2.JCREep)$

CheckPutfield? This check is performed when storing a value in a field.
$$CheckPutfield? : Object \times Obj_i \times RValue \to boolean.$$
For $(o_1, o_2, v) \in Object \times Obj_i \times RValue$, the access is authorized if and only if the context represented by o_1 is the context of the JCRE ($o_1.Owner.Id_p = JCRE$) or if the contexts of o_1 and o_2 are the same ($o_1.Owner.Id_p = o_2.Owner.Id_p$) and if the value is not a global object ($\neg v.global$) and is not a temporary JCRE entry point ($\neg v.tJCREep$).
CheckPutfield? $(o_1, o_2, v) =$
$(o_1.Owner.Id_p = JCRE) \vee ((o_1.Owner.Id_p = o_2.Owner.Id_p) \wedge (\neg v.global) \wedge$
  $(\neg v.tJCREep))$

CheckALoad? This check is performed when read access is made to an array.
$$CheckALoad? : Object \times Obj_a \to boolean.$$
For $(o, a) \in Object \times Obj_a$, the access is authorized if and only if the context represented by o is the context of the JCRE ($o.Owner.Id_p = JCRE$) or if the contexts of o and a are the same ($o.Owner.Id_p = a.Owner.Id_p$) or if the array represented by a is a global array ($a.global$).

The instruction `arraylength` performes exactly the same check, so for this instruction we use the *CheckALoad?* predicate.

CheckAStore? This check is performed when storing an element in an array.
$$CheckAStore? : Object \times Obj_a \times RValue \to boolean.$$
For $(o, a, v) \in Object \times Obj_a \times RValue$, the access is authorized if and only if the context represented by o is the context of the JCRE ($o.Owner.Id_p = JCRE$) or if the contexts of o and a are the same ($o.Owner.Id_p = a.Owner.Id_p$) or if the array represented by a is a global array ($a.global$) and if the value not represents a global array ($\neg v.global$) or a temporary JCRE entry point ($\neg v.tJCREep$).

CheckClass? This check is performed during a cast or an `instance_of` check.

$$CheckClass? : Object \times Object \times Id_i \rightarrow boolean.$$

For $(o_1, o_2, Id) \in Object \times Object \times Id_i$, the access is authorized if and only if the context represented by o_1 is the context of the JCRE ($o_1.Owner.Id_p = JCRE$) or if the contexts of o_1 and o_2 are the same ($o_1.Owner.Id_p = o_2.Owner.Id_p$) or if the object o_2 is global ($o_2.global$) or if the object o_2 is a JCRE entry point ($o_2.JCREep$) or if the object's class implements a *Shareable* interface (*Imp_Shareable?* ($o_2.Imp$)) and if the object being cast into or an instance of an interface that extends `Shareable` (*Ext_Shareable?* (*Id*)).

CheckGetfield? This check is performed when reading access on a field is made.

$$CheckGetfield? : Object \times Obj_i \rightarrow boolean.$$

For $(o_1, o_2) \in Object \times Obj_i$, the access is authorized if and only if the context represented by o_1 is the context of the JCRE ($o_1.Owner.Id_p = JCRE$) or if the contexts of o_1 and o_2 are the same ($o_1.Owner.Id_p = o_2.Owner.Id_p$).

CheckInterface? This check is performed during a call to an interface method.

$$CheckInterface? : Object \times Obj_i \times Id_i \rightarrow boolean.$$

For $(o_1, o_2, Id) \in Object \times Obj_i \times Id_i$, the access is authorized if and only if the context represented by o_1 is the context of the JCRE ($o_1.Owner.Id_p = JCRE$) or if the contexts of o_1 and o_2 are the same ($o_1.Owner.Id_p = o_2.Owner.Id_p$) or if the object o_2 is a JCRE entry point ($o_2.JCREep$) or if the object's class implements a *Shareable* interface (*Imp_Shareable?* ($o_2.Imp$)) and if the interface being invoked extends `Shareable` (*Ext_Shareable?* (*Id*)).

CheckPutstatic? This check is performed when storing a value in a static field.

$$CheckPutstatic? : Object \times RValue \rightarrow boolean.$$

For $(o, v) \in Object \times RValue$, the access is authorized if and only if the context represented by o is the context of the JCRE ($o.Owner.Id_p = JCRE$) or if the value is not a global array ($\neg v.global$) and is not a temporary JCRE entry point ($\neg v.tJCREep$).

4.2   The Semantics

The present semantics does not take visibility into account. Although the model has enough information to deal with visibility modifiers, we omit this for brevity.

Concerning the Java Card API, we only consider methods directly related to the firewall. These are `getAppletShareableInterfaceObject`, `getShareableInterfaceObject`, `getAID` and `getPreviousContextAID`. The static method `getAppletShareableInterfaceObject` that belongs to the `JCSystem` package is called by a client when it wants to obtain a shareable object from a server applet (cf. Section 2.1). The JCRE in turn invokes the method `getShareableInterfaceObject` that returns a shareable object based on the identity of the client. Thus, the modelling of a call to `getAppletShareableInterfaceObject` is a combination of a static and a virtual method call. The call to `getShareableInterfaceObject` is made directly by the rule of getAppletShareableInterfaceObject, the invoke-static is transformed into a invokevirtual if the call to getShareableInterface-Object is possible. The semantics contains a rule that treats the invocation of this method separately. Similarly, there is a separate semantic rule for the invocation of the two static methods of the JCSystem package getAID and getPreviousContextAID for accessing the AID of the applet that owns the currently executing object and the AID of the context in action before the switch to the current context, respectively. In addition, we give semantics to five bytecodes: getstatic, putfield, invokevirtual, goto and new.

getstatic The getstatic instruction loads a value stored in a static class or interface field and stores it in a local variable.

$$\frac{\begin{array}{c} I = (pc, NT := \text{ getstatic } C.f) \\ V' = V[NT \mapsto E_{ci}(C).FldS(C.f)] \\ I' \in Succ(I) \end{array}}{\langle\langle I, r, V\rangle :: A, mem, E_{ci}\rangle \Rightarrow \langle\langle I', r, V'\rangle :: A, mem, E_{ci}\rangle}$$

The class or the interface C must have a descriptor in E_{ci}. The field $C.f$ must exist in the set of static field of C. Then the value of the field $(E_{ci}(C).FldS(C.f))$ is loaded and stored into variable NT.

putfield The putfield instruction loads a value from a local variable and stores it into an instance field.

$$\frac{\begin{array}{c} I = (pc, \text{putfield } C.f\ T_1\ T_2) \\ o = mem(V(T_1)) \\ g = o.Fldv[C.f \mapsto V(T_2)] \\ o' = o[Fldv \mapsto g] \\ mem' = mem[V(T_1) \mapsto o'] \\ I' \in Succ(I) \\ [\ CheckPutfield?(mem(r), mem(V(T_1)), mem(V(T_2)))\ ] \end{array}}{\langle\langle I, r, V\rangle :: A, mem, E_{ci}\rangle \Rightarrow \langle\langle I', r, V\rangle :: A, mem', E_{ci}\rangle}$$

The value stored in T_1 must be a reference to a class object. This object must have a field $C.f$. Then the value stored in T_2 is stored in the field.

invokevirtual The invokevirtual instruction makes a call to an instance method.

$$\frac{\begin{array}{c} I = (pc, NT := \text{ invokevirtual } C.m\ T_0\ T_1\ \cdots\ T_n\ S_1 :: \cdots :: S_n) \\ desc = Lookup((m, S_1 :: \cdots :: S_n), mem(V(T_0)).Id_{ci}, C, E_{ci}) \\ V' = Init\_Var(desc.Param, V(T_0) :: \cdots :: V(T_n), desc.Varl) \\ I' = First(desc) \\ r' = V(T_0) \\ [\ CheckVirtual?(mem(r), mem(V(T_0)))\ ] \end{array}}{\langle\langle I, r, V\rangle :: A, mem, E_{ci}\rangle \Rightarrow \langle\langle I', r', V'\rangle :: \langle I, r, V\rangle :: A, mem, E_{ci}\rangle}$$

The value stored in T_0 must be a reference to a class instance. We search for the implementation of the method called using the function *Lookup*. We construct the new list of local variables with the variables set to the actual parameters.

goto The `goto` instruction makes a jump to an instruction labelled *label*.

$$I = (pc, \texttt{goto } label)$$
$$I' = Find(label)$$
$$\overline{\langle\langle I, r, V \rangle :: A, mem, E_{ci}\rangle \Rightarrow \langle\langle I', r, V \rangle :: A, mem, E_{ci}\rangle}$$

new The `new` instruction creates a new object in memory.

$$I = (pc, NT := \texttt{new } C)$$
$$O = (C, mem(r).Owner, false, false, Init\_Fields(C))$$
$$R \in Ref \setminus dom(mem)$$
$$V' = V[NT \mapsto R]$$
$$mem' = mem[R \mapsto O]$$
$$I' \in Succ(I)$$
$$\overline{\langle\langle I, r, V \rangle :: A, mem, E_{ci}\rangle \Rightarrow \langle\langle I', r, V' \rangle :: A, mem', E_{ci}\rangle}$$

A new object of class C is created in the memory with the flags for entry point and temporary entry point set to *false*. A reference to this object is stored in the variable NT.

getAID

$$I = (pc, NT := \texttt{invokestatic } JCSystem.getAID)$$
$$V' = V[NT \mapsto mem(r).Owner.AID]$$
$$I' \in Succ(I)$$
$$\overline{\langle\langle I, r, V \rangle :: A, mem, E_{ci}\rangle \Rightarrow \langle\langle I', r, V' \rangle :: A, mem, E_{ci}\rangle}$$

The AID of the currently active applet is the AID of the owner of the current object. A reference to the current object can be retrieved from the frame as r.

getPreviousContextAID

$$I_1 = (pc, NT := \texttt{invokestatic } JCSystem.getPreviousContextAID)$$
$$\forall i \in \{2, \cdots, n-1\}, Mem(r_i).Owner.Id_p = mem(r_1).Owner.Id_p$$
$$mem(r_n).Owner.Id_p \neq mem(r_1).Owner.Id_p$$
$$V' = V[NT \mapsto mem(r_n).Owner.AID]$$
$$I' \in Succ(I_1)$$
$$\overline{\langle\langle I_1, r_1 V_1 \rangle :: \cdots :: \langle I_n, r_n, V_n \rangle :: A, mem, E_{ci}\rangle \Rightarrow}$$
$$\langle\langle I', r_1, V' \rangle :: \langle I_2, r_2, V_2 \rangle :: \cdots :: \langle I_n, r_n, V_n \rangle :: A, mem, E_{ci}\rangle$$

The previous context is found by searching down the call stack for the most recent frame whose current object has an owner context that differs from the owner context of the current object on top of the call stack. If none such is found, *Null* is returned.

getAppletShareableInterfaceObject

$$I = (pc, NT := \texttt{invokestatic } JCSystem.getAppletShareableInterfaceObject$$
$$T_1 \, T_2)$$
$$server = V(T_1)$$
$$server \in Dom(Applet\_tbl)$$
$$class = Mem(Applet\_tbl(Server)).Id_{ci}$$
$$desc = Lookup((getShareableInterfaceObject, \texttt{AID} :: \texttt{byte}), class, \texttt{Applet}, E_{ci})$$
$$client = mem(r).Owner.AID$$
$$I' = First(desc)$$
$$r' = Applet\_tbl(server)$$
$$V' = Init\_Var(desc.Param, r' :: client :: mem(V(T_2)), desc.Varl)$$
$$\overline{\langle\langle I, r, V\rangle :: A, mem, E_{ci}\rangle \Rightarrow \langle\langle I', r', V'\rangle :: \langle I, r, V\rangle :: A, mem, E_{ci}\rangle}$$

This method is called by the *client* to get the *server* applet's shareable object. Although a static method call, it functions as a virtual call of the method `getShareableInterfaceObject` of the *server*. If the firewall conditions are not respected, the result is *Null*.

5   Related Works

There are several works on a formal semantics for Java [4,10]. The BALI project [2] provides an axiomatic semantics for a substantial subset of Java and Java Card but does not give an axiomation of the firewall. To formalize the language, they use a Hoare-style calculus [18,19]. All definitions and proofs are done formally with the theorem prover Isabelle/HOL. The resulting proof system can be proved sound, is easy to use, and complete. A similar goal is pursued in the LOOP project [3], where they develop an interface specification in JML of the Java Card API [14] and provide proofs that the current Java Card API classes satisfy these interface specifications [15]. The more comprehensive semantics was proposed by Bertelsen [5] and was taken as the starting point for the present work. This semantics models the stack-based Java bytecode. Our choice of passing to a variable-oriented language means that we no longer have an operand stack in the frames. Moreover, we had to add certain attributes to the run-time structures to keep track of the owner of objects, whether they are entry points *etc.* Pusch has formalised the JVM in HOL [16]. Like us, she considers the class file to be well-formed so that the hypotheses of rules are just assignments. The operational semantics is presented directly as a formalisation in HOL, whereas we have chosen (equivalently) to use inference rules. Several works have focussed on formalising aspects of the Java Card firewall. Motré has formalised the firewall in the B language [13]. She transforms the informal specification into an abstract machine which can then be refined into an actual implementation. Each operation of this machine corresponds to a specific object access. This description of the firewall provides a formal description of the security policy as defined in JCRE specification [12] and provides a reference implementation of the firewall.

She formally demonstrates that the firewall verifications of bytecodes are sufficient to fulfil the security policy and to ensure the memory integrity (that only an authorised operation can access the memory). Bieber *et al.* [7] propose a verification technique based on model checking for detecting illegal information flow between Java Card applets. They associate a level with each applet and the legal flow between applets are given as a lattice of levels. Each applet is abstracted into a set of call graphs. All call graphs that do not include an interface methods are discarded (the sharing mechanism uses interface method). All values of variables are abstracted by computed levels, a variable having the level of the applets which use it. They give an invariant that is a sufficient condition for the security property, and verify it by model checking. It would be worth examining how the semantics defined in this paper can be used to provide a formal proof of correctness of their analysis.

6 Summary

We have described a small-step operational semantics of a representative subset of byte codes pertaining to the Java Card firewall. In doing so, we have deliberately abstracted away certain aspects of the language; for example, numeric calculations are not modelled. The continuation of this work is to demonstrate that the level of abstraction chosen is suitable for constructing and arguing the correctness of verification techniques for the firewall.

References

1. Java Card 2.1.1. http://java.sun.com/products/javacard/javacard21.html. 95
2. The BALI project, Last visited 2001.
   http://www4.informatik.tu-muenchen.de/~isabelle/bali/. 108
3. The LOOP project, Last visited 2001. http://www.cs.kun.nl/~bart/LOOP/. 108
4. Jim Alves-Foss, editor. *Formal syntax and semantics of Java*, volume 1523 of *Lecture Notes in Computer Science*. Springer-Verlag, 1999. 404 pages. 108
5. Peter Bertelsen. Semantics of Java Byte Code. Technical report, Dep. of Information Technology, Technical University of Denmark, March 1997. Home page http://www.dina.kvl.dk/~pmb/. 99, 102, 108
6. Peter Bertelsen. Dynamic semantics of Java bytecode. In *Workshop on Principles on Abstract Machines*, September 1998.
   Home page http://www.dina.kvl.dk/~pmb/. 99, 102
7. Pierre Bieber, Jacques Cazin, Abdellah El Marouani, Pierre Girard, Jean-Louis Lanet, Virginie Wiels, and Guy Zanon. The PACAP prototype : a tool for detecting Java Card illegal flow. In Isabelle Attali and Thomas Jensen, editors, *Java Card Workshop (JCW)*, volume 2041 of *Lecture Notes in Computer Science*, September 2000. 109
8. Zhiqun Chen. *Java Card Technology for Smart Cards: Architecture and Programmer's Guide*. Addison Wesley, 2000. 95

9. Ewen Denney and Thomas Jensen. Correctness of Java Card method lookup via logical relations. In *9th European Symp. on Programming (ESOP)*, pages 104–118. Springer-Verlag, March 2000. 103
10. Stephen N. Freund and John C. Mitchell. A formal framework for the Java bytecode language and verifier. *Conf. on Object-Oriented Programming, Systems, Languages and Applications (OOPSLA)*, 34(10):147–166, November 1999. 108
11. James Gosling, Bill Joy, Guy Steele, and Gilad Bracha. *The Java Language Specification, Second Edition*. Addison Wesley, 2000. 896 pages, http://java.sun.com/docs/books/jls/index.html. 103
12. Sun Microsystems. Java Card 2.1.1 runtime environment (JCRE) specification, May 2000. Revision 1.0, 61 pages. 108
13. Stéphanie Motré. Modélisation et implémentation formelle de la politique de sécurité dynamique de la Java Card. In *Approches Formelles dans l'Assistance au Développement de Logiciel (AFADL)*, pages 158–172. LSR/IMAG, January 2000. 108
14. Erik Poll, Joachim van den Berg, and Bart Jacobs. Specification of the JavaCard API in JML. In J. Domingo-Ferrer, D. Chan, and A. Watson, editors, *4th Smart Card Research and Advanced Application Conf. (CARDIS)*, pages 135–154. Kluwer Acad. Publ., 2000. 108
15. Erik Poll, Joachim van den Berg, and Bart Jacobs. Formal specification of the JavaCard API in JML: the APDU class. *Computer Networks Magazine*, 2001. 108
16. Cornelia Pusch. Formalizing the Java Virtual Machine in Isabelle/HOL. Technical Report TUM-I9816, Institut für informatik, Technische Universtät München, 1998. 108
17. Soot: a Java optimization framework. http://www.sable.mcgill.ca/soot/. 98
18. David von Oheimb. Hoare logic for Java in Isabelle/HOL. *Concurrency: Practice and Experience*, 2001. 108
19. David von Oheimb and Tobias Nipkow. Machine-checking the Java specification: Proving type-safety. In Jim Alves-Foss, editor, *Formal Syntax and Semantics of Java*, volume 1523 of *Lecture Notes in Computer Science*, pages 119–156. Springer-Verlag, 1999. 108

CardS4:
Modal Theorem Proving on Java Smartcards

Rajeev Prabhakar Goré[1] * and Phuong Thê Nguyên[2] **

[1] Automated Reasoning Group, Computer Sciences Laboratory,
Res. Sch. of Inf. Sci. and Eng.
Institute of Advanced Studies, Australian National University
rpg@arp.anu.edu.au
arp.anu.edu.au/~rpg
[2] Formal Methods Group, Dept. of Computer Science, Fac. of Eng. and Inf. Tech.
The Faculties, Australian National University
ntp@cse.unsw.edu.au
www.cse.unsw.edu.au/~ntp

Abstract. We describe a successful implementation of a theorem prover
for modal logic **S4** that runs on a Java smart card with only 512 KBytes
of RAM and 32KBytes of EEPROM. Since proof search in **S4** can lead
to infinite branches, this is "proof of principle" that non-trivial modal
deduction is feasible even on current Java cards. We hope to use this
prover as the basis of an on-board security manager for restricting the
flow of "secrets" between multiple applets residing on the same card,
although much work needs to be done to design the appropriate modal
logics of "permission" and "obligations". Such security concerns are the
major impediments to the commercial deployment of multi-application
smart cards.

Keywords: security of mobile code, modal deduction

1   Introduction

Smart cards are credit-card sized pieces of plastic with an embedded silicon
chip. Smart cards are either memory cards, which cannot be programmed, or
microprocessor cards, which contain a small amount of RAM and disc (EEP-
ROM) on the card itself. A card reader/writer is required to provide power to
the card, to provide a clock signal, and to act as an interface between the card
and the terminal (a PC, an ATM machine, a public telephone, or even a mobile
telephone).

Java cards are smart cards that contain a (downsized) Java platform, installed
by the manufacturer, thus allowing users to download Java applets and run
them on the card. Java cards can therefore provide multiple applications such as

---

* Supported by a Queen Elizabeth II Fellowship from the Australian Research Council.
** Supported by an RSISE Summer Research Scholarship.

electronic purse, credit card, passport, loyalty programmes, all residing on the same card.

The Java cards used in this project were the GemXpresso RAD Protyping card, containing a 32-bit microprocessor with 512 bytes of RAM, 32 KBytes of Flash EEPROM and 8 KBytes of ROM.

Current Java cards are preprogrammed to contain applets by the manufacturer for the card vendor, typically a bank (for credit and debit cards), or an airline (for frequent flyer cards). But if Java cards are to succeed then a card carrier must be able to down-load new applets onto an existing card "just in time", or even merge existing cards into one card. This would mean that multiple applets from different vendors would reside on the same card.

The single biggest problem with this scenario is that of security. How can we guarantee that a simple query to the drivers licence section of the card for identification purposes (say) will not steal money from the card's electronic purse? If new applets are to be down-loaded then how can the vendor of applet A ensure that a competing vendor's applet will not be down-loaded at a later stage and steal information from applet A? Alternatively, applets A and B may trust each other to some extent, and therefore share some information. But if applets B and C enjoy a similar trust relationship, how can A be sure that B will not tell C information which it has obtained from A [Gir99,PB00] ?

Many methodologies for guaranteeing such security have been investigated, but almost all of them involve a trusted "third" party. For example, the bank applet may be signed using a digital signature obtained from the government that certifies that the applet really did originate from the bank in question. The digital certificate is decoded by the card's on-board digital signature chip and the applet is allowed to access the card's electronic purse. But the need for a certification agency and a certification procedure makes this avenue cumbersome.

An alternative methodology that involves no third parties is for card owners to implement a personal security policy using some international standard "language for security". The electronic purse applet installed on the card may come with such a built in security policy which the user is prompted to tailor to his or her needs. Another applet which wishes to access the electronic purse must now pass a challenge determined by the level of security chosen by the card user.

As new applets are added to the card, they are slotted into this set up either explicitly by the card user, or by some implicit default method. The simplest method is to use some form of access control list as is done by the Smart Card for Windows system (http://www.microsoft.com.smartcard), which uses simple propositional logic in its access control lists. A more sophisticated approach is to use a hierarchy with the "public" applets at the bottom, the "private" applets at the top, and the others in between these two extremes in some partial order [Gir99,PB00]. But this work does not address the problem of the dynamics of this partial order when a new applet is down-loaded. In particular, how can we be sure that all the previously checked "shared secrecy" conditions are satisfied by the new hierarchy ?

One way to define such a security policy is to use formal mathematical logic and to ensure that the permission granted to down-loaded applications meet certain rigorously defined security criteria expressed as formulae of logic. For example, notions like "agent i trusts agent j" are easily encoded as statements of multi-modal propositional logics, which are now well-established in artificial intelligence research as bases for defeasible reasoning [Shv90], logics of agents [RG93], and logics of authentication [BAN90,Mat97]. Multi-modal logics like Propositional Dynamic Logic [Gol87] have also been used to model the changing states of a program. Finally, propositional bi-modal tense logics give a very simple and elegant model of the flow of time [HC96].

Checking that a down-loaded applet meets the security criteria is now reduced to proving, **on-board**, that an appropriate formula is a theorem of the logic used to code the criteria, since this is the only computer that the customer should trust. Multi-modal logics are particularly well-suited to this task as most of them are decidable. Consequently, the ability to perform automated multi-modal deduction on Java smart cards may be of use in electronic commerce.

But surely multi-modal deduction is simply too difficult to perform on a smart card with extremely limited resources ? After all, even classical propositional logic is NP-complete, and most multi-modal logics are actually PSPACE-complete!

In [GNg00] automated deduction in bi-modal tense logics was shown to be feasible on a Java smart card. It is reasonably straightforward to extend this work to other multi-modal logics, and hence to logics of knowledge and belief, or to logics of authentication and security. But many of these logics (e.g. PDL) contain operators which are inherently transitive, and transitivity can lead to infinite loops. Here we show that transitivity is not insurmountable by implementing a prover for modal logic **S4**. Thus our work is "proof of principle" that a logic-based security policy could be implemented on current Java cards. As the resources and speed of Java cards skyrocket, the task will only become simpler.

The paper is set out as follows. Section 2 describes the logic **S4** and the basics of modal theorem proving using tableaux. Section 3 explains the design of our prover `CardS4`. Section 6 presents test results and Section 7 presents conclusions.

ACKNOWLEDGEMENTS: We are grateful to Didier Tollé of Gemplus Australia for donating the hardware necessary to carry out this project.

2   Syntax, Semantics and Tableaux for Modal Logic S4

2.1   Syntax and Semantics for S4

Given a denumerably infinite set of atomic formulae PRP $= \{p_0, p_1, p_2, \cdots\}$, a formulae φ of modal logic is defined using the following BNF grammar:

$$p ::= p_0 \mid p_1 \mid p_2 \mid \cdots$$
$$\varphi ::= \top \mid \bot \mid p \mid \neg\varphi_1 \mid \varphi_1 \wedge \varphi_2 \mid \varphi_1 \vee \varphi_2 \mid \varphi_1 \rightarrow \varphi_2 \mid \Diamond\varphi \mid \Box\varphi$$

$$
\begin{array}{llll}
w \models \top & \text{for every } w \in W & w \models \bot & \text{for no } w \in W \\
w \models p & \text{if } w \in V(p) & w \models \neg A & \text{if } w \not\models A \\
w \models A \wedge B \quad \text{if} \quad w \models A \text{ and } w \models B & & w \models A \vee B \quad \text{if} \quad w \models A \text{ or } w \models B \\
w \models A \rightarrow B \quad \text{if} \quad w \not\models A \text{ or } w \models B & & \\
w \models \Diamond A \qquad \text{if} \quad (\exists v \in R(w))(v \models A) & & w \models \Box A \qquad \text{if} \quad (\forall v \in R(w))(v \models A)
\end{array}
$$

Fig. 1. Kripke semantics for **S4**

The standard Kripke semantics for **S4** are as follows. A Kripke frame is a pair $\langle W, R \rangle$ where W is a non-empty set (of worlds) and R is a binary relation over W. A Kripke model $\langle W, R, V \rangle$ is a Kripke frame $\langle W, R \rangle$ augmented with a valuation $V : \text{PRP} \cup \{\top, \bot\} \mapsto 2^W$ mapping each atomic formula and atomic constant to the subset of W where they take the value "true". If $w \in V(p)$ we write $w \Vdash p$ and extend this satisfaction relation to arbitrary formulae in the usual way [HC96] as shown in Figure 1 where for any $w \in W$, $R(w) := \{v \in W \mid wRv\}$.

An **S4**-model is a Kripke model where R is both reflexive $(\forall w \in W)[wRw]$ and transitive $(\forall w_1, w_2, w_3 \in W)[w_1 R w_2 \ \& \ w_2 R w_3 \Rightarrow w_1 R w_3]$.

A formula φ is **S4**-satisfiable if there exists some **S4**-model with some $w \in W$ such that $w \Vdash \varphi$. A formula φ is **S4**-valid if $w \Vdash V(\varphi)$ for every $w \in W$ in every **S4**-model $\langle W, R, V \rangle$.

2.2 Proof Search in S4 Using Tableau Calculi

The problem of deciding whether or not a formula is **S4**-satisfiable is known to be **PSPACE**-complete [Lad77a,Lad77b] although the best known decision procedures use only $O(n^2.logn)$-space [Hud].

The most popular method for implementing theorem provers for **S4** is to use the tableau method [Fit83,Gor99]. In addition to the standard rules for classical propositional logic, we require only the following two rules, and their duals for $\neg\Box$ and $\neg\Diamond$ obtained via the equivalences $\neg\Box\varphi = \Diamond\neg\varphi$ and $\neg\Diamond\varphi = \Box\neg\varphi$:

$$
(\Box\mathbf{S4}) \ \frac{X, \Box\varphi}{X, \Box\varphi, \varphi} \qquad\qquad (\Diamond\mathbf{S4}) \ \frac{X, \Box Y, \Diamond\varphi}{\Box Y, \varphi}
$$

An **S4**-tableau for a finite set of formulae Z is a binary tree of nodes where: the root node contains Z and the children are obtained by an application of some tableau rules for **S4** to the parent node. The rules are applied systematically so that the $\Box\mathbf{S4}$ rule is applied only to a "saturated" node: a node to which all other rules have already been applied. A branch of such an **S4**-tableau is closed if its leaf node contains both φ and $\neg\varphi$ for some formula φ; otherwise the branch is open. The whole **S4**-tableau is closed if every branch in it is closed, otherwise it is open.

Theorem 1 (Soundness and Completeness). *The finite set* $\{\neg\varphi\}$ *has a closed* **S4***-tableau iff the formula* φ *is* **S4***-valid [Fit83,Gor99].*

Corollary 1. *If every* **S4**-*tableau for the finite set* $\{\neg\varphi\}$ *is open then the formula* φ *is* **S4**-*satisfiable.*

The completeness proof gives a systematic method for proof-search which consists of repeatedly applying all the rules of classical propositional logic, and the ($\Box$**S4**)-rule, until no more applications of these rules is possible. The resulting node then corresponds to a "saturated" world in the underlying Kripke model under construction; see [Gor99] for details. Some $\Diamond$-formula is then singled out for attention from this "saturated" node and a "successor" is created for it using the ($\Diamond$**S4**)-rule.

Naive proof search for a closed **S4**-tableau for some finite set of formulae Z using this systematic method can lead to infinite loops viz $Z = \{\Box\Diamond p, p\}$:

$$\frac{\dfrac{\dfrac{\Box\Diamond p, p}{\Box\Diamond p, \Diamond p, p}\ (\Box\mathbf{S4})}{\Box\Diamond p, p}\ (\Diamond\mathbf{S4})}{}$$

One solution for detecting loops involves storing certain nodes as they are encountered, checking for repetitions, and backtracking if necessary.

3   Algorithms

We now describe our algorithm and data structures in more detail.

3.1   Terms

Negated Normal Form: Input formulae are assumed to be in negated normal form (NNF): all implications $\varphi \to \phi$ are rewritten as $\neg\varphi\vee\phi$, and negations are pushed through all connectives so the negation symbol appears only before atomic formulae. This requirement is not restrictive since every formulae can be converted into a logically equivalent NNF formula in linear time [BG98]. The advantage of using NNF is that the formulae in the parse tree of the NNF formula constitute all of the formulae that can appear in any node of the search tree.

Parse tree: A formula is parsed as a tree, where each node has at most two children. The nodes are characterized as CONJ, DISJ, ALL, SOME if they are of type $\varphi\wedge\psi, \varphi\vee\psi, \Box\varphi, \Diamond\varphi$ respectively. At the leaves there are literals: atomic formulae or their negations. Each node represents a subformula of the original NNF formula, with the root representing the whole NNF formula. With the tableaux rules above, it can be shown that the subformulae that appear in the parse tree are all the formulae that can appear in the nodes of the search tree. Clearly, the number of nodes in the parse tree is less than or equal to the length of the formula (it is exactly the length of the formula less the number of negative symbols). The number of formulae in any node of the search tree is therefore less than the length of the original NNF formula.

The parse tree is indexed so that each parent node has a smaller index than its children. This simplifies the visit sequence of the parse tree, as can be seen below.

Search Tree: In the sequel we refer to the **S4** tableau as the search tree.

Model Tree: We refer to the underlying Kripke (tree-)model as the model tree. By "path" we mean an R-path in this model tree.

Good Nodes: A node of the search tree is "good" if no application of the $\Diamond$**S4** rule to this node gives a closed branch.

$n_\Diamond$, $n_\Box$, $n_\lor$, $n_\land$: The number of subformulae of the appropriate type in the original NNF formula.

3.2   Storing Nodes in the Search Tree

The parse tree provides access to the finite list of all formulae that can appear in the nodes of the search tree. Thus each node in the search tree can be represented as a bit string, whose bits indicate whether or not the corresponding formulae is present in the node. This bit string has length equal to the length of the original formula. Thus storing one node in the search tree requires n bits, where n is the length of the original formula.

3.3   Loop Checking

As shown in Section 2.2, an **S4**-tableau can contain an infinite branch. This problem can be solved by noticing that only a finite number of different nodes can appear in a search tree, and by avoiding examining any node twice. Thus if a node has ever been encountered before, it can be safely ignored.

The naive solution is to store each "saturated" node of the branch in a check list since these nodes correspond to worlds in the counter-model under construction, and to explicitly look for repeated worlds. When a world re-appears, we must terminate proof search along this (open) branch and backtrack to the previous application of the ($\Diamond$**S4**)-rule to choose a principal formula $\Diamond\psi$ different from the $\Diamond\varphi$ that lead to this loop; see the ($\Diamond$**S4**)-rule. If all such choices lead to open (or looping) branches, then we backtrack higher up to the previous application of the ($\Diamond$**S4**)-rule, and so on until all avenues have been explored, or a closed **S4**-tableau is found. This, however, is not a practical method, since it would require exponential space to store all the possible nodes of the search tree.

A better method is to check for repetitions of the nodes obtained by the application of the $\Diamond$**S4** rule since these contain the "core" of the new world. That is, the $\Diamond$**S4** rule is a transitional rule which goes from one world in the tree model to one of its successors. Thus the latter method looks for repetitions of the initial configuration of each newly generated world. This also guarantees the solution for the infinite branch problem, yet requires polynomial space. The price is that identical nodes on different branches now have to be treated separately.

3.4 A Straightforward Nondeterministic Algorithm

The following algorithm returns true if a given formula φ_0 of length n is **S4**-satisfiable, and false otherwise. It requires n^4 space.

$stack$ ::= empty
$checkList$ ::= empty
$currentWorld$ ::= $\{\varphi_0\}$
do
    while there are $\wedge$, $\vee$, $\square$ rules that can be applied **do**
        apply these rules to $currentWorld$
        if the rule applied is an $\vee$ rule **then**
            push ($checkListSize$, left child of the rule) onto $stack$
            $currentWorld$ ::= the right child of rule
        end if
    end while
    if $currentWorld$ is inconsistent **then**
        if the $stack$ is empty **then**
            return false
        else
            ($checkListSize$, $currentWorld$) ::= pop from $stack$
            resize $checkList$ to $checkListSize$
            continue
        end if
    end if
    if $currentWorld$ appears in $checkList$ **then**
        return true
    end if
    if no ($\Diamond$**S4**)-rules can be applied **then**
        return true
    end if
    non-deterministically pick a formula $\Diamond\varphi$ from $currentWorld$
    apply ($\Diamond$**S4**)-rule using $\Diamond\varphi$ to $currentWorld$ to get $newWorld$
    put $currentWorld$ into $checkList$
    $currentWorld$ ::= $newWorld$
while $stack$ is not empty

Space Complexity It can be seen that $stack$ grows by 1 only when the ($\vee$) rule is applied. Thus for one world, we may need to store the maximum of $n_\vee$ possible configurations. Also the transitional rule ($\Diamond$**S4**) which moves from one world to another preserves all the $\square$-formulae, thus the set of all $\square$-formulae (the core) in consecutive worlds in a branch of the search tree do not decrease. Therefore there are at most $n_\square$ different cores in the same branch of the search tree. Also the worlds that have the same core will form a chain in the branch. We need to find the maximum number of worlds in a chain that have the same core.

Since each new world is formed by taking all the $\Box$ formulae from the previous world together with one of the $\Diamond$ formulae, the maximum number of worlds in the chain that have the same core is $n_\Diamond$. Altogether, the maximum number of configurations that we need to store in the stack is $n_\lor \times n_\Box \times n_\Diamond \le n^3$ (a better approximation is $n^3/3$).

It can be seen that *checkList* contains only the node which is obtained by applying a ($\Diamond$**S4**) rule. It is also resized so that all the nodes it contains are the initial configurations of the worlds in the current search branch. Thus *checkList* is always smaller than or equal to *stack*. Overall, the maximum number of configurations we might need to store in *stack* and *checkList* is of order n^3. Given that a configuration needs n bits, the space complexity of this algorithm is n^4 [Lad77a,Lad77b].

3.5   An Improved Algorithm

First, the non-determinism must be eliminated. Note that a node in the search tree is good if every node that is obtained from it by applying the ($\Diamond$**S4**) rule is good. Thus non-determinism can be eliminated by examining every node obtainable from a node by the ($\Diamond$**S4**) rule. This can be done by storing the world configuration before applying the ($\Diamond$**S4**) rule and keeping the index of the last ($\Diamond$**S4**) rule applied to that configuration.

Second, it is not necessary to store all possible different configurations of a world since we can obtain some configurations from others. Notice that when applying an $\lor$ rule, choosing a different child of the $\lor$ formula gives a different possible configuration. Thus if each subformula of the original formula is named differently then it is possible to move from one node in the search tree to its sibling without storing them. This naming of the nodes of the parse tree forbids common sub-expressions and therefore introduces some redundancy. There may be duplications of the same subformula, but they are named with different indices, so they must be examined independently.

In the following algorithm, the stack stores only the configurations that have been fully expanded with non-($\Diamond$**S4**) rules.

checkList ::= empty
stack ::= empty
currentWorld ::= world consisting of the original formula
do
    while there are $\land$, $\Box$**S4** rules that can be applied **do**
        apply these rules to *currentWorld*
    end while
    if there are $\lor$ rules which can be applied **then**
        apply these rules to *currentWorld* such that
            if one child of the $\lor$ formula is already in *currentWorld* **then**
                take that child into *currentWorld*
            else
                take the first child of the $\lor$-formula in to *currentWorld*

        end if
        continue
    end if
    if *currentWorld* is inconsistent **then**
        mark *currentWorld* as *closed*
    end if
    if *currentWorld* is marked *closed* **then**
        if there is another sibling of *currentWorld* **then**
            take *currentWorld* to be that sibling
            reset *lastK_index* to indicate no $\Diamond$**S4** rules have been applied yet
            continue
        else if the *stack* is empty **then**
            return false
        else
            (*lastK_index*, *currentWorld*) ::= pop from *stack*
            pop from *checkList*
            mark *currentWorld* as *closed*
            continue
        end if
    end if
    if no more ($\Diamond$**S4**) rules can be applied **then**
        if *stack* is empty **then**
            return true
        else
            (*lastK_index*, *currentWorld*) ::= pop from *stack*
            pop from *checkList*
        end if
    end if
    lastK_index ::= the next $\Diamond$-formula from *currentWorld*
    apply the $\Diamond$**S4** rule to *currentWorld* to get *newWorld*
    if *newWorld* appears in *checkList* **then**
        continue
    end if
    put (*lastK_index*, *currentWorld*) into *stack*
    put *newWorld* into *checkList*
    currentWorld ::= *newWorld*
    continue
while *stack* is not empty

Note that now *checkList* and *stack* are of the same size. The *checkList* is actually the core of the world configuration stored at the corresponding location in *stack*. Thus it can be obtained from *stack* by generating the core of each world in *stack*. This gives a more efficient use of space. It can be seen that for one node in the search tree, we need only one location in *stack*. Thus the space requirement is reduced by a factor of $n_\vee$: the maximum number of configurations stored in *stack* at one time is $n_\square \times n_\lozenge \leq n^2$, and the space complexity of this algorithm is n^3 (a better approximation is $n_\square \times n_\lozenge \leq n^2/2$, and the space requirement is $n^3/2$).

4   Data Structures

4.1   The Parse Tree

The parse tree is stored in two byte arrays, one (*childs*) of length $2n$ and the other (*nature*) of length n. The $2i$ and $2i+1$ entries in the first array indicate the children of the i-th node in the parse tree (i.e. the indices of some other nodes in the parse tree, or the atom at that node), while the i-th entry in the second array indicates if the i-th node in the parse tree is a $\square$, $\lozenge$, $\vee$, $\wedge$, $\neg$ or PRP. The $\vee$ and $\wedge$ nodes have two children. The $\square$, $\lozenge$, $\neg$ and PRP nodes have one child, thus the second child for these node is redundant. This is not a severe problem, since the parse tree is fixed through the proving procedure. Note that in case of the $\neg$ and PRP nodes, the $2i$ entry of the *child* array contains the atom itself, not the index to another node in the parse tree.

4.2   The Nodes in the Search Tree

As discussed above, each node in the search tree can be represented as a bit string of length n. To examine all the ($\lozenge$**S4**)- rules that can be applied to a node (i.e all the $\lozenge$ formulae in that node), we need to store the index to the last $\lozenge$ formula that has been examined, requiring one more byte.

4.3   The Stack

Nodes are stored in a stack so that other branches in the search tree can be generated from the current branch, and so that a new node can be checked for duplication. This requires searching through all nodes in the stack, and also pushing and popping from the stack.

There are several possible implementations for the stack. The first two options store the stack as an array of bytes, and do not need extra memory for pointers. Since multidimensional arrays are not supported, access to elements of the stack will require some extra computations.

The upper bound of the size of the stack is known as seen above. Thus the stack can be allocated at the beginning of the procedure. We then need not worry about the growth of the stack. However, this is not a practical method, since the stack rarely grows to its theoretical upper bound size. Also, the limited amount of memory on the card will restrict the size of the input formulae. For example, with 512 bytes, the length of the formula will be less than 16 ($16^3/2$ bits $= 512$ byte). Allocating more than the card's RAM is possible, however it involves swapping to and from the EEPROM and will slow down the proof procedure. Consequently, the card reader usually cannot wait for the card and will throw an Exception.

Another way to implement the stack is to pre-allocate a small stack, and gradually increase its size by a large step when it becomes full. This ensures that the memory is used more effectively. However it still contains redundancy since it allocates more space than required each time it becomes full. Thus the longer formulae will result in larger redundancy. It also involves a lot of copying each time the stack grows.

The stack can also be implemented as a one way link list. Each node in the search tree is an element of the list. This requires extra memory for a pointer to the next element. However this extra memory becomes insignificant for long formulae. There is no redundancy. With this approach, the program has been tested for formulae of length up to 120.

5   Implementation

The program consists of two packages: `card` and `client`. The `client` package contains the classes for parsing the formula and converting it into NNF. Parsing is done by using Javacup (version 1.0j). We need a scanner (`scanner.java`) and a specification (`parser.cup`) for the formula, and Javacup automatically creates the parser. There is also a card proxy which manages the interactions with the card on behalf of the users. The class for testing is also in this package. Note that all of these operations are done off-board on a terminal (PC).

The `card` package contains an interface and two classes that are downloaded onto the card. These are classes `prover` and `State`, and the interface `proverInterface` The interface `proverInterface` provides access to the services offered by the prover. These include loading the formula onto the card and proving. The interface also defines constants that are used by the prover, and are also used in the parsing and converting procedures. The class `prover` contains the codes for the proving procedure. The `prover` object that is loaded onto the card reserves enough space to hold the longest formula. When the formula is put onto the card, it is stored in the object. The user then must explicitly call the `prove` procedures. The `prove` method reads the formula from the object, performs simplifications and then starts looking for a model for the formula. (Note that there is a separation between loading the formula and proving. This is due to the fact that loading is rather complicated, and it is discussed in the next paragraph).

Despite the limitations of the card, the prover is able to work for a number of long formulae. Tests have been conducted for formulae of length up to 120. Passing the input to the card and storing input in the card then requires greater care because communication with the card is not simple. There is an upper-bound for the amount of data that can be transfered in one transmission (approaching 64K is not recommended). Long formulae therefore need to be broken into small pieces. Here, the input arrays are split into pieces of length 32 bytes and each pieces is passed separately to the card, together with its length and position in the original array. Thus the maximum amount of data in one transmission is 34 bytes (one byte for the length and one for the position).

Since the inputs to the `prove` method are not ready in one pass, they need to be stored in the object `prover`, requiring the reservation of space for the longest input. Note that this also implies more time is required for copying the input from EEPROM to RAM in the `prove` procedure.

6   Results

This section shows the average time spent on the card in proving randomly generated formulae of various lengths (from 20 to 120). As can be seen, the time increases with the length of the formulae since longer formulae generally require more stack space, and require more arithmetic operations in the calculations.

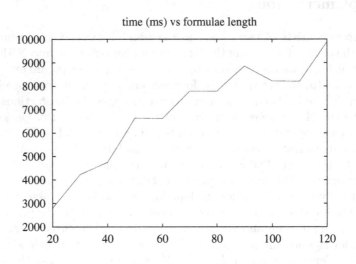

Fig. 2. Time (ms) vs formulae length

7   Conclusions and Further Work

We have shown that even modal logic **S4** can be handled on a Java card. Thus transitive modal logics are not necessarily beyond the scope of Java cards. We now need to invent appropriate logics of permissions and obligations to allow us to capture basic security notions like "trust". This is the subject of further work.

Another method for loop checking is to keep track of certain formula using a history mechanism [Heu99]. We intend to investigate whether such a history mechanism can be easily used in `CardS4`.

References

BAN90. M. Burrows, M. Abadi, and R. Needham. A logic of authentication. *ACM Transactions on Computer Systems*, 8:18–36, 1990. 113

BG98.   N. Bonnette and R. Goré. A labelled sequent system for tense logic Kt. In *AI98: Proceedings of the Australian Joint Conference on Artificial Intelligence*, LNAI 1502:71-82. Springer, 1998. 115

Fit83. M. Fitting. *Proof Methods for Modal and Intuitionistic Logics*, volume 169 of *Synthese Library*. D. Reidel, Dordrecht, Holland, 1983. 114

Gir99. Pierre Girard. Which security policy for multiapplication smart cards. In *Proceedings USENIX Workshop on Smartcard Technology*, pages 21–28, Chicago, USA, 1999. 112

Gol87. R. I. Goldblatt. *Logics of Time and Computation*. CSLI Lecture Notes Number 7, Center for the Study of Language and Information, Stanford, 1987. 113

Gor99. R. Goré. Chapter 6: Tableau methods for modal and temporal logics. In M. D'Agostino, D. Gabbay, R. Hänle, J. Posegga, editor, *Handbook of Tableau Methods*, pages 297–396. Kluwer Academic Publishers, 1999. 114, 115

GNg00. R Goré and L. D. Nguyen. CardKt: Automated Multi-modal Deduction on Javacards for Multi-application Security. In Proc. Java Card Workshop. Springer LNCS, to appear 2001. 113

Heu99. A. Heuerding. *Automated Deduction in Some Propositional Modal Logics*. Institut für Angewandte Mathematik und Informatik. Universitäte Bern, Switzerland, 1999. 122

HC96.   G. E. Hughes and M. J. Cresswell. *A New Introduction To Modal Logic*. Routledge, 1996. 113, 114

Hud.   J. Hudelmaier. Improved decision procedures for the modal logics K, T and S4. 114

Lad77a. R. Ladner. The computational complexity of provability in systems of modal propositional logic. *SIAM Journal of Computing*, 6(3):467–480, September 1977. 114, 118

Lad77b. Richard Ladner. The computational complexity of provability in systems of modal propositional logic. *SIAM Journal of Computing*, 6(3):467–480, 1977. 114, 118

Mat97. Anish Mathuria. *Contributions to Authentication Logics and Analysis of Authentication Protocols*. PhD thesis, School of Information Technology and Computer Science, University of Woolongong, Woolongong, Australia, 1997. 113

PB00.   P. Girard, J.-L. Lanet, V. Wiels, G. Zanon, P. Bieber, J Cazin. Checking secure interactions of smart card applets. Technical report, Gemplus R&D Centre, 2000. http://www.gemplus.com/smart/r_d/projects/pacap.htm. 112

RG93.   A. Rao and M. Georgeff. A model-theoretic approach to the verification of situated reasoning systems. In *Proceedings of the Thirteenth International Joint Conference on Artificial Intelligence (IJCAI-93)*, pages 318–324. Morgan-Kauffman, 1993. 113

Shv90. Grigori F. Shvarts. Autoepistemic modal logics. In Rohit Parikh, editor, *Theoretical Aspects About Reasoning About Knowledge*, pages 97–109, 1990. 113

iButton Enrolment and Verification Requirements for the Pressure Sequence Smartcard Biometric

Neil J. Henderson[1], Neil M. White[1], and Pieter H. Hartel[2]

[1] Department of Electronics and Computer Science, University of Southampton
Southampton SO17 1BJ, United Kingdom
{njh98r,nmw}@ecs.soton.ac.uk
[2] Department of Computer Science, University of Twente, The Netherlands
pieter@cs.utwente.nl

Abstract. With the growing number of smartcard applications there comes an increasing need to restrict access to the card itself. In previous work we proposed the pressure sequence biometric, within which a biometric sensor is integrated onto the card in a low-cost and mechanically compliant manner. Using an off-card verifier we demonstrated *reasonable* discrimination between users. In this paper we consider a number of on-card verification schemes, the best of which offers an equal error rate of 2.3%. On-card computational time requirements were found to be 3.1 seconds for enrolment and 0.12 seconds for verification. Incorporating our implementation into an existing applet used 684 bytes of program space. Whilst data memory requirements are estimated to be 1400 and 300 bytes for enrolment and verification, respectively. These time and size requirements demonstrate our biometric as a practical proposition for the protection of smart cards. Experiments were performed with the iButton's Java Card platform.

1 Introduction

In the rapidly growing world of the Internet and e-Commerce, smartcards offer the potential to protect data. This illustrates just one of the functions of a smartcard driving the motivation to protect and secure access to the smartcard itself. A number of schemes have been proposed whereby some device external to the smart card captures a biometric quantity, which is subsequently verified on a smartcard platform [19]. Off-card sensors suffer from the limitation that the external biometric device must be both present and trusted. This is hard to achieve [7]. In earlier work [8] we proposed the pressure sequence method, a novel biometric, which is both mechanically and economically compliant for incorporation onto the smartcard itself. In this paper we report on the implementation of enrolment and verification functions of our biometric on Dallas Semiconductor's iButton Java Card platform [18], thereby demonstrating the viability of our biometric from the perspective of available computational resources.

I. Attali and T. Jensen (Eds.): E-smart 2001, LNCS 2140, pp. 124–134, 2001.

The pressure sequence method measures the differences with which a user taps a sequence, or rhythm, upon a simple polymer pressure sensor. The recognition of people from a series of taps or pulses has some precedent. For example early telegraphic operators recognised other operators by the way in which they keyed information. Operators developed a distinctive 'fist' or telegraphic style that could be recognised [4]. Indeed much work has been reported on the use of a person's typing style, or keystroke dynamics [9], as a route to identity verification. Rumelhart and Norman [17] offer an explanation for the discriminating basis of keystroke dynamics, suggesting that differences in typing style are due to both the physical characteristics of the hand - such as finger length and agility - and the level of motor control of a person.

The pressure sequence method seeks recognition by the pattern of pressure pulses between fingertip and pressure sensor, resulting to some measure from the biomechanical characteristics of a person's hand and wrist. The human hand is complex and offers scope for discrimination between people. This is demonstrated in its composition of 19 bones, 19 joints and 20 muscles, combining to give 22 degrees of freedom [11].

For the pressure sequence method to gain merit as a verifier, a high level of discrimination must be demonstrated. Since there are strong similarities between the pressure sequence method and that of keystroke dynamics, the discrimination methods of keystroke dynamics have been investigated for their potential to discriminate between people, based only on a sequence of taps on a single pressure sensor. This is justified in that both result from similar neurophysiological and biomechanical mechanisms and that, at a minimum, both consider time intervals between finger taps.

2   Experimental Method

To validate the pressure sequence biometric, 34 students and staff from the Electronics and Computer Science department in Southampton participated in an experiment. Each volunteer was asked to choose a short tapping sequence (typically lasting between 2 and 4 seconds), and to tap that rhythm 30 times. Data collection from each volunteer was collected in one single session in a supervised manner at all times. For further details see our earlier work [8]. Figure 1 shows the analogue waveform of a pressure sequence. It is with these macro features; Pulse Heights, Pulse Widths and Interval Durations, that the pressure sequence method aims to discriminate between a valid and an invalid user. A feature extraction algorithm was devised to pre-process the analogue waveform, generating a single column feature vector comprising of (PulseHeight(1), PulseWidth(1), IntervalDuration(1) , ... , IntervalDuration(n-1), PulseHeight(n), PulseWidth(n)), where n is the number of pulses in a sequence. Table (1) represents the sequence presented in figure 1 as a feature vector.

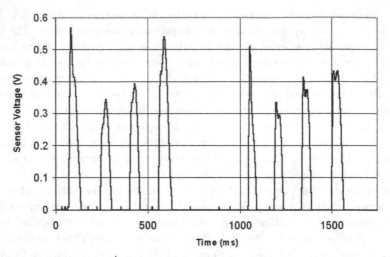

Fig. 1. Unprocessed Pressure Sequence

Table 1. Corresponding Feature Vector

Pulse1 Height	Pulse1 Width	Interval1 Duration	Pulse2 Height	Pulse2 Width	...	...	Interval7 Duration	Pulse8 Height	Pulse8 Width
52.13	115.63	215.5	36.5	105.38	...	...	246.5	48.25	129.38

3   System Architecture

The pre-processing of raw pressure sequence data occurs within a separate biometrics module, comprising of analogue to digital conversion block, alongside feature extraction circuitry. We envisage this module being implemented in a small piece of silicon providing the interface between the analogue sensor and the smartcard's processor. Figure 2 outlines this architecture. This implies that the smartcard's processor will only be presented with the feature vector representation of the pressure sequence, and will not be required to monitor live real-time data.

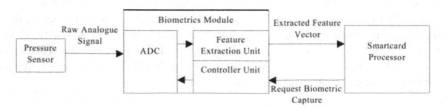

Fig. 2. Biometric System Schematic

This paper assess the viability of using a standard processor for much of the hard work; future work will be to assess the integration of the electronics comprising the biometrics module; for example signal conditioning circuitry, analogue to digital conversion unit and how to protect the wiring on the card.

4 Verification Schemes

A number of authors have reported on the successful use of keystroke dynamics as a route to identification verification [20,14,2,10,1,3,13,16,12,6,21]. The process of verification is essentially the comparison of a live biometric sample to a stored reference template, calculated during the process of enrolment. If the live sample is sufficiently close to the stored reference, then the user's identity will be considered valid. If not, the user will be rejected and denied access to the services or facilities on offer. Due to the similarities, in terms of hand physiology and motor control, responsible for underlying mechanisms of both keystroke dynamics and the pressure sequence method, successful keystroke verification schemes have been assessed (in MatLab V5.3) for their success in recognising a pressure sequences. Table 2 shows our results.

Table 2. Pressure Sequence Error Rates with Verification Scheme

Verification Scheme Keystroke Dynamics Reference(s)	EER %	FRR at 1% FAR
ℓ_1 norm - Fixed Threshold [10]	9.7	80
ℓ_2 norm - Fixed Threshold [21,3,16]	5	41
Component-Wise Linear [12]	7.2	32
MICD - Fixed Threshold [1]	5.2	37
Component-Wise non-Linear [12,16]	3.7	20
ℓ_1 norm - User Specific [10]	2.3	10
ℓ_2 norm - User Specific	3	18
Mahalanobis - Fixed Threshold [16]	3.4	42
Mahalanobis User Specific	2.4	10
MICD - User Specific	2.8	11

Figure 3 shows the effect of the acceptance tolerance on the false acceptance and false rejection rates, whilst figure 4 plots the false acceptance rate against the false rejection rate, or the Receiver Operating Curve (ROC), for the ℓ_1 norm Method. This demonstrates the inverse relationship between False Acceptance Rates (FAR) and False Rejection Rates; as the acceptance threshold for a verifier is tightened, the number of false acceptances decreases. The penalty to pay is an increase in false rejections. This property allows the designer of a verification system the flexibility to match the verifier's performance with the security requirements of an application. The third column in table 2 shows the false rejection penalties incurred in tightening the acceptance threshold to allow only 1% false acceptances.

Table 2 shows that the two best verification schemes; namely the user specific ℓ_1 norm and Mahalanobis Distance, demonstrate impressive discrimination properties. The next section deals with these verifiers in detail, outlining their implementation on the iButton.

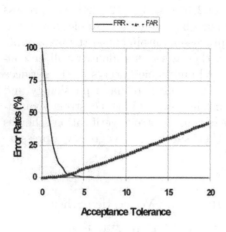
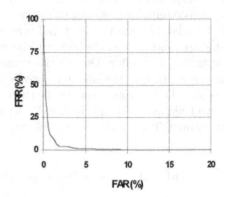

Fig. 3. FAR & FRR with Acceptance Tolerance

Fig. 4. ROC for L1 Norm with User Specific Threshold

5 Implementing Verifiers on the Java-Enabled iButton

A self-contained verification system embedded onto a smartcard must be capable of performing both the enrolment and verification of a user in a *reasonable* time. We accept one-off enrolment times of a few seconds, and per-transaction verification times of less than one second. To test the suitability of our verification schemes, all 10 schemes above have been translated to Java and executed on a Dallas Semiconductor Java-Enabled iButton [18]. The iButton was chosen as a test-platform, being comparable to the latest generation Java-Powered smartcards, in terms of both processing and memory resources, whilst offering accessible simulation and debug facilities. Applets were compiled using Sun Microsystem's JDK2.1.1 under version 1.10 of Dallas Semiconductor's iButton Development environment (iB-IDE). The resulting Java-Code was run on the JavaCard 2.0 compliant Java-Virtual-Machine (JVM) of the iButton. The enrolment and verification functions of each verifier were implemented in a skeletal applet, containing basic functionality to allow PC Host to iButton communication and the timing of enrolment and verification functions. The structure of our test applet is as follows:

- Retrieve and store pre-processed enrolment vectors from PC
- Record start time
- Perform enrolment (a number of times)
- Record finish time
- Send total enrolment time and reference vector to PC

Verification times were measured in the same way as enrolment times, with the verification function called in place of enrolment. Times were recorded using the iButton's real time clock, which has a resolution of only 1 second. The applet executes by firstly loading a user's enrolment feature vectors, pre-processed from their enrolment sequences, to the iButton. The enrolment process is then repeated a number of times. Time is recorded using the iButton's clock value, before and after a number of calls to the enrolment process. From these values an average execution time is calculated. Total time required, along with the computed reference vector, is transmitted to the Host PC. Implementing the process in this way avoids lengthy PC to iButton communications which are not involved in the enrolment (or verification process). This simulation assumes that the enrolment samples have already been captured, pre-processed, and are now available to the processor. Data capture and feature extraction pre-processing is the responsibility of the biometrics module, outlined in figure 2.

5.1   Specific Implementation Issues

There are two fundamental limitations to running our verifiers on the JavaCard platform; the restriction to 32-bit integers and hence the lack of floating-point data-types; and the lack of elementary mathematical functions, such as square-roots.

The fixed threshold version of one of the most successful verification schemes, the ℓ_1 norm is defined as:

$$\|\mathbf{M} - \mathbf{T}\|_1 = \sum_{i=1}^{d} |m_i - t_i| \qquad (1)$$

where $\mathbf{M}$ is the d dimensional reference-vector, generated from the mean of each of the components in the user's enrolment vectors, $\mathbf{T}$ is a d dimensional test vector, and m and t are the components of $\mathbf{M}$ and $\mathbf{T}$ respectively.

The identity of a user will be accepted if:

$$\|\mathbf{M} - \mathbf{T}\|_1 \leq \theta \qquad (2)$$

where θ is the acceptance threshold.

Calculation of the ℓ_1 norm is achievable with no loss of precision under the restriction of the 32-bit integer data type. Using a fixed acceptance threshold, however, resulted in a rather uninspiring equal error rate (EER) of 9.7% (see Table 2), since the same acceptance threshold is used for all users irrespective of their natural variance.

To improve upon this rate, the variation of a user's enrolment vectors from their reference vector can be taken into account. This is performed in the manner of Joyce [10]. If each of the enrolment vectors are S_1, S_2, ..., S_n, respectively, then the ℓ_1 norm between the reference vector, M and S_j is calculated for j = 1 to the number of enrolment vectors. The mean deviation $\overline{D}_{Enrolment}$, and standard deviation, $\sigma_{Enrolment}$, of these distances are calculated and used to decide an acceptance threshold on a per user basis. This results in acceptance of the user's identity if:

$$\|M - T\|_1 \leq |\overline{D}_{Enrolment} - \tau \cdot \sigma_{Enrolment}| \tag{3}$$

where τ is the globally-set acceptance tolerance.

The problem for the integer-only Java Card system is that calculation of $\sigma_{Enrolment}$, the standard deviation of the distance between enrolment vectors and reference vector, requires calculation of a square root:

$$\sigma_{Enrolment} = \sqrt{\frac{\sum_{j=1}^{n}(S - M)^2}{(n - 1)}} \tag{4}$$

Whilst the immediately obvious method for calculation of square roots, the Newton-Raphson method [15], is well known and used, it suffers from a number of problems. Firstly, it is an iterative method, whose efficiency depends upon the quality of the initial guess. Secondly, applied to integers in its native form, the Newton-Raphson method will infinitely oscillate between two integers, above and below a real non-integer root [5]. Crenshaw [5] has devised a simple algorithm for the calculation of square roots. His method is essentially a search through all possible integers until the integer part of a non-integer root is found. The simplest form of this is to search all possible integer square roots, x, for $\sqrt{N}$ until $x^2 \geq N$. The integer root of N is then the exit value of x, minus one. Crenshaw provides a more efficient implementation, arising from the observation:

$$(x + 1)^2 = x^2 + (2x + 1) \tag{5}$$

This means that to check each new possible square root, $(2x + 1)$ merely has to be added to the previous square. The Java code implementation for this is presented as follows:

Java Code for Integer Square Root Function

```
public static int SQRT(int a) {
    int square = 1;            // x=1: 1st Integer Square Root
    int delta = 3;             // (2x+1), for x=1

    while(square<=a) {
        square+=delta;         // (x+1)^2 = x^2 + (2x+1)
        delta +=2;             // Next value for (2x+1)
    }
    return (delta/2 - 1);      // square is now > a, so find
                               // previous value of x

}
```

Although faster fixed cycle-length square root functions exist [5], the time required for execution of the enrolment process using this implementation was measured to be 3.1 seconds - well within the bounds of a *reasonable* duration. 20 square roots were required for the enrolment process, each iterating 49 times. Verification required only 0.12 seconds for completion.

Although the final values for the mean distance and its standard deviation between enrolment vectors and the user's reference vector will be truncated to integer levels, the fractional loss is small relative to the distances involved and is not expected to cause any significant reduction in the verifier's accuracy. Table 3, presenting the floating point and integer results from one user, illustrates this point.

Table 3. Comparison of Floating Point and Integer Results

...	Mean Distance	Standard Deviation
Floating Point Result	221	49.29
iButton's Integer Result	222	48

The second most discriminating method; the Mahalanobis distance verifier is defined as follows:

$$(\mathbf{M} - \mathbf{T}) \cdot \mathbf{V}^{-1} \cdot (\mathbf{M} - \mathbf{T}) \leq |\overline{D}_{Enrolment} - \tau \cdot \sigma_{Enrolment}| \qquad (6)$$

where $\mathbf{M}$, $\mathbf{T}$, $\overline{D}_{Enrolment}$, τ and $\sigma_{Enrolment}$ are as defined in (1) and (3), above. $\mathbf{V}^{-1}$ is defined as the inverse of a square $d \times d$ matrix whose leading diagonal is composed of the variances from each dimension of the enrolment vectors and all other elements are zero.

This leads us to the problem that multi-dimensional arrays are not supported under Java Card 2.0, and as a result matrix manipulation will be both convoluted and time consuming. The solution rests with the analytical reduction of the left-hand side of (6) to give:

$$(\mathbf{M} - \mathbf{T}) \cdot \mathbf{V}^{-1} \cdot (\mathbf{M} - \mathbf{T}) = \sum_{i=1}^{d} \frac{(m_i - t_i)^2}{v_i} \tag{7}$$

where v_i is the variance of the component of the enrolment vectors. Equation (7) now offers a route to the direct computation of the Mahalanobis distance verifier. There is one further catch, however. v_i as the variance of each vector component, is the square of the standard deviation for that component. It is hence likely to be of comparable magnitude to that of the component values. The integer division, therefore, of $(m_i - t_i)^2$ by v_i is extremely likely to result in the loss of a significant fractional part of the result, further compounded by the sum across all components. Pre-multiplying each numerator by $10^{RequiredPrecision}$ and post-dividing the sum by the same enables retention of the fractional information. Table (4) provides the floating point, the integer and the pre-multiplied integer results.

Table 4. Comparison of Floating Point, Integer and Pre-Multiplied Integer Results

...	Mean Distance	Standard Deviation
Floating Point Result	17.5	5.56
iButton's Integer Result	10	4
iButton's Pre-Multiplied Integer Result	17	5

Execution of the Mahalanobis enrolment process required 4.5 seconds, whilst verification required 0.16 seconds.

5.2   Further Results

The enrolment and verification times for the other verification schemes were also measured on the iButton. In addition the program size for enrolment and verification functions, combined was recorded. Table (5) presents a comparison of these quantities, along with a repetition of the Equal Error Rates, for convenience.

6   Conclusions

The Java Card 2.0 platform does not support floating-point arithmetic. We show that 32-bit integer arithmetic offered by the iButton implementation of Java Card 2.0 is sufficient to implement on-card verification and enrolment for our

Table 5. Results for all Verifiers

Verification Scheme	Enrolment Time (Seconds)	Verification Time (Seconds)	Program Size (bytes)	EER%
ℓ_1 norm - Fixed Threshold	1.2	0.12	296	9.7
ℓ_2 norm - Fixed Threshold	1.2	0.26	356	5
Component-Wise Linear	1.2	0.19	285	7.2
MICD - Fixed Threshold	1.2	0.15	319	5.2
Component-Wise Non-Linear	2.9	0.29	524	3.7
ℓ_1 norm - User Specific	3.1	0.12	684	2.3
ℓ_2 norm - User Specific	4.2	0.25	707	3
Mahalanobis - Fixed Threshold	2.4	0.16	550	3.4
Mahalanobis User Specific	4.5	0.16	752	2.4
MICD - User Specific	8.5	0.16	704	2.8

pressure sequence biometric. We develop the necessary mathematics and estimate the errors introduced by representing real data as integer data.

We measure the execution times and space requirements required by our implementation of verification and enrolment and show that they are within reach for a typical Java Card platform.

We present an architecture for a complete on-card pressure sequence biometric. In a previous paper we presented a method of integrating the physical sensor the plastic substrate of the smart card. In this paper we show that the processing capabilities required can be provided by a standard smart card. Future work includes an investigation into integrating the analogue electronics and the wiring on a standard smart card.

References

1. S. Bleha, C. Slivinsky, and B. Hussien, *Computer access security systems using keystroke dynamics*, IEEE Transactions on Pattern Analysis and Machine Intelligence **12** (1990), no. 12, 1217–1222. 127
2. S. A. Bleha and M. S. Obaidat, *Computer user verification using the perceptron algorithm*, IEEE Transactions on Systems, Man and Cybernetics **23** (1993), no. 3, 900–902. 127
3. M. Brown and S. J. Rogers, *User identification via keystroke characteristics of typed names using neural networks*, International Journal of Man-Machine Studies **39** (1993), 999 – 1014. 127
4. W. L. Bryan and N. Harter, *Studies in the physiology and psychology of the telegraphic language*, Psychological Review **4** (1897), 27–53. 125
5. J. Crenshaw, *Integer square roots*, Embedded Systems Programming (1998), no. 2. 130, 131
6. J. D. Garcia, *Personal identification apparatus*, US Patent 4 621 334, November 1986. 127

7. G. Hachez, F. Koeunne, and J-J. Quisquater, *Biometrics, access control, smart-cards: A not so simple combination*, Smart Card Research and Advanced Applications (Bristol, UK), IFIP/TC8 Fourth Working Conference on Smart Card Research and Advanced Applications, Kluwer Academic Publishers, September 2000, ISBN: 0-7923-7953-5, pp. 273–288. 124

8. N. J. Henderson and P. H. Hartel, *'pressure sequence' - a novel method of protecting smart cards*, Smart Card Research and Advanced Applications (Bristol, UK), IFIP/TC8 Fourth Working Conference on Smart Card Research and Advanced Applications, Kluwer Academic Publishers, September 2000, ISBN: 0-7923-7953-5, pp. 241–256. 124, 125

9. A. Jain, R. Bolle, and S. Pankanti, *Biometrics: Personal identification in networked society*, Kluwer, Boston, 1998, ISBN 0792383451. 125

10. R. Joyce and G. Gupta, *Identity authentication based on keystroke dynamics*, Communications of the ACM **33** (1990), no. 2, 168–176. 127, 130

11. E. R. Kandel, *Principles of neural science*, Elsevier, North Holland, 1981. 125

12. J. Leggett and G. Williams, *Verifying identity through keystroke characteristics*, International Journal of Man-Machine Studies **28** (1988), 67–76. 127

13. F. Monrose and A. D. Rubin, *Keystroke dynamics as a biometric for authentication*, Future Generation Computer Systems **16** (2000), 351–359. 127

14. M. S. Obaidat and B. Sadoun, *Verification of computer users using keystroke dynamics*, IEEE Transactions on Systems, Man and Cybernetics - Part B - Cybernetics **27** (1997), no. 2, 261 – 269. 127

15. W. H. Press, S. A. Teukolsky, W. T. Vetterling, and B. P. Flannery, *Numerical recipies in c*, Cambridge University Press, Cambridge, United Kingdom, 1993. 130

16. J. A. Robinson, V. M. Liang, J. A. M. Chambers, and C. L. MacKenzie, *Computer user verification using login string keystroke dynamics*, IEEE Transactions on Systems, Man and Cybernetics - Part A - Systems and Humans **28** (1998), no. 2, 236 – 241. 127

17. D. E. Rummelhart and D. A. Norman, *Simulating a skilled typist: A study of skilled cognitive-motor performance*, Cognitive Science **6** (1982), no. 1, 1–36. 125

18. Dallas Semiconductor, http://www.ibutton.com/, March 2001. 124, 128

19. Siemens, http://www.silicon-trust.com/, March 2001. 124

20. D. Umphress and G. Williams, *Identity verification through keyboard characteristics*, International Journal of Man-Machine Studies **23** (1985), 67–76. 127

21. J. R. Young and W. Hammond, *Method and apparatus for verifying an individual's identity*, US Patent 4 805 222, February 1989. 127

SIMspeak – Towards an Open and Secure Application Platform for GSM SIMs

Roger Kehr and Hendrik Mieves

Databases and Distributed Systems Group
Darmstadt University of Technology, Germany
kehr@informatik.tu-darmstadt.de
mieves@rbg.informatik.tu-darmstadt.de

Abstract. Today mobile operators are in the possession of the SIM
application toolkit technology available in their GSM SIM smartcards
plugged into the mobile handsets of their subscribers. Although there
are roughly 500 mio. SIMs deployed all over the world, they are not
integrated into the Internet yet. With the WebSIM approach [6] we have
demonstrated how SIMs can be integrated into the Internet by means
of a tiny HTTP server implemented in a SIM to provide value-added
services running on top of the SIM toolkit.

In this contribution we propose to further extend this approach by making SIMs accessible as open and secure execution platforms for mobile
code. Here, *open* means that virtually anybody in the Internet can use
this mobile code platform, and *secure* means that both – platform and
subscriber – cannot be harmed by malicious code. Such a platform can
be provided by operators upon which third-party service providers can
build their applications which would benefit from the security context of
the smartcard they run inside.

The SIMspeak system is comprised of an off-card compiler, a verifier,
and a corresponding card-resident interpreter, which can interpret code
that has been pushed by an Internet service provider into a customer's
SIM. We describe the underlying trust model of SIMspeak, its architecture, language, and protocols. Furthermore we present approaches for
end-to-end security that influence the design of the compiler, verifier,
and interpreter and we give an overview on the current status of our
implementation.

1 Motivation

Imagine you were participating in an on-line auction with eBay.com and you
were bidding for an antique watch. After registering and placing a bid with
your favourite browser, you fill in eBay's form asking whether you are SIMspeak
equipped. After entering the phone number of your SIMspeak-enabled SIM, you
tell eBay to continue to push subsequent information and communication to your
SIM. Until the end of the bidding phase you receive SMS messages at regular
intervals from eBay containing small SIMspeak scripts that are interpreted on-
the-fly upon arrival in your SIM. These scripts inform you about the current

I. Attali and T. Jensen (Eds.): E-smart 2001, LNCS 2140, pp. 135–149, 2001.
© Springer-Verlag Berlin Heidelberg 2001

highest bid in the auction, asking whether you want to place a new bid, enable you to enter a new bid and return the new digitally signed bid to eBay via SMS. Since you were equipped with SIMspeak, you were able to place a final bid just two minutes before the end of the auction while sitting in a train, and you are now a proud owner of the antique Rolex you dreamed of since the early days of GSM...

Lessons learned from the WebSIM approach. The core idea behind our motivation is that a GSM SIM [4] is an ideal platform for communicating with mobile subscribers from the Internet in a secure push-based style of communication as motivated above. We have already demonstrated with the WebSIM [6] how to integrate GSM SIMs into the Internet by an appropriate proxy architecture. There, each SIM has its unique URL to which HTTP requests can be sent containing SIM application toolkit commands (SAT) [3] that allow for user interaction. The proxy forwards the requests embedded into short messages (SMS) to the SIM. The requests are interpreted by a small Web server in the SIM triggering the SIM toolkit commands specified in the URL. The responses of, e.g. a SAT *SelectItem* command, are returned to the originator of the request.

> *Basically, the WebSIM brings the GSM security infrastructure into the Internet upon which various protocols can be implemented, e.g. for authentication of Internet users via their mobile phones (cf. [9]).*

Unfortunately, the WebSIM does not allow for interaction as presented above in the mobile auction scenario for two reasons:

- It lacks the possibility of launching more than one SIM application toolkit command at a time, thus it is not possible to encode some kind of user interaction in a request, and
- it does not offer any end-to-end security between a service provider and the SIM.

Our approach overcomes these drawbacks by opening the SIM in a flexible though secure manner for third-party application providers, mobile operators, and subscribers. We think that it should be possible for virtually anybody in the Internet with basic knowledge of Internet technology to develop SIMspeak applications called *scripts* and send them via an operator's gateway to the mobile subscriber's SIM. The key approach is to send *mobile code* and *data* to a SIM for instant execution. Furthermore we are interested in confidential transmission of such scripts from the service provider to the SIM avoiding *content-recoding* problems as known from the Wireless Application Protocol (WAP) or the WebSIM which leads to a breach of end-to-end security.

Comparison with Related Work. The WebSIM and the SIMspeak systems share some similarity with several other technologies.

WAP Push [15] defines the architecture underlying the future push-based technology in the WAP protocol family. Content is pushed via an appropriate gateway architecture to a WAP-enabled terminal, hence it is targeted towards the mobile handset in contrast to the SIM.

SIM toolkit browsers [12,13] provide a browsing technology on top of the SIM application toolkit. Applications are driven by a gateway usually hosted by a mobile operator. It also offers some means for end-to-end encryption of confidential data between the service provider and the SIM. In contrast, SIM-speak less addresses a browsing-like type of interaction initiated by the user but a push-based style of communication driven by an Internet client also aiming at true end-to-end security of transmitted scripts.

The draft specification of the 3GPP USAT interpreter working group [1] comes the most close to our envisioned platform. This group defines the USAT interpreter that makes use of the SIM toolkit commands available in the future USIM. It does not only define a browser-based model but also allows for push-style communication from the gateway, which in turn can be triggered from the Internet. The byte-codes used there reflect the group's idea of a *page*-based style of subscriber interaction similar to the SIM toolkit browsers. As such they support pages as the elementary containers that can be linked by a web of anchors for navigation. Within a page, variables can be used to store page-local information and exchange data between different pages. Contained in a page are USAT commands encoded as tag-length-value data (TLV) structures providing a generic approach to subscriber and handset interaction.

Although USAT interpreter and SIMspeak target similar application domains the actual approaches differ substantially: The SIMspeak platform is programmable in terms of control-flow, arithmetics, Boolean expressions, response message formats, etc. The USAT interpreter, though, follows a more operator-centric model that has similar drawbacks as the SIM toolkit browsers w.r.t. end-to-end security, an issue further discussed in Section 4. Generally, a browser-based style of communication is suitable for many applications but the ability to perform local computations as envisioned in SIMspeak is of equal importance and not supported in the USAT interpreter model.

The rest of this paper is organised as follows: In Section 2 we analyse the essential requirements of the envisioned platform. Section 3 describes the overall SIMspeak architecture, its language, and investigates the core components compiler and interpreter. Issues around end-to-end security are described in Section 4. Section 5 describes a sample script and illustrates a number of possible application domains and Section 6 discusses future work and draws final conclusions.

2 Requirements Analysis

The mobile auction example has motivated the need for an open and secure means to download mobile code and data into a GSM SIM for instant interpretation. In the sequel we discuss general requirements that should be guaranteed by the involved components and underlying protocols.

Roles and Trust Model. The envisioned trust model needs to support at least the following roles:

- **Subscriber** or **user** is the owner of the mobile phone and target of all input and output facilities offered by the platform.
- **Service providers** interact with subscribers by means of applications that are dynamically loaded into the provider's platform.
- **Platform provider** is the role that manages and controls the platform that provides means for interaction between service providers and subscribers. It should be noted that there is no general assumption that the SIM issuer also plays the role of the platform provider.

In the traditional GSM world the SIM is basically *trusted by* (the mobile) *operator* which means, that the mobile operator decides which applications to load onto the SIM. This mostly occurs at the time of card personalisation, sometimes afterwards.

We argue that the SIM can be opened up for third-party service providers while preserving integrity and security of the SIM. This can be achieved by a platform operator who offers an execution platform inside the SIM that service providers can use to run applications that interact with subscribers. Therefore, the trust model must be extended in a way that both – service providers and mobile subscribers – trust the provider's runtime platform in the SIM. Furthermore, the operator does in general not trust the mobile code sent to the platform for execution. This problem is comparable to some extent with the issues around *host security* in mobile code systems (cf. [5]) and the problem of security of *mobile agents* where a mobile agent distrusts the platform it is running on (cf. [14]) and we will apply common solutions known from this community.

Platfrom Security Properties. We approach the problem by designing a platform such that all necessary security properties are decidable without human intervention, i.e. non-interactively. In the rest of this paper we discuss technical approaches to yield such a trustworthy platform without, however, giving formal proofs. We have identified the following security-relevant properties:

- **Application Provider Authentication:** For a mobile subscriber it is of vital importance to identify the provider of the application running in her SIM. For example, consider the case of a script masquerading as a banking application that asks the subscriber for a personal identification and transaction number, and subsequently uses this "stolen" information to issue a malicious transaction on the subscriber's behalf. Therefore, the platform must offer suitable facilities to make the subscriber aware of the identity of the sender.
- **Code and Data Confidentiality and Integrity:** Obviously, the transport of the mobile application comprised of the actual program and its data must be protected. Integrity of the shipped data is needed under all circumstances. Whether confidentiality of the program, its data, or both is needed, depends on the particular application, and appropriate means to implement

a required level of security should be offered to applications. Hence, a flexible management of symmetric and asymmetric keys is mandatory.

- **Code Verification:** Besides the integrity of the shipped program it must be guaranteed that malicious code does not compromise the platform's security. Basically, well-formedness according to certain security properties can be checked in the card prior or parallel to execution, or off-line in some kind of trusted verifier. Typical properties include:

  - **Syntactic integrity** of the program.
  - **Stack behaviour** to avoid over- and underflow of the runtime stack.
  - **Data typing** to avoid type errors in the language's type system.
  - **Guaranteed termination** of an application. Since smartcards cannot be interrupted during execution except resetting them, the platform is responsible for not allowing applications to run forever.

  Ideally, all of the above properties should be verified in advance to avoid cancelling an application upon a property violation at runtime.

- **Non-Repudiation:** For the application provider it is of vital importance to have a proof on the inputs performed by a subscriber, e.g. entering the amount of money for the new bid the subscriber places in the on-line auction. This evidence must be created by the runtime platform, e.g. in the form of an electronic signature (cf. [2]).

The previous list is by no means exhaustive and more requirements such as *persistent storage*, *transactions*, etc. could optionally be considered.

3   Architecture and Implementation

The requirements presented in the previous section have shaped the approach taken in our architecture and implementation.

Components. The overall SIMspeak architecture is depicted in Figure 1. Basic components are an Internet node, e.g. a Web server, to which SIMspeak scripts can be uploaded by means of HTTP(S) from any node in the Internet. This Web server acts as a gateway from the Internet into the GSM world. Script pushing can be made subject to extensive access control, e.g. disabling access for any parties not authenticated. Furthermore the gateway can be used as a starting point for any

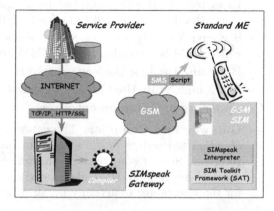

Fig. 1. SIMspeak architecture

kind of billing mechanism implemented by the platform operator.[1] This architecture is directly derived from the one described in [6].

The SIMspeak compiler parses the uploaded script and checks for a number of security properties described later. Afterwards the byte-code for the SIM-resident interpreter is generated and packaged into a number of short messages (SMS) sent to the target SIM.

Upon arrival in the SIM the interpreter collects the SMS until the script is complete. Then script execution starts and the script's instructions are subsequently interpreted. Possible responses from the SIM to the gateway are sent back to the gateway which can be delivered via an asynchronous or synchronous communication style back to the original sender, e.g. the response can be sent as the HTTP response of the initial script submission or by an appropriate notification mechanism.

Language. A suitable domain-specific language for interpretation in a GSM SIM must at least offer primitives for control flow, data processing, and access to the SIM toolkit. We have chosen a stack-based interpretable programming language in the spirit of Forth [7] from which we have borrowed the stack model. Control structures and arithmetic operations have been added, and additional support for registers and bindings for SIM toolkit commands are available. The instruction set can be classified as follows:

- **Stack:** pop, dup, swap, and push
- **Registers:** load, store
- **Control-flow:** nop, exit, if...goto, goto, call, return
- **Boolean:** and?, or?, not?, eq?, le?, etc.
- **Arithmetics:** add, sub, mul, div, mod
- **Cryptography:** encode, decode, sign, digest, verify
- **SIM application toolkit:** sat.select, sat.display, sat.input, sat.loci, etc.

Data types. The following data types are supported:

- **Integers:** At the moment the language supports only 8-bit arithmetics which should be extended to at least 32/64-bit for monetary applications.
- **Strings:** We only support 8-bit strings for displaying and entering data which could be extended to 7-bit GSM and ISO-UCS2 encodings.
- **Boolean:** Used for Boolean expressions and flow control.
- **Mark** and **Null:** Used for stack element marking and a bottom type.

Components and Implementation.

- **Gateway and Compiler:** The gateway is responsible for the compilation of submitted scripts into a format understandable by the SIM-resident interpreter. Since resources on a smartcard in terms of processing power and memory are limited, the code generation should make it as easy as possible for the interpreter to actually perform the interpretation.

---

[1] Naturally, this conflicts with the idea of an *open* application platform but we consider such business issues beyond the scope of this paper.

- **Interpreter and Verifier:** The byte-code instruction set has been designed to obtain a very efficient encoding of scripts – both for small number of SMS and for easy interpretation in the SIM. We have tried to eliminate most data movements within the implementation to get reasonable performance and avoid the problem of memory management on top of the Java Card runtime environment.

- **User Interface Aspects:** Since the platform controls any user interaction this "direct" link to the subscriber can be used for several purposes:

  - **Script starting:** Before a script actually starts, the subscriber can be notified, e.g. by playing a tone and displaying some information that a script has been received for execution. The platform can furthermore display the originator of the script and the user can accept the script's execution, postpone it to later, or completely reject.

  - **Location information:** Access to location information can be given only after the user has explicitly accepted. Hence, a suitable menu can be displayed, querying the subscriber, whether the information may be given to the script, or not.

  - **Response:** Before a script sends responses back to the gateway, the subscriber can be asked to first authorise this process.

- **Implementation:** The interpreter consists of about 1.500 lines of Java Card code compiling to roughly 15 kBytes of class files. The SIMspeak applet size is about 4,4 kBytes. The interpreter was built on top of Bull's SIM Rock Java Card Toolkit based on the Java Card 2.1 API.

  The compiler is written in Java 2 and consists of about 4.200 lines of code including documentation of which approximately 50 % are devoted to the script parsing code generated with the JavaCC parser generator[2].

  After compilation the compiler yields a set of script segments ready for transmission to the SIM in any order. Each segment contains a header that identifies the current session and segment number to manage the arrival of SMS in a different order. A script is executed after all segments have arrived in the SIM. The gateway is based on the version implemented in [6] with extensions for sending more than one SMS.

This architecture still suffers from the problem of *end-to-end security* since the compiler at the gateway performs a translation of the submitted code. In the next section we elaborate concepts to overcome this drawback.

4   Towards End-to-End Security

Although in the previous paragraphs we implicitly assumed that the compiler and verifier are placed at the operator's gateway, they can also be placed at different locations as Table 2 illustrates:

---

[2] Available at www.metamata.com/javacc/.

If the compiler is placed with the service provider, the operator (**1**) or the platform itself (**2**) must host the verifier. Another option is to place compiler and verifier at the operator (**3**). Furthermore the verifier can be implemented on the platform (**4**). Options (**2**), (**4**), and (**5**) are of particular interest since they aim at an on-card code verification. Option (**2**) is the most appealing since it opens up for

	1	2	3	4	5
Provider	C	C	–	–	–
Operator	V	–	C,V	C	–
Platform	–	V	–	V	C,V

Fig. 2. Compiler and verifier placement

end-to-end encryption of the whole application – program *and* data – not only data as in (**4**). Therefore, we have decided to approach end-to-end security using option (**2**) and aim at an on-card verifier implementation.

4.1 Compiler

A compiler translates an input language into a compiled form intended for direct execution on a target processor or for interpretation. Within SIMspeak the compiler essentially aims at two major goals: (a) generate a compact encoding of scripts for bandwidth-saving over-the-air transmission, and (b) simplify the implementation of the on-card interpreter as much as possible in terms of code-size and execution speed, e.g. completely remove resource-intensive parsing of the input language. Following option (**2**) the compiler can be hosted and run by the service provider in addition to the gateway host (**4**).

4.2 Verifier

The verifier checks whether the generated code satisfies certain properties. The most common example of such a component is the Java byte-code verifier [11]. The verifier has to check for at least the following properties:

- **Syntactic integrity:** Syntactic integrity of the byte-code is easy to check in advance as long as the representation is simple enough.
- **Data stack behaviour:** The data stack is used for temporary storage of data and parameter passing to SIM toolkit library calls. It can be statically checked whether at any point of execution a stack violation occurs.
- **Data typing:** At the moment we support only strings and integers as data types.

Our approach is essentially a simplified version of the Java byte-code verification since, for example, we do not support user-defined types and exceptions which introduce an additional overhead for on-card verification (cf. [10]).

Verification of Control-flow and Termination. One of the most problematic issues w.r.t. security is the fact that scripts running in the SIM always must terminate and that they are interruptible at any point of execution. Control-flow primitives are available through the if. . . goto statements and the primitives call, and return manipulating the control stack. We place the following restrictions on the control-flow graph of a script:

i. Subroutines can only be called. No goto from outside a subroutine to a label inside a subroutine is allowed. This yields closed subroutines.

ii. Each path of execution within a subroutine must pass a return or exit statement to ensure proper termination.

iii. The subroutine call-graph must be acyclic to avoid simple and mutual recursion.

iv. The control-flow graph of the application or a subroutine may have cycles, *iff* along each cycle there exists a call to an interruptible interaction primitive. Currently, those are the SIM toolkit primitives display, select, and input. This ensures that an application or subroutine cannot loop without subscriber's notice, thus a user is able to interrupt execution.

Figure 3 illustrates the last property. It shows an example of a legal jump (indicated by an arrow) in the control-flow graph. Numbers indicate maximum distance to end of application (bottom-most node). Jump of interest is from node c to node n and is allowed since all possible paths from n to c pass a user interaction.

These restrictions yield a very constrained domain-specific language that does not allow for, e.g. iteration over a fixed set of numbers without subscriber interaction. Furthermore, there is no support for dynamic data structures such as sets or lists. Despite these limitations we have found the resulting language very flexible for our application domain and we are still looking for interesting examples that cannot be encoded with the current set of language primitives and control flow restrictions which would need further support from the platform.

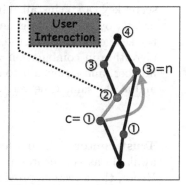

Fig. 3. Control flow example

About Java Card. Very naturally the question arises *"Why not use Java Card [8] applets for this purpose?"*

First of all we wanted to demonstrate the feasibility of our approach by starting *top-down*, i.e. to explore, what is the minimal language needed to do useful things and how much in terms of on-card resources do we need to implement this functionality? Furthermore we were interested in performing a complete implementation with all the necessary functionality on-card.

The object-orientation of Java is not a mandatory requirement for the intended application domain and just adds complexity without yielding concrete benefits. Furthermore, some properties, e.g. termination, require knowledge of the semantics of operations and library calls currently not inherently subject to Java byte-code verification.

SIMspeak on the other hand follows a minimal approach that simplifies checking of properties in most cases but introduces further checks needed for its open platform approach. Our first results indicate that the verification of the termination alone is rather complex to implement efficiently.

Summing up, we consider Java Card to be a very flexible platform and language for card-resident applications. In contrast, SIMspeak is meant as a domain-specific language targeting towards simple and short applications transmitted over-the-air that not only require special transport and loading protocols, but also have a different life-cycle which does not necessarily fit with Java Card. However, this does not imply that Java Card could not be a suitable language for implementing our approach in the future especially, if we consider recent work by Leroy [10] who reports promising progress in on-card verification techniques for Java Card byte-code.

4.3   End-to-End Security Protocols and Key Management

To support the above end-to-end approach, suitable communication protocols are needed. We propose to use public-key cryptography to enable secure end-to-end communication between a service provider and the platform as follows:

– **Public-key pair:** Each card C owns a *platform key pair* (S_C, P_C). The secret key can be installed in the platform at time of issuance by operator M, or later by on-card key generation.[3] In the latter case a subscriber can trigger the key generation and the mobile operator can use the GSM authentication algorithm in combination with the SIM's secret key Ki, its *IMSI* identity number, and a nonce n to securely obtain the public key P_C from the card and at the same time verify its authenticity as follows:

$$C \to M : sig\{IMSI, P_C, n\}_{Ki}.$$

– **Trust center:** The platform operator makes the public keys of the SIMs available as certificates in a central directory, e.g. Web or LDAP server. Hence, the directory provides a mapping $P \to P_C$ from a phone number P to the platform's public key P_C.[4]

– **Secret key installation:** The platform offers each service provider S mechanisms to install a secret symmetric key K_S into the platform. Each provider generates a unique key for each individual platform. This results not only in end-to-end confidentiality but also provides for authentication. Key installation requires that the service provider authenticates first with the operator, e.g. using a PKI. The following protocol achieves this goal:[5]

$$S \to M : \{P, enc\{K_S, i, k, n\}_{P_C}\},$$
$$M : D = sig\{enc\{K_S, i, k, n\}_{P_C}, id_S, m\}_{Ki},$$
$$M \to C : \{enc\{K_S, i, k, n\}_{P_C}, D\}.$$

---

[3] Several SIM smartcard manufacturers are planning to integrate RSA key generation into future products.
[4] If platform and mobile operators are different authorities, appropriate agreements must be established.
[5] Here again, n and m are nonces.

First the service provider sends to the operator the phone number P of the target SIM, the secret key K_S along with a sequence number i for replay prevention, a key store number k, and a nonce n, encrypted with P_C. The operator completes the message with the identity id_S of the service provider and a nonce m, and signs it appropriately with Ki. The message and its signature are then sent to the platform and after signature verification, K_S can be safely stored into the service provider's key store at position k.

- **Secure end-to-end communication:**
  Upon successful installation of the service provider's key K_S, secure communication can be achieved as follows:

  - $S \rightarrow C : \{id_S, enc\{prog, i, n\}_{K_S}, k\}$,
    i.e. S encrypts its data with K_S and annotates its identity id_S for correct decoding. The platform decrypts the message with the secret key K_S stored as key number k from the sender's key store. This step not only decrypts the message but also achieves achieves provider authentication which has been identified as a major requirement for the platform.
  - $C \rightarrow S : \{IMSI, enc\{E\}_{K_S}, k\}$,
    i.e. data E is simply encrypted with K_S. The $IMSI$ (or another suitable identifier for the platform) and k are used to look up the appropriate key for decryption. Encryption can be achieved with the interpreter operation encrypt that performs encryption of the topmost stack element with a key from the key store. Since K_S is only known to the card and the service provider, it also achieves authentication of the card.[6]

In the above protocols we have not made concrete assumptions about the underlying public- and symmetric-key protocols. For usage in a GSM SIM, data blocks should generally be as small as possible which could give Elliptic Curve Cryptography (ECC) an advantage over, e.g. RSA. On the other hand we do not know of any ECC-capable GSM SIM at the moment.

The protocols above also assume that the operator or platform provider has no means to access the service provider's secret keys K_S or the secret key S_C of the card. Otherwise, the whole chain of trust would be compromised. Furthermore it is not explicitly stated that operator and platform provider must be the same body, e.g. the platform could be a separate application in a multi-application card offered by another third-party. If not, the operator might be responsible for the key pair generation and trust center responsibilities only, into which the platform provider must have sufficient confidence.

Non-Repudiation. As outlined in the requirements analysis, assurance of non-repudiation is necessary for business-critical services and applications. We follow a straightforward approach by offering service providers the primitive sign that first displays a note that some data has to be digitally signed, then displays the actual data, e.g. D, and finally signs the cryptographic hash of the data $h(D)$ with the subscriber's signature key S_S which can be configured similar to the

---

[6] E may contain additional information, e.g. to prevent replay attacks.

platform key S_C. The digital signature obtained is pushed back onto the stack and can be subsequently sent to the service provider.

4.4 Status of Implementation

We have implemented an off-card verifier which is currently being ported onto a Java Card 2.1 SIM. We still experiment with different algorithms and encodings to obtain an efficient on-card implementation. In particular our approach is based on a scheme comparable to a simplified version of the Java byte-code verification focusing on byte-code encodings that allow for linear scanning of the whole application that are cheaply implementable on-card while leaving computationally expensive operations to the off-card compiler.

5 Sample Applications

The Mobile Auction Example. The implementation of the illustrative eBay auction client example described in Section 1 is shown in Figure 4.

A script starts with header information about the name of the script and its provider. The implementation part contains the actual program.

Lines 14–16 demonstrate how to display an initial message about the latest news of the online auction. Lines 18–22 show how the arguments for a SAT *SelectItem* are pushed onto the stack marked by the initial marker set in line 18. After the selection has been performed the arguments including mark are removed from the stack and the number of the selected item is available on the stack.

Lines 24–26 check, whether the subscriber selected the second item in which case a jump to the label at the end is performed. Otherwise an input dialogue is opened in lines 28–29 and the input from the subscriber is returned on the topmost stack position. Then a mark is pushed and swapped with the subscriber's response in lines 30–31.

Finally a return token is pushed onto the stack and the response containing all elements up to the mark are returned to the gateway. Depending on the kind of response – synchronous or asynchronous – the data is returned to eBay.

The script compiles to exactly 198 bytes of which 156 bytes (80 %) are text strings. This indicates that the chosen byte-code is very compact in relation to the overall data that needs to be transported anyhow. The codes fits into two segments (payload size of 112 bytes) that can be transported in two short messages.

Further Application Domains. SIMspeak allows platform operators to offer of an *open* and *secure* platform to Internet service providers such as shops, banks, etc. It offers secure interaction of these providers with their customers in a push-based style of communication. To some extent one can view SIMspeak as a secure interpreter running in a smartcard inserted into the wireless card reader (*mobile phone*) that happens to be equipped with a keyboard and a display. The content pushed is not only data – as it would be the case for a hard-wired application

```
 1 simspeak script {
 2
 3   scriptname "ebay_auction_client";
 4   provider "ebay.com";
 5
 6   implementation {
 7     sat.playtone;
 8     push("News_from_ebay.com:\nBid_in_auction_#3576_(Antique_watch):_$63.");
 9     sat.display;
10
11     push(mark);               // Mark following entries on stack
12     push("Place_new_bid?");   // This is the title of the menu
13     push("New_bid...");       // First item
14     push("Cancel");           // Second item
15     sat.select;               // Pushes number of selected item onto stack
16
17     push( 2 );                // Number of choice of interest
18     eq?;                      // Check for selected item == #2
19     if (true) goto end;       // Branch to end if selected "Cancel"
20
21     push("Enter_new_bid_(>$64):");
22     sat.input;                // pushes entered value onto stack
23     push(mark);
24     swap();
25     push("ebay.com:_123456"); // Unique identifier for response
26     sat.response();           // Send input on stack back to ebay. Stack
27                               // contents are identifier and newly entered bid
28 end:
29     exit;
30   }
31 }
```

Fig. 4. Listing of the SIMspeak implementation of the eBay example from Sect. 1

in the SIM – but rather code and data, which makes it much more flexible. The following examples should give an impression on the types of applications that could be thought of:

– **Push-based brokerage, stock trading:** A broker application is similar to the auction client. The subscriber could be informed about new stock watch-points that could be used in addition to stop-loss. It could provide more subscriber feedback to what is going on at the stock market and provide means to react on current trends in a matter of seconds.

– **Internet-based authentication:** Possibly one of the most interesting class of applications is authentication of mobile subscribers to the Internet. Currently, Internet servers accessed by HTTPS/SSL authenticate themselves via certificates whereas in practice client authentication is not used due to the lack of a global PKI infrastructure. SIMspeak can be used to implement various protocols how a service provider can send a script executing, e.g. a menu selection, whether the intended transaction or order should actually be performed, or not. Further protocols and approaches are described in [6] and [9].

- **Secure enterprise applications:** Enterprises with a strong demand for secure and application-specific mobile transactions are likely to invest into customisable solutions. Especially flexible mechanisms for end-to-end secure communication between an enterprise and its mobile employees could be of particular importance.

- **Loyalty-points application:** Smartcards offer secure persistent storage that could be used by loyalty point systems that manage the bonus points via GSM. This would provide a complete off-line light-weight loyalty system that uses the distributed secure storage of SIMs for management.

Summing up, the SIMspeak architecture provides an open and secure platform upon which various other applications can be built on top of.

6   Conclusions and Future Work

The SIM is the security module of the largest security infrastructure the world has seen so far. The experiences gained from the WebSIM project have shown that the idea of integrating a GSM SIM into the Internet with suitable protocols such as HTTP can enable more secure business between subscribers and service providers.

In the SIMspeak approach we have tried to overcome some of the existing limitations in the WebSIM approach by designing an open application platform inside the SIM that providers can use for implementing their own services. We have extended the Web server in the SIM by a platform for the execution of mobile code in a secure and safe way – from the provider's, subscriber's, and platform's point of view. This platform allows a service provider to implement its own policies for security-sensitive transactions, e.g. in the fields of mobile commerce or business-to-employee applications.

The most notable achievements are secure end-to-end communication between service provider and subscriber, server-side application execution that allows for much more flexibility and interactivity, and the management of persistent storage for service providers.

Acknowledgements

We would like to thank J. Posegga, M. Rohs, H. Vogt, F. Gärtner, and U. Wilhelm for giving valuable comments on earlier versions of this paper and discussing some of the key management protocols. Furthermore we thank S. Guthery for pointing us to the 3GPP working group for the USAT interpreter and the anonymous referees for their valuable comments on our paper.

References

1. 3GPP. *3rd Generation Partnership Project; Technical Specification Group Terminals; US AT Interpreter Byte Codes (Release 4)*, January 2001. Available at *www.3gpp.org.* 137
2. Directive 1999/93/EC of the European Parliament and of the Council of 13 December 1999 on a Community framework for electronic signatures. Available at *http://www.ict.etsi.org/eessi/e-sign-directive.pdf*, 1999. 139
3. European Telecommunications Standard Institute. *Digital cellular telecommunications system (Phase 2+); Specification of the SIM Application Toolkit for the Subscriber Identity Module - Mobile Equipment (SIM-ME) interface (GSM 11.14)*, 1998. 136
4. European Telecommunications Standard Institute. *Digital cellular telecommunications system (Phase 2+); Specification of the Subscriber Identity Module -Mobile Equipment (SIM-ME) interface (GSM 11.11)*, 1998. 136
5. Philip W. L. Fong. Viewer's discretion: Host security in mobile code systems. Technical Report SFU CMPT TR 1998-19, School of Computing Science, Simon Erascr University, Burnaby, B.C., Canada, 1998. Available at *http://www.cs.sfu. ca/ ~pwfong/personal/.* 138
6. Scott Guthery, Roger Kehr, and Joachim Posegga. How to turn a GSM SIM into a Web server. In Josep Domigo-Ferrer, David Chan, and Anthony Watson, editors, *Proceedings of Fourth IFIP TC8/WG8.8 Smart Card Research and Advanced Application Conference CARDIS'2000, Bristol, UK*, pages 209-222. Kluwer Academic Publisher, September 20-22, 2000. 135, 136, 140, 141, 148
7. International Standardization Organization, JTC 1/SC 22. *ISO/IEC 15145:1997 Standard Information technology - Programming languages - FORTH*, 1997. 140
8. Java Card Technology. Specifications are available at *http://java.sun.com/ products/javacard/.* 143
9. Roger Kehr, Joachim Posegga, Roland Schmitz, and Peter Windirsch. Mobile security for Internet applications. In *Proceedings of Kommunikationssicherheit KSI'2001*, DuD Fachbeitrage. Vieweg Verlag, March 27-28, 2001. 136, 148
10. Xavier Leroy. On-card bytecode verification for Java Card. In *Proceedings of eSmart '2001, Cannes, France*, Lecture Notes in Computer Science. Springcr-Vcrlag, September 2001. 142, 144
11. Tim Lindholm and Frank Yellin. *The Java Virtual Machine Specification.* Sun Microsystems Inc., Mountain View, second edition, 1999. 142
12. Across Wireless (now Sonera Smart Trust), *www.acrosswireless.com.* 137
13. SIMalliance. *www.simalliance.org.* 137
14. U. G. Wilhelm, L. Buttyan, and S. Staamann. On the problem of trust in mobile agent systems. In *Symposium on Network and Distributed System Security*, pages 114-124, San Diego, CA, USA, March 1998. Internet Society. 138
15. Wireless Application Protocol Forum, Ltd. *WAP Push Architectural Overview Version 1999-11-08*, November 1999. Available at *www.wapforum.org.* 136

On-Card Bytecode Verification for Java Card

Xavier Leroy

Trusted Logic
5, rue du Bailliage, 78000 Versailles, France
Xavier.Leroy@trusted-logic.fr

Abstract. This paper presents a novel approach to the problem of byte-code verification for Java Card applets. Owing to its low memory require-ments, our verification algorithm is the first that can be embedded on a smart card, thus increasing tremendously the security of post-issuance downloading of applets on Java Cards.

1 Introduction

The Java Card architecture for smart cards [4] bring two major innovations to the smart card world: first, Java cards can run multiple applications, which can communicate through shared objects; second, new applications, called *applets*, can be downloaded on the card post issuance. These two features bring considerable flexibility to the card, but also raise major security issues. A malicious applet, once downloaded on the card, can mount a variety of attacks, such as leaking confidential information outside (e.g. PINs and secret cryptographic keys), modifying sensitive information (e.g. the balance of an electronic purse), or interfering with other honest applications already on the card, causing them to malfunction.

The security issues raised by applet downloading are well known in the area of Web applets, and more generally mobile code for distributed systems [23,11]. The solution put forward by the Java programming environment is to execute the applets in a so-called "sandbox", which is an insulation layer preventing direct access to the hardware resources and implementing a suitable access control policy [7]. The security of the sandbox model relies on the following three components:

1. Applets are not compiled down to machine executable code, but rather to bytecode for a virtual machine. The virtual machine manipulates higher-level, more secure abstractions of data than the hardware processor, such as object references instead of memory addresses.
2. Applets are not given direct access to hardware resources such as the se-rial port, but only to a carefully designed set of API classes and methods that perform suitable access control before performing interactions with the outside world on behalf of the applet.
3. Upon downloading, the bytecode of the applet is subject to a static analysis called bytecode verification, whose purpose is to make sure that the code

I. Attali and T. Jensen (Eds.): E-smart 2001, LNCS 2140, pp. 150–164, 2001.

of the applet is well typed and does not attempt to bypass protections 1 and 2 above by performing ill-typed operations at run-time, such as forging object references from integers, illegal casting of an object reference from one class to another, calling directly private methods of the API, jumping in the middle of an API method, or jumping to data as if it were code [8,24,10].

The Java Card architecture features components 1 and 2 of the sandbox model: applets are executed by the Java Card virtual machine [22], and the Java Card runtime environment [21] provides the required access control, in particular through its "firewall". However, component 3 (the bytecode verifier) is missing: as we shall see later, bytecode verification as it is done for Web applets is a complex and expensive process, requiring large amounts of working memory, and therefore believed to be impossible to implement on a smart card.

Several approaches have been considered to palliate the lack of on-card bytecode verification. The first is to rely on off-card tools (such as trusted compilers and converters, or off-card bytecode verifiers) to produce well-typed bytecode for applets. A cryptographic signature then attests the well-typedness of the applet, and on-card downloading is restricted to signed applets. The drawback of this approach is to extend the trusted computing base to include off-card components. The cryptographic signature also raises delicate practical issues (how to deploy the signature keys?) and legal issues (who takes liability for a buggy applet produced by faulty off-card tools?).

The second workaround is to perform type checks dynamically, during the applet execution. This is called the defensive virtual machine approach. Here, the virtual machine not only computes the results of bytecode instructions, but also keeps track of the types of all data it manipulates, and performs additional safety checks at each instruction. The drawbacks of this approach is that dynamic type checks are expensive, both in terms of execution speed and memory requirements (storing the extra typing information takes significant space). Dedicated hardware can make some of these checks faster, but does not reduce the memory requirements.

Our approach is to challenge the popular belief that on-card bytecode verification is unfeasible. In this paper, we describe a novel bytecode verification algorithm for Java Card applets that is simple enough and has low enough memory requirements to be implemented on a smart card. A distinguishing feature of this algorithm is to rely on off-card bytecode transformations whose purpose is to facilitate on-card verification. Along with auxiliary consistency checks on the CAP file structure, not described in this paper for lack of space, the bytecode verifier described in this paper is at the heart of the Trusted Logic on-card CAP file verifier. This product – the first and currently only one of its kind – allows secure execution with no run-time speed penalty of non-signed applets on Java cards.

The remainder of this paper is organized as follows. Section 2 reviews the traditional bytecode verification algorithm, and analyzes why it is not suitable to on-card implementation. Section 3 presents our bytecode verification algorithm and how it addresses the issues with the traditional algorithm. Section

4 describes the off-card code transformations that transform any correct applet into an equivalent applet that passes on-card verification. Section 5 gives preliminary performance results. Related work is discussed in section 6, followed by concluding remarks in section 7.

2   Traditional Bytecode Verification

In this section, we review the traditional bytecode verification algorithm developed at Sun by Gosling and Yellin [8,24,10].

Bytecode verification is performed on the code of each non-abstract method in each class of the applet. It consists in an abstract execution of the code of the method, performed at the level of types instead of values as in normal execution. The verifier maintains a stack of types and an array associating types to registers (local variables). These stack and array of registers parallel those found in the virtual machine, except that they contain types instead of values.

2.1   Straight-Line Code

Assume first that the code of the method is straight line (no branches, no exception handling). The verifier considers every instruction of the method code in turn. For each instruction, it checks that the stack before the execution of the instruction contains enough entries, and that these entries are of the expected types for the instruction. It then simulates the effect of the instruction on the stack and registers, popping the arguments, pushing back the types of the results, and (in case of "store" instructions) updating the types of the registers to reflect that of the stored values. Any type mismatch on instruction arguments, or stack underflow or overflow, causes verification to fail and the applet to be rejected. Finally, verification proceeds with the next instruction, until the end of the method is reached.

The stack type and register types are initialized to reflect the state of the stack and registers on entrance to the method: the stack is empty; registers $0, \ldots, n-1$ holding method parameters and the **this** argument if any are given the corresponding types, as given by the descriptor of the method; registers $n, \ldots, m-1$ corresponding to uninitialized registers are given the special type $\top$ corresponding to an undefined value.

2.2   Dealing with Branches

Branch instructions and exception handlers introduce forks (execution can continue down several paths) and joins (several such paths join on an instruction) in the flow of control. To deal with forks, the verifier cannot in general determine the path that will be followed at run-time. Hence, it must propagate the inferred stack and register types to all possible successors of the forking instruction. Joins are even harder: an instruction that is the target of one or several branches or exception handlers can be reached along several paths, and the verifier has to make sure that the types of the stack and the registers along all these paths agree (same stack height, compatible types for the stack entries and the registers).

Sun's verification algorithm deals with these issues in the manner customary for data flow analyses. It maintains a data structure, called a "dictionary", associating a stack and register type to each program point that is the target of a branch or exception handler. When analyzing a branch instruction, or an instruction covered by an exception handler, it updates the type associated with the target of the branch in the dictionary, replacing it by the least upper bound of the type previously found in the dictionary and the type inferred for the instruction. (The least upper bound of two types is that smallest type that is assignment-compatible with the two types.) If this causes the dictionary entry to change, the corresponding instructions and their successors must be re-analyzed until a fixpoint is reached, that is, all instructions have been analyzed at least once without changing the dictionary entries. See [10, section 4.9] for a more detailed description.

2.3 Performance Analysis

The verification of straight-line pieces of code is very efficient, both in time and space. Each instruction is analyzed exactly once, and the analysis is fast (approximately as fast as executing the instruction in the virtual machine). Concerning space, only one stack type and one set of register types need to be stored at any time, and is modified in place during the analysis. Assuming each type is represented by 3 bytes, this leads to memory requirements of $3S + 3N$ bytes, where S is the maximal stack size and N the number of registers for the method. In practice, 100 bytes of RAM suffice. Notice that a similar amount of space is needed to execute an invocation of the method; thus, if the card has enough RAM space to execute the method, it also has enough space to verify it.

Verification in the presence of branches is much more costly. Instructions may need to be analyzed several times in order to reach the fixpoint. Experience shows that few instructions are analyzed more than twice, and many are still analyzed only once, so this is not too bad. The real issue is the memory space required to store the dictionary. If B is the number of distinct branch targets and exception handlers in the method, the dictionary occupies $(3S + 3N + 3) \times B$ bytes (the three bytes of overhead per dictionary entry correspond to the PC of the branch target and the stack height at this point). A moderately complex method can have $S = 5$, $N = 15$ and $B = 50$, for instance, leading to a dictionary of size 3450 bytes. This is too large to fit comfortably in RAM on current generation Java cards.

Storing the dictionary in persistent rewritable memory (EEPROM or Flash) is not an option, because verification performs many writes to the dictionary when updating the types it contains (typically, several hundreds, even thousands of writes for some methods), and these writes to persistent memory take time (1-10 ms each); this would make on-card verification too slow. Moreover, problems may arise due to the limited number of write cycles permitted on persistent memory.

3   Our Verification Algorithm

3.1   Intuitions

The novel bytecode verification algorithm that we describe in this paper follows from a careful analysis of the shortcomings of Sun's algorithm, namely that a copy of the stack type and register type is stored in the dictionary for each branch target. Experience shows that dictionary entries are quite often highly redundant. In particular, it is very often the case that stack types stored in dictionary entries are empty, and that the type of a given register is the same in all or most dictionary entries.

These observations are easy to correlate with the way current Java compilers work. Concerning the stack, all existing compilers use the stack only for evaluating expressions, but never store the values of Java local variables on the stack. Consequently, the stack is empty at the beginning and the end of every statement. Since most branching constructs in the Java language work at the level of statements, the branches generated when compiling these constructs naturally occur in the context of an empty stack. The only exception is the conditional expression e_1 ? e_2 : e_3, which indeed generates a branch on a non-empty stack. As regards to registers, Java compilers very often allocate a distinct JCVM register for each local variable in the Java source. This register is naturally used with only one type, that of the declaration of the local variable.

Of course, there is no guarantee that the JCVM code given to the verifier will enjoy the two properties mentioned above (stack is empty at branch points; registers have only one type throughout the method), but these two properties hold often enough that it is justified to optimize the bytecode verifier for these two conditions.

One way to proceed from here is to design a data structure for holding the dictionary that is more compact when these two conditions hold. For instance, the "stack is empty" case could be represented specially, and differential encodings could be used to reduce the dictionary size when a register has the same type in many entries.

We decided to take a more radical approach and *require* that all JCVM bytecode accepted by the verifier is such that

- **Requirement R1**: the stack is empty at all branch instructions (after popping the branch arguments, if any), and at all branch target instructions (before pushing its results). This guarantees that the stack is consistent between the source and the target of any branch (since it is empty at both ends).
- **Requirement R2**: each register has only one type throughout the method code. This guarantees that the types of registers are consistent between source and target of each branch (since they are consistent between any two instructions, actually).

To avoid rejecting correct JCVM code that happens not to satisfy these two requirements, we will rely on a general off-card code transformation that transforms correct JCVM code into equivalent code meeting these two additional requirements. The transformation is described in section 4. We rely on the fact that the violations of requirements R1 and R2 are infrequent to ensure that the code transformations are minor and do not cause a significant increase in code size.

3.2   The Algorithm

Given the two additional requirements R1 and R2, our bytecode verification algorithm is a simple extension of the algorithm for verifying straight-line code outlined in section 2.1. As previously, the only data structure that we need is *one* stack type and *one* array of types for registers. As previously, the algorithm proceeds by examining in turn every instruction in the method, in code order, and reflecting their effects on the stack and register types. The complete pseudo-code for the algorithm is given in Fig. 1. The significant differences with straight-line code verification are as follows.

- When checking a branch instruction, after popping the types of the arguments from the stack, the verifier checks that the stack is empty, and rejects the code otherwise. When checking an instruction that is a branch target, the verifier checks that the stack is empty. (If the instruction is a JSR target or the start of an exception handler, it checks that the stack consists of one entry of type "return address" or the exception handler's class, respectively.) This ensures requirement R1.
- When checking a "store" instruction, if τ is the type of the stored value (the top of the stack before the "store"), the type of the register stored into is not replaced by τ, but by the least upper bound of τ and the previous type of the register. This way, register types accumulate the types of all values stored into them, thus progressively determining the unique type of the register as it should apply to the whole method code (requirement R2).
- Since the types of registers can change following the type-checking of a "store" instruction as described above, and therefore invalidate the type-checking of instructions that load and use the stored value, the type-checking of all the instructions in the method body must be repeated until the register types are stable. This is similar to the fixpoint computation in Sun's verifier.
- The dataflow analysis starts, as previously, with an empty stack type and register types corresponding to method parameters set to the types indicated in the method descriptor. Locals not corresponding to parameters are set to $\perp$ (the subtype of all types) instead of $\top$ (the supertype of all types) for reasons that are explained in section 3.4 below.

The correctness of our verifier was formally proved using the Coq theorem prover. More precisely, we developed a mechanically-checked proof that any code that passes our verifier does not cause any run-time type error when run through a type-level abstract interpretation of a defensive JCVM.

Global variables:

> N_r number of registers
> N_s maximal stack size
> $r[N_r]$ array of types for registers
> $s[N_s]$ stack type
> sp stack pointer
> chg flag recording whether r changed.

```
Set sp ← 0
Set r[0],...,r[n − 1] to the types of the method arg.
Set r[n],...,r[Nr − 1] to ⊥
Set chg ← true
While chg:
  Set chg ← false
  For each instruction i of the method, in code order:

    If i is the target of a branch instruction:
      If sp ≠ 0 and the previous instruction falls through, error
      Set sp ← 0
    If i is the target of a JSR instruction:
      If the previous instruction falls through, error
        Set s[0] ← retaddr and sp ← 1
    If i is a handler for exceptions of class C:
      If the previous instruction falls through, error
        Set s[0] ← C and sp ← 1
    If two or more of the cases above apply, error

    Determine the types a1,...,an of the arguments of i
    If sp < n, error (stack underflow)
    For k = 1,...,n:  If s[sp − n − k − 1] is not subtype of ak, error
    Set sp ← sp − n
    Determine the types r1,...,rm of the results of i
    If sp + m > Ns, error (stack overflow)
    For k = 1,...,m:  Set s[sp + k − 1] ← rk
    Set sp ← sp + m
    If i is a store to register number n:
      Determine the type t of the value written to the register
      Set r[n] ← lub(t, r[n])
      If r[n] changed, set chg ← true

    If i is a branch instruction and sp ≠ 0, error

  End for each
End while
Verification succeeds
```

Fig. 1. The verification algorithm

3.3   Performance Analysis

Our verification algorithm has the same low memory requirements as straight-line code verification: $3S + 3N$ bytes of RAM suffice to hold the stack and register types. In practice, it fits comfortably in 100 bytes of RAM. The memory requirements are independent of the size of the method code, and of the number of branch targets.

Time behavior is similar to that of Sun's algorithm: several passes over the instructions of the method may be required; experimentally, most methods need only two passes (the first determines the types of the registers and the second checks that the fixpoint is reached), and quite a few need only one pass (when all registers are parameters and they keep their initial type throughout the method).

3.4   Initialization of Registers

Unlike Sun's, our verification algorithm cannot guarantee that registers are initialized (stored into) before use. The reason is that since we have only one set of register types for the whole method, we cannot analyze precisely the situation where a register is initialized on one branch of a conditional and not on the other branch.

The JVM and JCVM specifications do not require the virtual machine to initialize non-parameter registers on entry to a method. Hence, a method that reads (using the ALOAD instruction) from such a register before having stored a valid value in it could obtain an unspecified bit pattern (whatever data happens to be in RAM at the location of the register) and use it as an object reference. This is a serious security threat.

There are two ways to avoid this threat. One is to verify register initialization (no reads before a store) statically, as part of the bytecode verifier. The other is to rely on the virtual machine to initialize, on entry to a method, all registers that are not method parameters to the bit-pattern representing the null object reference. This way, incorrect code that perform a read before write on a register does not break type safety: all instructions operating on object references test for the null reference and raise an exception if appropriate; integer instructions can operate on arbitrary bit patterns without breaking type safety. (A dynamic check must be added to the RET instruction, however, so that a RET on a register initialized to null will fail instead of jumping blindly to the null code address.)

Clearing registers on method entrance is inexpensive, and it is our understanding that several implementations of the JCVM already do it (even if the specification does not require it) in order to reduce the life-time of sensitive data stored on the stack. In summary, register initialization is a rare example of a type safety property that is easy and inexpensive to ensure dynamically in the virtual machine. Hence, we chose not to ensure it statically by bytecode verification.

Since the bit pattern representing null is a correct value of any JCVM type (short, int, array and reference types, and return addresses), it semantically belongs to the type $\perp$ that is subtype of all other JCVM types. Hence, assuming initialization to `null` in the virtual machine, it is semantically correct to assign the initial type $\perp$ to registers that are not parameters, like our verification algorithm does.

3.5 Subroutines

Subroutines are shared code fragments built from the JSR and RET instructions and used for compiling the `try...finally` construct in particular [10]. Subroutines complicate Sun-style bytecode verification tremendously. The reason is that a subroutine can be called from different contexts, where registers have different types; checking the type-correctness of subroutine calls therefore requires that the verification of the subroutine code be polymorphic with respect to the types of the registers that the subroutine body does not use [10, section 4.9.6]. This requires a complementary code analysis that identifies the method instructions that belong to subroutines, and match them with the corresponding JSR and RET instructions. See [19,17] for formalizations of this approach.

All these complications (and potential security holes) disappear in our bytecode verification algorithm: since it ensures that a register has the same type throughout the method code, it ensures that the whole method code, including subroutines, is monomorphic with respect to the types of all registers. Hence, there is no need to verify the JSR and RET instructions in a special, polymorphic way: JSR is treated as a regular branch that also pushes a value of type "return address" on the stack; and RET is treated as a branch that can go to any instruction that follows a JSR in the current method. No complementary analysis of the subroutine structure is required.

4 Off-Card Code Transformations

As explained in section 3.1, our on-card verifier accepts only a subset of all type-correct applets: those whose code satisfies the two additional requirements R1 (stack is empty at branch points) and R2 (registers have unique types). To ensure that all correct applets pass verification, we could compile them with a special Java compiler that generates JVM bytecode satisfying requirements R1 and R2, for instance by expanding conditional expressions e_1 ? e_2 : e_3 into if...then...else statements, and by assigning distinct register to each source-level local variable.

Instead, we found it easier and more flexible to let applet developers use a standard Java compiler and JavaCard converter of their choice, and perform an off-card code transformation on the compiled code to produce an equivalent compiled code that satisfies the additional requirements R1 and R2 and can therefore pass the on-card verifier (see Fig. 2).

Two main transformations are performed: stack normalization (to ensure that the stack is empty at branch points) and register reallocation (to ensure that a given register is used with only one type).

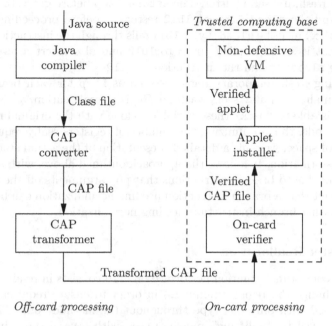

Off-card processing   *On-card processing*

Fig. 2. Architecture of the system

4.1   Stack Normalization

The idea underlying stack normalization is quite simple: whenever the original
code contains a branch with a non-empty stack, we insert stores to fresh registers before the branch, and loads from the same registers at the branch target.
This effectively empties the stack into the fresh registers before the branch, and
restore the stack to its initial state after the branch. Consider for example the
following Java statement: C.m(b ? x : y);. It compiles down to the JCVM
code fragment shown below on the left.

```
          sload Lb                        sload Lb
          ifeq lbl1                       ifeq lbl1
          sload Lx                        sload Lx
          goto lbl2                       sstore Ltmp
    lbl1: sload Ly                        goto lbl2
    lbl2: invokestatic C.m          lbl1: sload Ly
                                          sstore Ltmp
                                    lbl2: sload Ltmp
                                          invokestatic C.m
```

Here, Lx, Ly and Lb are the numbers for the registers holding x, y and b. The
result of type inference for this code indicates that the stack is non-empty across
the goto to lbl2: it contains one entry of type short. Stack normalization
therefore rewrites it into the code shown above on the right, where Ltmp is the

number of a fresh, unused register. The `sstore Ltmp` before `goto lbl2` empties the stack, and the `sload Ltmp` at `lbl2` restore it before proceeding with the `invokestatic`. Since the `sload Ly` at `lbl1` falls through the instruction at `lbl2`, we must treat it as an implicit jump to `lbl2` and also insert a `sstore Ltmp` between the `sload Ly` and the instruction at `lbl2`.

(Allocating fresh temporary registers such as `Ltmp` for each branch target needing normalization may seem wasteful. Register reallocation, as described in section 4.2, is able to "pack" these variables, along with the original registers of the method code, thus minimizing the number of registers really required.)

By lack of space, we omit a detailed presentation of the actual stack normalization transformation. It follows the approach outlined above, with some extra complications due to branch instructions that pop arguments off the stack, and also to the fact that a branch instruction needing normalization can be itself the target of another branch instruction needing normalization.

4.2   Register Reallocation

The second code transformation performed off-card consists in re-allocating registers (i.e. change the register numbers) in order to ensure requirement R2: a register is used with only one type throughout the method code. This can always be achieved by "splitting" registers used with several types into several distinct registers, one per use type. However, this can increase markedly the number of registers required by a method.

Instead, we use a more sophisticated register reallocation algorithm, derived from the well-known algorithms for global register allocation via graph coloring. This algorithm tries to reduce the number of registers by reusing the same register as much as possible, i.e. to hold source variables that are not live simultaneously and that have the same type. Consequently, it is very effective at reducing inefficiencies in the handling of registers, either introduced by the stack normalization transformation, or left by the Java compiler.

Consider the following example (original code on the left, result of register reallocation on the right).

```
sconst_1          sconst_1
sstore 1          sstore 1
sload 1           sload 1
sconst_2          sconst_2
sadd              sadd
sstore 2          sstore 1
new C             new C
astore 1          astore 2
 . . .             . . .
```

In the original code, register 1 is used with two types: first to hold values of type **short**, then to hold values of type C. In the transformed code, these two roles of register 1 are split into two distinct registers, 1 for the **short** role and 2 for the C role. In parallel, the reallocation algorithm notices that, in the original code, register 2 and the short role of register 1 have disjoint live ranges and have the same type. Hence, these two registers are merged into register 1 in the transformed code. The end result is that the number of registers stays constant.

The register reallocation algorithm is essentially identical to Briggs' variant of Chaitin's graph coloring allocator [3,1], with additional type constraints reflecting requirement R2. More precisely, we add edges in the interference graph between live ranges that do not have the same principal type, thus guaranteeing that they will be assigned different registers.

5 Experimental Results

5.1 Off-Card Transformation

The table below shows results obtained by transforming 6 packages from Sun's Java Card development kit.

Package	Code size (bytes)			Resident size (bytes)			Registers
	Orig.	Transf.	Incr.	Orig.	Transf.	Incr.	
java.lang	92	91	-1%	320	319	-0.3%	0.0%
javacard.framework	4047	4142	+2.3%	5393	5488	+1.8%	+0.3%
com.sun.javacard.HelloWorld	100	99	-1%	220	219	-0.5%	0.0%
com.sun.javacard.JavaPurse	2558	2531	-1%	3045	3018	-0.8%	-8.3%
com.sun.javacard.JavaLoyalty	207	203	-1.9%	365	361	-1%	0.0%
com.sun.javacard.installer	7043	7156	+1.6%	8625	8738	+1.3%	-7.5%
Total	14047	14222	+1.2%	17968	18143	+0.9%	-4.2%

The code size increase caused by the transformation is almost negligible: the size of the Method component increases by 1.2%; the resident size (total size of all components that remain on the card after installation) increases by 0.9%. The requirements in registers globally decreases by about 4%.

To test a larger body of code, we used a version of the off-card transformer that works over Java class files (instead of Java Card CAP files) and transformed all the classes from the Java Runtime Environment version 1.2.2, that is, about 1.5 Mbyte of JVM code. The results are very similar: code size increases by 0.7%; registers decrease by 1.3%.

The transformer performs clean-up optimizations (branch tunneling, register coalescing) whose purpose is to reduce inefficiencies introduced by other transformations. These optimizations are also quite effective at reducing inefficiencies left by the Java compiler, resulting in code size decreases of up to 1.9% for some packages. Similarly, the packing of registers actually reduces the maximal number of registers in most packages.

5.2 On-Card Verifier

We present here preliminary results obtained on an implementation of our bytecode verifier running on a Linux PC. A proper on-card implementation is in progress, but we are not in a position to give results concerning this implementation.

Bytecode verification proper (ensuring that method code is type-safe), written in ANSI C, compiles down to 11 kilobytes of Intel IA32 code, and 9 kilobytes of Atmel AVR code. A proof-of-concept reimplementation in hand-written ST7 assembly code fits in 4.5 kilobytes of code.

In addition to verifying the bytecode of methods, our implementation also checks the structural consistency of CAP file components. Since the CAP file format is extremely complex [22, chapter 6], CAP file consistency checking takes a whopping 12 kilobytes of Intel IA32 code. However, when integrating the verifier with an actual Java Card VM, many of these consistency checks become redundant with checks already performed by the VM or the installer, or useless because they apply to CAP file information that the VM ignores. Programming tricks such as table-driven automata can also be used to reduce further the code size of consistency checking, at some expense in execution speed.

The PC implementation of the verifier, running on a 500 Mhz Pentium III, takes approximately 1.5 ms per kilobyte of bytecode. Extrapolating this figure to a typical 8-byte smartcard processor (e.g. 8051 at 5 Mhz), we estimate that an on-card implementation should take less than 1 second per kilobyte of bytecode, or about 2 seconds to verify an applet the size of JavaPurse. Notice that the verifier performs no EEPROM writes and no communications, hence its speed benefits linearly from higher clock rates or more efficient processor cores.

Concerning the number of iterations required to reach the fixpoint in the bytecode verification algorithm, the 6 packages we studied contain 7077 JCVM instructions and require 11492 calls to the function that analyzes individual instructions. This indicates that each instruction is analyzed 1.6 times on average before reaching the fixpoint. This figure is surprisingly low; it shows that a "perfect" verification algorithm that analyzes each instruction exactly once, such as [18], would only be 38% faster than ours.

6   Related Work

The work most closely related to ours is the lightweight bytecode verification of Rose and Rose [18], also found in the KVM architecture [20] and in [9]. Inspired by proof-carrying code [12], lightweight bytecode verification consists in sending, along with the code to be verified, pre-computed stack and register types for each branch target. Verification then simply checks the correctness of these pre-computed types, using a simple variant of straight-line verification, instead of inferring them by fixpoint iteration, as in Sun's verifier.

The interest for an on-card verifier is twofold. The first is that fixpoint iteration is avoided, thus making the verifier faster. (As mentioned at the end of section 5.2, the performance gain thus obtained is modest.) The second is that the stack and register types at branch targets can be stored temporarily in EEPROM, since they do not need to be updated repeatedly during verification.

The RAM requirements of the verifier become similar to those of our verifier: only the current stack type and register type need to be kept in RAM.

There are two problems with Rose and Rose's lightweight bytecode verification. One is that it currently does not deal with subroutines, more specifically with polymorphic typing of subroutines as described in section 3.5. Subroutines are part of the JCVM specification, and could be useful as a general code sharing device for reducing bytecode size. The second issue is the size of the "certificate", that is, the pre-computed stack and register types that accompany the code. Our experiments indicate that, using a straightforward representation, certificates are about the same size as the code. Even with a more complex, compressed representation, certificates are still 20% of the code size. Hence, significant free space in EEPROM is required for storing temporarily the certificates during the verification of large packages. In contrast, our verification technology only requires at most 1–2% of extra EEPROM space.

Challenged by the lack of precision in the reference publications of Sun's verifier [8,24,10], many researchers have published rational reconstructions, formalizations, and formal proofs of correctness of various subsets of Sun's verifier [5,16,15,17,6,13]. These works were influential in understanding the issues, uncovering bugs in Sun's implementation of the verifier, and generating confidence in the algorithm. Unfortunately, most of these works address only a subset of the verifier. In particular, none of them proves the correctness of Sun's polymorphic typing of subroutines in the presence of exceptions.

A different approach to bytecode verification was proposed by Posegga [14] and further refined by Brisset [2]. This approach is based on model checking of a type-level abstract interpretation of a defensive Java virtual machine. It trivializes the problem with polymorphic subroutines and exceptions, but is very expensive (time and space exponential in the size of the method code), thus is not suited to on-card implementation.

7   Conclusions

The novel bytecode verification algorithm described in this paper is perfectly suited to on-card implementation, due to its low RAM requirements. It is superior to Rose and Rose's lightweight bytecode verification in that it handles subroutines, and requires much less additional EEPROM space (1–2% of the code size vs. 20–100% for lightweight bytecode verification).

On-card bytecode verification is the missing link in the Javacard vision of multi-application smart cards with secure, efficient post-issuance downloading of applets. We believe that our bytecode verifier is a crucial enabling technology for making this vision a reality.

References

1. P. Briggs, K. D. Cooper, and L. Torczon. Improvements to graph coloring register allocation. *ACM Trans. Prog. Lang. Syst.*, 16(3):428–455, 1994. 161
2. P. Brisset. Vers un vérifieur de bytecode Java certifié. Seminar given at École Normale Supérieure, Paris, Oct 2nd 1998. 163
3. G. J. Chaitin. Register allocation and spilling via graph coloring. *SIGPLAN Notices*, 17(6):98–105, 1982. 161
4. Z. Chen. *Java Card Technology for Smart Cards: Architecture and Programmer's Guide*. The Java Series. Addison-Wesley, 2000. 150
5. R. Cohen. The defensive Java virtual machine specification. Technical report, Computational Logic Inc., 1997. 163
6. S. N. Freund and J. C. Mitchell. A type system for object initialization in the Java bytecode language. *ACM Trans. Prog. Lang. Syst.*, 21(6):1196–1250, 1999. 163
7. L. Gong. *Inside Java 2 platform security: architecture, API design, and implementation*. The Java Series. Addison-Wesley, 1999. 150
8. J. A. Gosling. Java intermediate bytecodes. In *Proc. ACM SIGPLAN Workshop on Intermediate Representations*, pages 111–118. ACM, 1995. 151, 152, 163
9. G. Grimaud, J.-L. Lanet, and J.-J. Vandewalle. FACADE – a typed intermediate language dedicated to smart cards. In *Software Engineering - ESEC/FSE '99*, volume 1687 of *LNCS*, pages 476–493. Springer-Verlag, 1999. 162
10. T. Lindholm and F. Yellin. *The Java Virtual Machine Specification*. The Java Series. Addison-Wesley, 1999. Second edition. 151, 152, 153, 158, 163
11. G. McGraw and E. Felten. *Securing Java*. John Wiley & Sons, 1999. 150
12. G. C. Necula. Proof-carrying code. In *POPL'97*, pages 106–119. ACM Press, 1997. 162
13. T. Nipkow. Verified bytecode verifiers. In *Foundations of Software Science and Computation Structures (FOSSACS'01)*, volume 2030 of *LNCS*, pages 364–378. Springer-Verlag, 2001. 163
14. J. Posegga and H. Vogt. Java bytecode verification using model checking. In *OOPSLA Workshop Fundamental Underpinnings of Java*, 1998. 163
15. C. Pusch. Proving the soundness of a Java bytecode verifier specification in Isabelle/HOL. In W. R. Cleaveland, editor, *TACAS'99*, volume 1579 of *LNCS*, pages 89–103. Springer-Verlag, 1999. 163
16. Z. Qian. A formal specification of Java virtual machine instructions for objects, methods and subroutines. In J. Alves-Foss, editor, *Formal syntax and semantics of Java*, volume 1523 of *LNCS*. Springer-Verlag, 1998. 163
17. Z. Qian. Standard fixpoint iteration for Java bytecode verification. *ACM Trans. Prog. Lang. Syst.*, 22(4):638–672, 2000. 158, 163
18. E. Rose and K. Rose. Lightweight bytecode verification. In *OOPSLA Workshop Fundamental Underpinnings of Java*, 1998. 162
19. R. Stata and M. Abadi. A type system for Java bytecode subroutines. *ACM Trans. Prog. Lang. Syst.*, 21(1):90–137, 1999. 158
20. Sun Microsystems. Java 2 platform micro edition technology for creating mobile devices. White paper, 2000. 162
21. Sun Microsystems. Java Card 2.1.1 runtime environment specification, 2000. 151
22. Sun Microsystems. Java Card 2.1.1 virtual machine specification, 2000. 151, 162
23. G. Vigna, editor. *Mobile Agents and Security*. Number 1419 in Lecture Notes in Computer Science. Springer-Verlag, 1998. 150
24. F. Yellin. Low level security in Java. In *Proc. 4th World Wide Web Conference*, pages 369–379. O'Reilly, 1995. 151, 152, 163

Towards a Full Formal Specification of the JavaCard API

Hans Meijer and Erik Poll

Computing Science Institute, University of Nijmegen
Toernooiveld 1, 6525 ED Nijmegen, The Netherlands
{hans,erikpoll}@cs.kun.nl

Abstract. This paper reports on ongoing work to develop a formal specification of the JAVACARD API using the specification language JML. It discusses the specification of the JCSystem class, which deals with the JAVACARD firewall, (atomic) transactions and transient objects. The JCSystem class seems to be the hardest class in the API to specify, and it is closely connected with some of the peculiarities of JAVACARD as opposed to JAVA.

1 Introduction

There has been a lot of work on formalisations of the JAVA(CARD) platform. (For a comprehensive overview see [4].) However, most of the work has concentrated on the JAVA(CARD) Virtual Machine, and there has only been very little work on formalisations of the other component of the JAVACARD platform, the JAVACARD API. This paper reports on an ongoing effort to develop a formal specification of the JAVACARD API using the specification language JML. Our ultimate goal is to use a formal specification of the API to verify API implementations and to use it as a basis for the verification of JAVACARD applets. But of course a formal specification of the API is of wider interest, notably to improve and clarify existing informal documentation. For verification we want to use the LOOP tool developed in Nijmegen [1], which gives a formal semantics to JAVA programs and acts as a front-end to the theorem prover PVS. The first —very modest— steps to verify JML-annotated JAVACARD code using the LOOP tool and the theorem prover PVS are reported in [2].

Earlier work on 'lightweight' formal JML specifications for the JAVA-CARD API is reported in [13,14]. This paper discusses the specification of the JCSystem class, which is the class in the API that deals with the JAVACARD firewall, (atomic) transactions and transient objects. The JCSystem class seems to be the most difficult class in the API to specify, as it cannot be described completely independently of some basic features of the JAVACARD Virtual Machine. The class is closely connected with some of the peculiarities of JAVACARD as opposed to JAVA.

This work is part of the EU-sponsored VERIFICARD-project which aims to provide formal descriptions of the JAVACARD platform and to provide tools

I. Attali and T. Jensen (Eds.): E-smart 2001, LNCS 2140, pp. 165–178, 2001.
© Springer-Verlag Berlin Heidelberg 2001

for applet verification based on these formal descriptions. (For more details see
`http://www.verificard.org`.)

2   JML

JML [8,9] is a behavioural interface specification language tailored to JAVA. It
can be used to specify JAVA classes and interfaces by annotating code with invariants and pre- and postconditions of methods, in the style of Eiffel, also known
as 'Design by Contract' [10]. JML annotations are a special kind of JAVA comments: they are preceded by //@, or enclosed between /*@ and @*/, so that they
are simply ignored by a JAVA compiler.

Methods can be specified in JML by so-called normal behaviours. These are
of the form:

```
/*@ normal_behavior
  @    requires: <precondition> ;
  @    ensures: <postcondition> ;
  @*/
```

Such a 'normal behaviour' specification states that if the precondition holds at
the beginning of a method invocation, then the method terminates normally
(i.e. without throwing an exception) and the postcondition will hold at the end
of the method invocation.

Pre- and postconditions are simply standard Java boolean expressions, extended with several additional operators, for example \forall for universal
quantification and ==> for implication. A few more of these additional operations will be explained as we go along.

Java methods can terminate abruptly, by throwing exceptions. If a method
can throw an exception, then a more general form of method specification than
the normal behaviour above is needed:

```
/*@ behavior
  @    requires: <precondition> ;
  @    ensures: <postcondition>;
  @    signals: (Exception1) <condition1>;

  @      :
  @    signals: (Exceptionn) <conditionn>;
  @*/
```

Such a 'behaviour' specification states that if the precondition holds at the beginning of a method invocation, then the method either terminates normally
or terminates abruptly by throwing one of the listed exceptions; if the method
terminates normally, then the postcondition will hold; if the method throws an
exception, then the corresponding condition will hold.

More than one (normal) behaviour can be specified for a single method. This
simply means that the method has to satisfy all of the given (normal) behaviours.

This is a convenient way to specify different cases in the behaviour of a method. The default pre- and postconditions are `requires: true` and `ensures: true`, and these may be omitted in specifications.

In addition to `requires`, `ensures` and `signals` clauses, methods specifications can also include `modifiable` clauses. These clauses specify so-called frame conditions, which say that only certain fields may have their values changed by a method. For example, `modifiable:x` specifies that a method changes only field `x`.

One feature of JML that is of particular importance for this paper is the possibility of using so-called *model fields* (or *model variables*). Model fields are declared in JML annotations and provide specification-only variables: they can not be used in program code, but only in JML assertions. Typically, model fields are introduced to refer to some part of the 'state' encapsulated by objects of a class, a 'piece of state' on which the informal specification implicitly relies, and on which the formal JML specification will explicitly rely. As far as the class `JCSystem` discussed in this paper is concerned, the main difficulty in developing formal JML specifications is introducing appropriate model fields.

Ultimately, there should be a relation between the model variables used in the specification and variables actually used in the implementation, and this relation can again be stated as a JML annotation. Of course, if a method is native, which is the case for many methods of `JCSystem`, there is no concrete implementation to which the models variables can be related.

Normally a model variable and the way its value changes in response to invocations of certain methods is completely described by the specifications of these methods. However, as will be discussed later, for some model variables used in the specification of `JCSystem` this is not the case. The value of some model variables does not only change in response to certain method invocations, but can also change as a side-effect of basic JAVACARD language constructs.

3 The JavaCard API

Together with the JAVACARD virtual machine (JCVM), the JAVACARD API forms the JAVACARD runtime environment, or JCRE, as illustrated in Figure 1. The JCVM provides the interpretation of the basic JAVACARD language, i.e. of all the JAVACARD language constructs. The API is a collection of classes and interfaces providing additional functionality that can be used in JAVACARD programs. The JAVACARD API (version 2.1.1) [5] comprises 18 classes for exceptions, 16 interfaces for working with cryptographic keys and only 10 fundamental classes (in the package `javacard.framework`). Of these ISO7816, `Util`, `Applet` and `Shareable` are elementary from a specification perspective, `PIN` and `OwnerPIN` facilitate working with PIN-codes, and `AID` is a datatype for the identification of applets.

Part of the JAVACARD API – namely the classes `APDU` and `JCSystem` – can be understood as an interface to the miniature operating system running on the smart card. The class `APDU` is the interface of the device driver handling

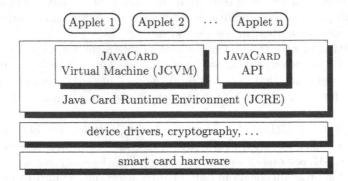

Fig. 1. The JAVACARD Platform

communication of the smart card and the card reader, aka the Card Acceptance Device (CAD). A (still incomplete) formal specification for APDU is discussed in [14]. The class JCSystem provides an interface to the core of the operating system, dealing with the firewall, (atomic) transactions and transient objects. Its specification is the topic of this paper.

A diagram such as Figure 1 is somewhat misleading, as it suggests a clear division between the JCVM and the API, whereas there is a close connection: some parts of the API concern features that are an integral part of the JCVM. It would be more accurate to have some overlap between the API and JCVM boxes in Figure 1. The one class in the API that would be in this overlap is JCSystem, as the functionality it provides is intimately connected with the JCVM. A complicating factor in understanding the connection between JCVM and API is that the specification of the JCVM [7] is given at byte-code level, whereas the specification of the API [5] is given at source-code level. The additional JCRE specification [6], which gives the most detailed description of the connection between JCVM and API, uses byte code level in some parts and source code in others.

4   JCSystem

The JCSystem class offers the functionality for 3 basic ingredients of the JAVA-CARD platform:

1. the creation of objects in transient memory which are cleared when the applet is deselected or when the card is reset;
2. atomic transactions enabling the undoing of certain (partial) updates when power is lost;
3. the firewall which restricts the access of an applet's objects by other applets unless explicitly granted.

This functionality is embodied in 15 methods (not counting the method getVersion which yields the current version number), listed in Figure 2 below. These methods may be considered as the *system calls* of the JAVACARD operating system by which applets have access to the basic features of JAVACARD. We will discuss the formal specification of transience and the firewall in some detail, and sketch that of atomicity.

As far as the three features listed above are concerned it is hard to draw a line between the API and the JAVACARD language (or the JCVM). Unlike the other API classes the class JCSystem does not provide a piece of functionality that provides an addition to the bare JCVM and that can be understood in isolation, as the three features are really an integral part of the JAVACARD language. This is what makes the specification of JCSystem essentially more difficult than the specification of the other API classes. Indeed, the class JCSystem is not only specified in SUN's API specification [5], but is also extensively discussed in the JAVACARD Runtime Environment (JCRE) specification [6]. A still more detailed description is given by SUN's JAVA reference implementation of the JAVACARD API. In particular, the reference implementation of SUN includes a class Dispatcher that does not contain any public fields or methods and is therefore not included in the API specification. It contains the main method which performs card initialization (creates fundamental objects like the APDU buffer and installs built-in applets; it is called only once) and card reset (at each power up), and drives the main loop of the card, which processes APDUs resulting in the (de)selection of applets or the dispatching of APDUs to or from the currently selected applet.

The basis for our formal JML specification of JCSystem is provided by the three sources of information mentioned above: the (informal) JAVACARD API specification [5], the JAVACARD Runtime Environment (JCRE) specification [6], and SUN's reference implementation of the API. The following sections discuss the different parts of JCSystem, dealing with transient objects, the firewall, and the transaction mechanism, in more detail.

4.1 Transient Objects

The JAVACARD platform assumes the presence of both persistent memory which retains data even if power is lost, and transient memory which is cleared upon power loss. When objects are created by the new operator, they are allocated in persistent memory. The class JCSystem provides methods for creating objects in transient memory; these objects are always arrays.

The method

    makeTransientBooleanArray (short length, byte event)

creates (allocates) an array of booleans of the given length in transient memory. The array is persistent in the sense that it survives card resets, but its *contents* are cleared (i.e. set to false) when the card is reset (e.g. after power loss), or when the applet which created it is deselected. This choice is determined by the parameter event, which can be CLEAR_ON_RESET or CLEAR_ON_DESELECT.

```
public final class JCSystem {

  public static short getVersion();

  /* methods for transient objects */

  public static native byte isTransient(Object theObj);

  public static native boolean[] makeTransientBooleanArray(short length,
                                                           byte event);
  public static native byte[] makeTransientByteArray(short length,
                                                     byte event);
  public static native short[] makeTransientShortArray(short length,
                                                       byte event)
  public static native Object[] makeTransientObjectArray(short length,
                                                         byte event) ;


  /* methods for the transaction mechanism */

  public static native void beginTransaction() throws TransactionException;
  public static native void abortTransaction() throws TransactionException;
  public static native void commitTransaction() throws TransactionException;
  public static native byte getTransactionDepth();
  public static native short getUnusedCommitCapacity();
  public static native short getMaxCommitCapacity();

  /* methods for the firewall */

  public static AID getAID();
  public static AID lookupAID( byte[] buffer, short offset, byte length );
  public static AID getPreviousContextAID();
  public static Shareable getAppletShareableInterfaceObject(AID serverAID,
                                                            byte parameter);
}
```

Fig. 2. The methods of JCSystem

The methods makeTransientByteArray, makeTransientShortArray, make-
TransientObjectArray are completely analogous. The method isTransient
(Object theObj) yields a byte with value NOT_A_TRANSIENT_OBJECT,
CLEAR_ON_RESET or CLEAR_ON_DESELECT with the obvious meaning.

For a formal specification, we first note that a normal behavior of make-
TransientBooleanArray requires a restriction on the values of its parameters:
$0 \leq$ length $\leq$ *free* where *free* is the amount of available free transient memory,
and event $\in$ {CLEAR_ON_RESET, CLEAR_ON_DESELECT}. The firewall imposes additional restrictions. The firewall relies on a partitioning of the object system into
separate objects spaces called *contexts*. The JCRE manages a context for each applet, and the firewall restricts access across boundaries between these contexts.
Because of the firewall, the normal behavior of makeTransientBooleanArray
requires that if event equals CLEAR_ON_DESELECT, the currently active context
should equal the currently selected context.

These conditions together constitute the precondition of the normal behavior of the method. Each possible way to negate this precondition represents
a precondition of an exceptional behavior, where an exception is thrown. For

instance, if `length` > *free*, a `SystemException` is thrown with reason code `SystemException.NO_TRANSIENT_SPACE`.

The postcondition of `makeTransientBooleanArray`'s normal behavior should express that its result is a non-null transient Boolean array with the correct length, event and contents (viz. all `falses`), that *free* decreases by an amount of `length`[1]. Finally, the JML operation `\fresh` can be used to say that the result is a 'freshly' allocated object. Before writing the actual JML-code of this specification, we should note that the variable *free*, the notions 'currently active context' and 'currently selected context', and the 'event' property of a (transient) object are not directly available when the method is applied. Therefore, we introduce JML model variables for *free* (which we call `_freeTransient`) as well as for the contexts, and assume that each object has an 'event' model field telling whether that object is `NOT_A_TRANSIENT_OBJECT`, or else `CLEAR_ON_RESET` or `CLEAR_ON_DESELECT`.

We must make sure when verifying the API and applets that the values of these model variables and properties are properly maintained. For instance, the increase and decrease of the run-time stack of the JCVM will influence `_freeTransient`. The 'currently active context' can change with a method call, and is (in)directly registered in the JCVM run-time-stack. The 'currently selected context' changes with the (de)selection of applets by the dispatcher. In some cases (the changes in) the values of model variables and properties can be maintained in the JML-specification itself. For instance, one could imagine that the value of the 'currently selected context' is maintained in the `select`- and `deselect`-methods of the `Applet`-class. Otherwise, the maintenance has to be built in into the semantics of the relevant JAVACARD statements.

We will not resolve this issue here, and just assume that the appropriate (model) variables and properties are available and properly maintained. By conventions, their names are distinguished by an initial underscore.

This then results in the JML-specification for `makeTransientBooleanArray` in Figure 3.

The JAVACARD documentation does not specify the behavior in the case where `length` < 0. Whatever class declares `_freeTransient` should specify the invariant 0 <= `_freeTransient` (possibly also giving an upper limit by means of a constant `_MAX_SIZE_OF_TRANSIENT`). The question may be raised whether it is necessary to specify that the allocation is not actually done in persistent memory (as is required by the informal specification), or even that the allocation does not use memory which is already allocated to other objects.

The actual clearing of transient arrays should be specified in the dispatcher. This may call for a detailed administration of all created transient arrays, necessitating an extension of our specification. For instance, we might use a model variable `_transientMemory` modelling the whole transient memory and specify the precise allocation in the `ensures`-clause of the normal behavior (and make `_freeTransient` a field of `_transientMemory`). Alternatively, one could model

---

[1] Here we possibly oversimplify things a bit, e.g. we ignore any fixed overhead to record the length of the array.

```
public static native boolean[] makeTransientBooleanArray(short length,
                                                         byte event)
throws SystemException;

/*@ normal_behavior
  @   requires: 0 <= length && length <= _freeTransient &&
  @             (event == CLEAR_ON_RESET || event == CLEAR_ON_DESELECT) &&
  @             (event == CLEAR_ON_DESELECT
  @                          ==> _selectedContext == _activeContext);
  @ modifiable: _freeTransient;
  @   ensures: \result != null && \result.length == length &&
  @            \result._event == event && \fresh(\result) &&
  @            _freeTransient == \old(_freeTransient) - length &&
  @            \forall (byte i) 0 <= i < length ==> \result[i] == false;
  @ also
  @ behavior
  @   signals: (SystemException e)
  @            (e.getReason() == SystemException.ILLEGAL_VALUE &&
  @            (length < 0 ||
  @             (event != CLEAR_ON_RESET && event != CLEAR_ON_DESELECT)))
  @        ||
  @            ( e.getReason() == SystemException.NO_TRANSIENT_SPACE &&
  @            _freeTransient < length)
  @        ||
  @            (e.getReason() == SystemException.ILLEGAL_TRANSIENT &&
  @            event == CLEAR_ON_DESELECT &&
  @            _selectedContext != _activeContext);
  @*/
```

Fig. 3. JML specification of `makeTransientBooleanArray`

a separate transient memory for 'clear_on_reset' arrays and separate transient memories for 'clear_on_deselect' arrays for each possible applet, identified by its AID.

The specification of `isTransient` is rather trivial:

```
public static native byte isTransient(Object theObj);

/*@  behavior
  @      ensures: \result == theObj._event;
  @*/
```

4.2   The Firewall

The firewall mechanism prohibits an applet's access to objects owned (created) by other applets. The rules as detailed in the JAVACARD Runtime Environment (JCRE) specification are quite elaborate. The main principles are that the JCRE can access any object, but applets can only access objects owned by applets in the same package, objects designated as JCRE entry-point objects, and 'shareable' objects to which access is explicitly granted by their owners.

Applets have a certain context, which is basically the package they belong to, and the JCRE is considered to have no context. As long as an applet is selected, that applet's context is the currently selected context. When a method of an applet is called, that applet's context becomes the currently active context.

```
public static Shareable getAppletShareableInterfaceObject(AID  serverAID,
                                                        byte parameter)
/*@ normal_behavior
  @   requires: _previousContext == _jcreContext &&
  @             _registeredAIDs.has(serverAID);
  @     ensures: \result ==
  @             (_appletTable.apply(serverAID)).getShareableInterfaceObject
  @                                     (null,parameter);
  @ also
  @ normal_behavior
  @   requires: _previousContext != _jcreContext &&
  @             _registeredAIDs.has(serverAID);
  @   ensures: \result ==
  @             (_appletTable.apply(serverAID)).getShareableInterfaceObject
  @                             (getPreviousContextAID(),parameter);
  @ also
  @ normal_behavior
  @   requires: !_registeredAIDs.has(serverAID);
  @     ensures: \result == null;
  @*/
```

Fig. 4. JML specification of `getAppletShareableInterfaceObject`

There is also a 'previous context' which is the context of the applet which called
the currently active method, possibly via intermediate JCRE methods.

JCSystem provides a method

```
public static Shareable getAppletShareableInterfaceObject
                    (AID serverAID, byte parameter)
```

by which an applet may ask permission to access an object owned by
the applet identified by the given `serverAID`. It follows from the informal API specification [5] (from the specifications of `getAppletShareable-`
`InterfaceObject` of the class `JCSystem` and of `getShareableInterface-`
`Object` of class `Applet`, to be precise) that this method calls the method
`getShareableInterfaceObject` of the applet identified by `serverAID`, passing it the `AID` of the calling applet (or `null` if the caller is a JCRE-method) and
the given `parameter`. The `AID` of the calling applet can be obtained using the
method `getPreviousContextAID`. If the `serverAID` is invalid, `null` is returned.
Therefore, if the server is valid, and the caller is valid (or the JCRE), the specification of `getAppletShareableInterfaceObject` will be that of the server's
`getShareableInterfaceObject`.

This is formalized in the JML-specification for `getAppletShareable-`
`InterfaceObject` in Figure 4. It requires the introduction of more model variables, as discussed below.

The model variable `_previousContext` is akin to the model variables
`_selectedContext` and `_activeContext` introduced in Section 4.1. The
`_selectedContext` is set and reset when applets are selected and deselected.
The other two have to be maintained as part of the semantics of the method
call. In fact, their values could be extracted from the run-time stack. The related
model constant `_jcreContext` represents the context of the JCRE; it is different
from any applet's context.

Two model variables used in the specification of `getAppletShareable-InterfaceObject` are of more complicated types than the model variables seen so far. First, there is a model variable `_registeredAIDs`, which is the set of all the AID's of installed applets. Second, there is a model variable `_appletTable`, which is a partial function from AID's to applets, that, given an AID, returns the applet with that AID, if such an applet is installed. So the domain of `_appletTable` will be `_registeredAIDs`, and this could in fact be included as an invariant. The values of these model variables will change in response to invocations of the method `register` of an applet.

In specifications one often needs model variables that represents sets and functions, such as `_registeredAIDs` and `_appletTable` above. For this reason the JML distribution comes with a package `edu.iastate.cs.jml.models` that implements many mathematical notions that are frequently needed in specifications. This package provides suitable classes for `_registeredAIDs` and `_appletTable`:

```
public model JMLObjectSet        _registeredAIDs;
public model JMLObjectToObjectMap _appletTable;
```

The method `has` for `JMLObjectSet` and `apply` for `JMLObjectToObjectMap` used in the specification of `getAppletShareableInterfaceObject` in Figure 4 have the obvious interpretations. A detailed description of these classes is given as part of the JML release that can be obtained at `http://www.cs.iastate.edu/~leavens/JML.html`.

Sun's reference implementation of the JAVACARD API provides a particular representation of the information in `_registeredAIDs`, `_appletTable`, and `_previousAID`. In fact, it uses an array of objects `theAppletTable` to record the mapping `_appletTable`. Internally, the reference implementation does not use AIDs but indexes in this array to identify applets. To ensure that the specification is in agreement with this implementation one would use the standard technique of establishing an invariant that expresses the correspondence between the abstract model variable and the concrete implementation.

The method `lookupAID`, by which an applet can obtain AIDs to pass to `getAppletShareableInterfaceObject` accesses the internal applet table in much the same way as `getAppletShareableInterfaceObject` and is easy to specify.

The two remaining methods related to the firewall, `getAID` and `getPreviousContextAID`, return the AIDs associated with the current and the previous applet context, respectively. They could be specified by introducing model variables `_currentContextAID` and `_previousContextAID`, and then specifying

```
public static AID getPreviousContextAID()

/*@ normal_behaviour
  @   ensures: \result == _previousContextAID;
  @*/
```

and similarly for `getAID`. But observe that there is then effectively no difference between `getPreviousContextAID()` and the method variable `_previousContextAID`. One could simply do away with the model variable and use the method instead. (Indeed, the specification of `getAppletShareableInterfaceObject` in Figure 4 already uses the method invocation `getPreviousContextAID()` rather than some model variable `_previousContextAID`.) Essentially the methods `getAID` and `getPreviousContextAID` are too fundamental for an interesting specification in JML.

Something interesting that could still be specified is the relation between contexts and AIDs. A model variable for this relation could be introduced in order to express the invariants that hold between `_currentContext` and `_currentContextAID` and `_previousContext` and `_previousContextAID`.

4.3   Atomic Transactions

All updates of single array elements, object fields and class fields in persistent memory are atomic. If a failure or power loss occurs during an update, the field is restored to its previous value. With modern hardware it is not difficult to obey this requirement, and in formal specifications atomic updates are in fact silently assumed. The `Util`-class of the JAVACARD API provides methods for atomic and non-atomic updates of arrays.

For more complicated updates, the `JCSystem`-class provides the methods `beginTransaction()`, `abortTransaction()` and `commitTransaction()`. A (hidden) variable `transactionDepth`, which is 0 initially, is incremented by `beginTransaction()`, decremented by `abortTransaction()` and `commitTransaction()`, but should always have a value of 0 or 1, otherwise a `TransactionException` is thrown. This outlines a behavior specification of these methods.

Essentially, `beginTransaction()` should create a 'backup' of persistent memory in a second persistent memory, and `abortTransaction()` should 're-store' it. However, this is not feasible as the amount of persistent memory is severely restricted and writing to it is expensive. Therefore, a *commit buffer* is provided, the size of which is implementation-dependent. The use of this buffer may follow different schemes (as outlined in [12]), of which we just choose one ('old value logging', as opposed to 'new value logging') for our specification.

For each update of a byte of persistent memory, if `transactionDepth` > 0, the value to be overwritten is recorded in the commit buffer, provided that no value is yet recorded for that byte. The buffer is cleared by `commitTransaction()`, but `abortTransaction()` restores the old values. Also, `abortTransaction()` is implicitly called when the JCRE regains control, upon applet deselection, card reset (e.g. after a power loss), or any kind of failure. This may happen even if `abortTransaction()` is in progress. Consequently, from the perspective of the applets, the result of such a transaction is always consistently the collection of new values or the collection of old values. The atomicity of transactions ultimately relies on the fact that the decrease of `transactionDepth` is atomic, and the last action of `abortTransaction()`.

Moreover, any object created during a transaction, either in persistent or in transient memory, is deleted and has its memory freed upon `abortTransaction()`. Each reference to such an object, even on the run-time stack, is set to `null`.

In the specification we introduce a (rather complicated) model variable `_theCommitBuffer`. We assume that the semantics of updates and object creation is extended so as to include the recording of old values and pointers in this model object. The specification of `abortTransaction()` will state that the values of all object fields and array elements recorded in the commit buffer equal those recorded, that any references to newly created objects are set to `null` and that the memory of these objects is freed.

The specification of three other methods dealing with atomic transactions, `getTransactionDepth`, `getUnusedCommitCapacity` and `getMaxCommitCapacity` are quite straightforward. The latter two extract properties from `_theCommitBuffer`.

5   Related Work

Most of the work on formalising the JAVACARD platform has focussed on the JCVM rather than the API. Still, some (formal) models of transaction mechanism, firewall, and transient memory have been given. For example, transaction mechanisms are described in [15] (using B), [12] and [3] (using Z), and the firewall in [11] (using B). As mentioned earlier, as far as firewall, atomic actions, and transient memory are concerned it is hard to draw a line between the API and JCVM, so this work is not unrelated to what we have done. The model variables we need in our JML specifications should have counterparts in formal descriptions of the JCVM, as explained in more detail below.

6   Conclusion

Although some details of the specification of the JAVACARD API are somewhat subtle, the specification as a whole turns out to be rather small. All methods have a specification which is not essentially larger than that of `makeTransientBooleanArray` as given in Figure 3.

The model variables that have to be introduced in our JML specifications make explicit many of the informal notions used in the existing informal documentation. This can help to clarify and improve these informal specifications.

Normally, the values of model variables and the way these change in response to methods invocations is completely described by the JML specifications. However, for many model variables used in the specification of `JCSystem` this is not the case. Maintaining the correct values of these model variables is an integral part of the semantics of normal JAVACARD statements. For example, any assignment to a persistent object field that occurs during a transaction affects _theCommitBuffer, so the semantics of assignment should include this side-effect on _theCommitBuffer. Or, to give another example, the variable _activeContext may need to be changed at every method invocation, so the semantics of method invocation should include a side-effect on _activeContext. Note that a comprehensive account of all such examples comes down to a specification of the differences between JAVA and JAVACARD.

All this means that ultimately a specification of the JAVACARD API cannot be considered on its own, but has to be considered together with a formalisation of the JAVACARD language itself, e.g. a formal description of the JCVM or —in our case— our denotational semantics of JAVACARD in PVS. The 'side-effects' mentioned above should then be made part of the implementation of certain virtual machine instructions (e.g. *invoke* bytecodes) c.q. be included in the semantics of JAVACARD source code statements. The list of model variables needed in a formal JML specification gives a good overview of the variables that have to be maintained by a JCVM in order to, say, implement the firewall.

When verifying JAVACARD source code using the LOOP tool and PVS, verifying any properties that depend on (the model variables of) JCSystem will require some mechanism by which (JML) model variables can be associated with the external operations they are subject to. How this should be accomplished is a matter of further investigation. Note that this issue is not particular to our approach to verification using the LOOP tool and PVS: whenever one wants to adapt an existing approach of JAVA-verification to JAVACARD the question of how to deal with the peculiarities of JAVACARD as opposed to JAVA arises.

References

1. J. van den Berg and B. Jacobs. The LOOP compiler for Java and JML. In T. Margaria and W. Yi, editors, *Tools ans Algorithms for the Construction and Analysis of Software (TACAS)*, number 2031 in LNCS, pages 299–312. Springer, Berlin, 2001. 165

2. J. van den Berg, B. Jacobs, and E. Poll. Formal Specification and Verification of JavaCard's Application Identifier Class. In I. Attali and T. Jensen, editors, *Proceeding of the first JavaCard Workshop (JCW'2000)*, LNCS. Springer Verlag, 2001. To appear. 165

3. P. H. Hartel, M. J. Butler, E. de Jong, and M. Longley. Transacted memory for smart cards. In *10th Formal Methods for Increasing Software Productivity (FME)*, LNCS. Springer Verlag, 2001. 176

4. P. H. Hartel and L. A. V. Moreau. Formalizing the safety of Java, the Java virtual machine and Java Card. *ACM Computing Surveys*, 2001. to appear. 165

5. *The Java Card 2.1.1 Application Programming Interface (API)*. Sun Microsystems, 2000. 167, 168, 169, 173

6. *The Java Card 2.1.1 Runtime Environment (JCRE) Specification*. Sun Microsystems, 2000. 168, 169

7. *The Java Card 2.1.1 Virtual Machine (JCVM) Specification*. Sun Microsystems, 2000. 168

8. G. T. Leavens, A. L. Baker, and C. Ruby. JML: A notation for detailed design. In H. Kilov and B. Rumpe, editors, *Behavioral Specifications of Business and Systems*, pages 175–188. Kluwer, 1999. 166

9. G. T. Leavens, A. L. Baker, and C. Ruby. Preliminary design of JML: A behavioral interface specification language for Java. Techn. Rep. 98-06, Dep. of Comp. Sci., Iowa State Univ. (http://www.cs.iastate.edu/~leavens/JML.html), 1999. 166

10. B. Meyer. *Object-Oriented Software Construction*. Prentice Hall, 2nd rev. edition, 1997. 166

11. Stéphanie Motré. Formal model and implementation of the Java Card dynamic security policy. Technical Report SM-99-09, Gemplus Research Lab, 1999. Presented at AFADL'2000. 176

12. Marcus Oestreicher. Transactions in Java Card. In *15th Annual Computer Security Applications Conference (ACSAC'99)*, pages 291–298. IEEE, 1999. 175, 176

13. E. Poll, J. van den Berg, and B. Jacobs. Specification of the JavaCard API in JML. In J. Domingo-Ferrer, D. Chan, and A. Watson, editors, *Fourth Smart Card Research and Advanced Application Conference (CARDIS'2000)*, pages 135–154. Kluwer Acad. Publ., 2000. 165

14. E. Poll, J. van den Berg, and B. Jacobs. Formal Specification of the JavaCard API in JML: The APDU class. *Computer Networks*, 2001. To appear. 165, 168

15. Denis Sabatier and Pierre Lartigue. The use of the B formal method for the design and the validation of the transaction mechanism for smart card applications. *Formal Method in System Design*, 17(3):145–272, 2000. Special issue on FM'99. 176

Protection Profiles and Generic Security Targets for Smart Cards as Secure Signature Creation Devices - Existing Solutions for the Payment Sector

Gisela Meister and Michael Vogel

Giesecke & Devrient,
Prinzregentenstr. 159, D-81677 Munich, Germany
{Gisela.Meister,Michael.Vogel}@gdm.de

Abstract. This paper describes European standardisation activities for the evaluation of Secure Signature Creation Devices (SSCDs) focussing on smart cards. These standards were delivered this year to the Article 9 committee in accordance to requirements of the "DIRECTIVE 1999/93/EC OF THE EUROPEAN PARLIAMENT AND OF THE COUNCIL of 13 December 1999 on a Community framework for electronic signatures". Further on an example of a German payment card usable as SSCD is presented which will be evaluated at the end of the year.

1 Introduction

One main issue of standardisation work for smart cards is the interoperability of smart card applications.This issue especially applies for electronic signature applications on smart cards:

An electronic signature of one user, performed inside a smart card, should be verifiable by another user.
A smart card with signature application should be accepted by different environments, in the user's home environment, in the office and /or in a public environment (e.g. hotel, airport).
National specifications are already in use which describe signature formats and smart card interfaces (e.g. see[1]).

Another important issue of standardisation work has legislative importance:

The quality of signatures should be comparable, because verifier as well as signer have to rely on their trustworthiness.

Our paper describes related European standardisation activities and presents a smart card application in the payment field.
The EU standardisation activities do not focus on electronic signatures on smart cards but describe requirements for *advanced electronic signatures* on product neutral tokens: *Secure Signature Creation Devices.*

I. Attali and T. Jensen (Eds.): E-smart 2001, LNCS 2140, pp. 179-187, 2001.
© Springer-Verlag Berlin Heidelberg 2001

According to the EU Directive [3] *Secure Signature Creation Devices* (SSCD) are able to store private signature keys of a card holder without delivering the key to the outside world. Therefore the calculation of the signature algorithm as well as its storage is performed inside the SSCD.

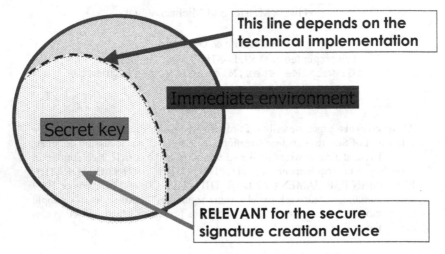

Fig. 1. Structure of a SSCD according to [4]

An *advanced electronic signature* is a high quality electronic signature, the exact definition is presented in the next chapter.

In the CEN/ISSS Workshop on Electronic Signatures (*WS/E-Sign*), an initiative founded by European standardisation bodies CEN, CENELEC and ETSI, recent standardisation work for this type of signatures has been accomplished (see Fig. 1).

Especially for smart cards two documents are relevant:

One documents contains a protection profile and requirements for SSCDs (designed by E-SIGN WG F), the second one describes the requirements for the environment and the signature creation application (SCA (designed by E-Sign WG G1) [5].

The *German Geldkarte* with operating system SECCOS (**Se**cure **C**hip **C**ard **O**perating **S**ystem) is an example of a smart card which has been influenced by the German and European standardisation work and will be evaluated according the related generic security target specified for smart cards [8] (level : ITSEC E4) by G&D at the end of the year.

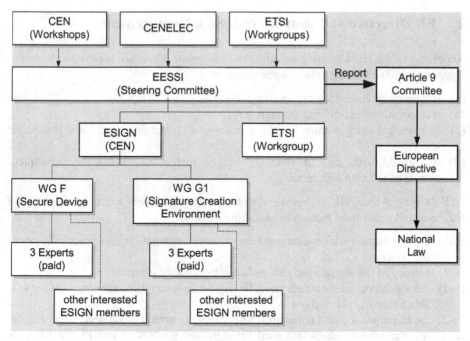

Fig. 2. Overview of Workgroups

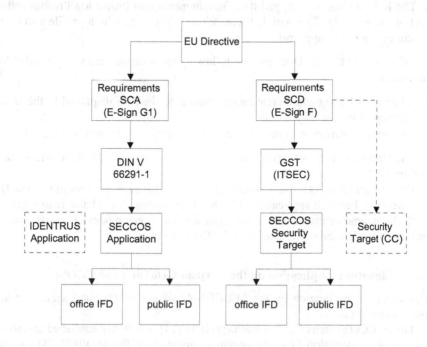

Fig.3. Hierarchies of the Security Target for SECCOS

2   EU Directive and Respective E-Sign Requirements

According to the EU Directive an *advanced electronic signature* means an electronic signature which meets the following requirements:

(a) it is uniquely linked to the signatory;
(b) it is capable of identifying the signatory;
(c) it is created using means that the signatory can maintain under his sole control; and
(d) it is linked to the data to which it relates in such a manner that any subsequent change of the data is detectable.

Following Annex III, 1: Secure signature-creation devices must, by appropriate technical and procedural means, ensure at the least that:

(a-1) the signature-creation-data used for signature generation can practically occur only once,
(a-2) secrecy of the signature-creation-data is reasonably assured;
(b-1) the signature-creation-data used for signature generation cannot, with reasonable assurance, be derived
(b-2) the signature is protected against forgery using currently available technology;
(c) the signature-creation-data used for signature generation can be reliably protected by the legitimate signatory against the use of others.

The E-Sign Group F mapped these requirements into Protection Profiles following EAL 4 res. EAL 4+. The Article 9 committee will decide which profile will be referenced by the EU as appropriate.

According to the EU Directive the following requirements are to be fulfilled for the environment:

• data used for signature creation correspond to the data displayed to the signatory (comp. Annexes III 2, IV a)
• signature creation is an act of volition of the signatory (comp. Article 5.1)

The Directive does not cover the IT security requirements for the entire system environment.

The E-Sign group G1 defined requirements for the Environment of the SSCD and the interfaces between application and SSCD enhancing these basic requirements.

Both documents are an important input for the development of smart card applications following the requirements of the EU Directive.

2.1   Signature Application on the German Geldkarte (SECCOS)

The signature application on the SECCOS *Geldkarte* is designed according to the *DIN Vornorm* [1].

The SECCOS Smart Card operating system [14] is recently published together with a signature application [15]. Its design is oriented on the ISO/IEC 7816 series for smart cards. Especially the cryptographic command set is based on ISO/IEC 7816-8, following the DIN Vornorm. The access conditions are specified according to ISO/IEC 7816-9.

The G1 specification [5] distinguishes 2 different types of environments – a private or office environment which is controlled by the signer and a public environment controlled by a service provider (see. Fig. 4). In case of a public environment the protection of the interaction sequences may be performed by means of a trusted channel in the public environment. There is no special technique mentioned to achieve this trusted path. The G1 specification suggests to replace the trusted path by organisatoric means, if the environment is trusted, e.g. in a private environment.

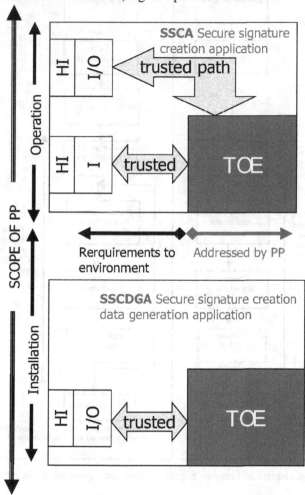

Fig. 4. Trusted path between Signature Creation Application (SCA) and SSCD according to [4]

184   Gisela Meister and Michael Vogel

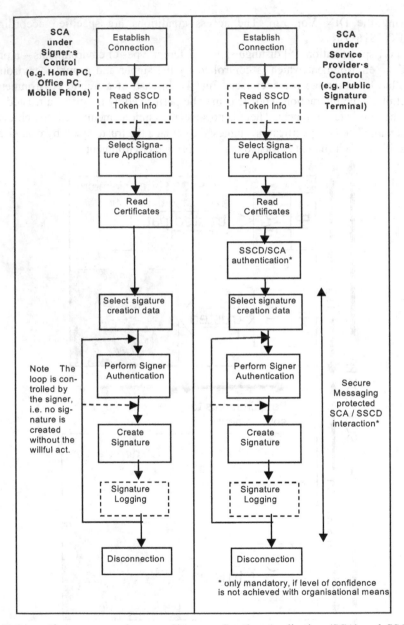

Fig. 5. Interaction sequences between Signature Creation Application (SCA) and SSCD according to [5]

In agreement with this specification the SECCOS Signature Application supports two different security environment (SE) settings for use with private IFDs (SE1) and public IFDs (SE2).

This may be demonstrated by the referenced example in the introduction: The electronic signature generation may be performed in a private environment (at home or at the office under the control of the user, 'private IFD') or public environment (e.g. at an airport, 'public IFD').

According to [15] based on [1] the card, may be used in these two different scenarios. In case of the public environment the interaction between terminal and card is protected by mutual device authentication with secure messaging.

Thereby, for the purpose of interoperability, a mutual device authentication protocol is specified for different mechanisms as RSA, DSA and Elliptic Curves. Hereby the algorithm, implemented on the card is indicated by a corresponding certificate and is sent to the terminal for the purpose that this algorithm is to be used by the terminal as well.

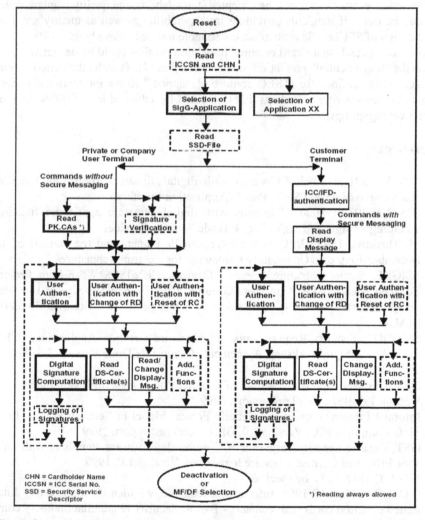

Fig. 6. Interaction sequences between card and terminal used in a private environment or public environment according to [1]. The same interaction sequences are realised within SECCOS

The mutual authentication method with key exchange also used in [15] fulfils the requirements of a trusted path between SSCD and the *Secure Application environment (SCA)* (see Fig. 5).The sequences shown in Fig. 5 are realised using ISO commands exclusively [9], [10], [11].

The comparison between Fig. 4 and 5 exhibits, that the signature application on the card exactly represents an example of a SSCD according to [4] together with [5].

The key generation process for SECCOS follows as well DIN V66291 as one possible solution of [4].

The key is generated in the card, the public key is transported by a trusted path to *the Certifcate Service Provider* (CSP) using Secure Messaging functions on the card.

Electronic signatures can only be accepted if availability and quality is guaranteed. This may be done, if standards providing interoperability as well as quality are used for the design of SSCDs . Smart cards are a suitable tool to achieve both.

Moreover, special smart card oriented protection profiles could be designed which base on the "token neutral" protection profile defined in [4]. Thereby the generic security target of [8] defined for ITSEC could be "mapped " to the internationally more accepted Common Criteria. Perhaps this task could be achieved in EUROSMART or related working groups.

References

[1]   DIN V66291-1: 1999, Chipcards with digital signature application/function according to SigG and SigV, Part 1: Application Interface
[2]   DIN V66291-4: 2000, Chipcards with digital signature application/function according to SigG and SigV, Part 4: Basic Security Services
[3]   EU Directive 1999/93/EC of the European Parliament and the council of 13 December 1999 on a Community framework for electronic signatures
[4]   ESIGNF, Secure Signature Creation Devices, CEN/ISSS WS/E-Sign Project Team on Area F, CEN Agreement Group F, CEN/ISSS WS/E-Sign N 136 Berlin/2001-03-01 (EAL 4), CEN/ISSS WS/E-Sign N 137 Berlin/2001-03-01 (EAL 4+)
[5]   ESIGNG1, Security Requirements for Signature Creation Applications, CEN /ISSS WS/E-Sign Workshop Agreement Group G1, Draft Version 3.5, February, 2001
[6]   GFM-Din, Generic Formal Model of Security Policy for a SigG Compliant ICC, Version 1.0, BSI-, TeleTrust-report, 1999
[7]   Informal Interpretation of the Generic Formal Model of Security Policy for a SigG Compliant ICC, Version 1.0, BSI-, TeleTrust-report, 1999
[8]   GST, Generic Security Target for ICC embedded software compliant with DIN V 66391-1 and German signature legislative, Version 1.0, 1999
[9]   ISO/IEC 7816-4: To be specified.
[10] ISO/IEC 7816-8: IS 1998, Information technology - Identification cards - Integrated circuit(s) cards with contacts - Part 8: Security related interindustry commands [ISO/IEC 7816-9]

[11] ISO/IEC 7816-9: IS 2000, Information technology - Identification cards - Integrated circuit(s) cards with contacts - Part 9: Additional interindustry commands and security attributes

[12] SigG97, German digital signature law - Gesetz zur digitalen Signatur (Signaturgesetz - SigG) vom 22.07.1997 (BGBl. I S. 1870, 1872), verkündet als Artikel 3 des "Gesetzes zur Regelung der Rahmenbedingungen für Informations- und Kommunikationsdienste (Informations- und Kommunikationsdienste-Gesetz - IuKDG), 2. Version expected May 2001

[13] German signature regulations -Verordnung zur digitalen Signatur (Signaturverordnung - SigV), 22.10.1997, 2. Version expected May 2001

[14] SECCOS, Secure Chip Card Operating System, Schnittstellenspezifikation für die ZKA-Chipkarte, Vers.0.9., March 2001

[15] Signatur-Anwendung der Schnittstellenspezifikation für die ZKA-Chipkarte, Version Entwurf 0.6, September 2000

A Flexible Invocation Framework
for Java Card

Michael Montgomery and Ksheerabdhi Krishna

Austin Product Center, Schlumberger, 8311 North FM 620 Rd, Austin, TX 78726, USA
mmontgomery@slb.com, kkrishna@slb.com

Abstract. The Java Card Specification specifies a framework suitable for most tasks that interface with ISO-7816 protocols. However, this framework limits Java Card applets to only handling tasks that are supported by this protocol. Tasks such as physical security using the standard Wiegand protocol, cards which test ISO-7816 card readers by pushing the limits of the protocol, and applications that depend on interfacing to different communication mechanisms, such as full duplex serial, USB, TCP/IP, or Bluetooth are among the many applications that cannot be handled within the Java Card Framework. In this paper we describe an approach that maintains backwards compatibility with the current Java Card framework, while enabling applications a means to escape from some of the constraints of the framework when necessary.

1 Introduction

The Java Card Specification [1] presents an architecture for interoperable Java Cards. The specification consists of three parts. The Java Card Virtual Machine Specification outlines the characteristics of the interpretation engine accompanied with file format layouts for execution and interfaces. The Java Card Runtime Environment (JCRE) Specification describes the features of the card runtime such as communications, method sharing, transactions, installation, and invocation mechanisms of Java Card applets. The Java Card API specification describes the on-card API used by the Java Card applet programmer to write Java Card applets.

To enforce interoperability, the JCRE lays out certain firm rules to describe runtime behaviour. This necessarily limits the kinds of applets that can be run within this framework. Furthermore, there is no way specified to escape the framework constraints when necessary to do so to implement specific applications, thus rendering those applications unimplementable with the current Java Cards.

In this paper, *applet* always implies a card application, and often will be used without qualification for brevity.

I. Attali and T. Jensen (Eds.): E-smart 2001, LNCS 2140, pp. 188-199, 2001.

2   Java Card Runtime Environment

The Java Card assumes that the underlying application level protocol between an on-card applet and the host application is performed by exchanging data packets known as APDUs (Application Protocol Data Units). This protocol for communication between a smart card and a host application is specified in ISO 7816-4 [2] and comprises two primary structures, one to send commands to the card (C-APDU) and another to send a response back from the card (R-APDU).

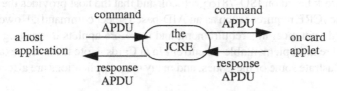

Figure 1. Applet Communication with the JCRE

Data sent to the card is first received by the JCRE. As shown in Figure 1, the JCRE routes the APDUs targeted to the card to the appropriate applet [3]. Hence, the JCRE assumes a particular structure for the incoming data to parse it appropriately. When the host application wants to select an applet to run, it sends an APDU that specifies the SELECT command and the AID of the requested applet. The JCRE searches its internal table to find the AID that matches the one specified in the APDU and if found, selects the corresponding applet to run. All subsequent APDUs are forwarded to the selected applet until a new applet is selected. Access to the contents of the APDU are made available via an on card API as shown in Figure 2.

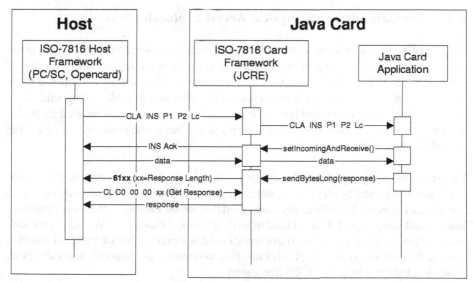

Figure 2. Typical ISO-7816 Communication Framework

The framework contains a set of communication methods needed for handling the ISO 7816-4 protocol. Applets can access high level functions that handle data exchange at a buffer level, with underlying protocol details handled automatically.

3   Motivating Applications

Although the JCRE framework provides high level services that ease development of applications that utilize ISO-7816 protocol, it presumes interaction with a host that also uses a framework based on ISO-7816 protocol, and that the host provides the particular commands the JCRE requires (such as an AID-based select command). However, some host systems do not meet this requirement, and therefore applets interacting with such host systems are unimplementable on current Java Cards. Note that these examples are intended to illustrate some of the issues, and many more applications are affected by this limitation.

3.1   Compatibility with Legacy Smart Card Terminals

The current JCRE framework depends upon receiving APDUs which are understood by the JCRE, since all communications are first received by the JCRE. The JCRE then determines which applet will receive the APDU, if any. However, many legacy terminals do not provide APDUs which are recognized by the JCRE framework, and therefore will not be passed on to any applet. Such terminals include vending machines, parking meters, ticket dispensers, and banking terminals. It is not practical to change the terminals, which are already in the field. Yet it is impossible to introduce Java Cards into such an environment unless they can handle these legacy terminals, and to handle these terminals, the applications must bypass the framework.

3.2   Compatibility with Physical Access Protocols

As part of a campus solution, many times a smart card is desired to handle physical access issues such as building or room entry, along with other applets which are easily support by Java Card. The physical access protocols are often already determined by an installed system. A potential customer would be motivated to replace magnetic stripe entry terminals with smart card terminals so that the same card could be used for building entry as well as information technology purposes, but would probably not be willing to replace their entire security system.

By far the most popular physical security protocol is the Wiegand protocol. This protocol is generally used by all of the remote terminals and sensors to report information to the security system. Therefore, any smart card that would interact with this system must understand this protocol. It is not hard to write a protocol handler for Wiegand protocol; however, the current Java Card framework could not execute such a protocol handler. Again, the problem is that the JCRE must first understand the protocol, and there is no provision for bypassing the JCRE framework.

3.3   Smart Card Reader or Terminal Testing

To test smart card acceptance devices, such as readers and terminals it is desirable to create several kinds of test smart cards which stress the limits of the ISO-7816 protocol. The test cards ensure that the readers are fully behaving according to ISO-7816 specifications, by presenting test cases which are at the limits of the protocol, and making sure that the reader still performs correctly. One such example are the test cards for PC/SC reader compliance testing.

Because the JCRE controls the interface to the reader, it is not possible to present test cases with unusual timing, intentionally induced protocol errors, legal but unusual protocol choices, and many other test cases.

3.4   High Performance Communication Protocols

It is clear that the current half-duplex protocol currently standardized by ISO-7816 must continue to be supported for legacy terminals and applications, but it will be supplemented with high performance protocols such as USB, TCP/IP, full duplex serial, and Bluetooth, to name a few [5]. The current Java Card framework is ill-prepared for these protocol additions. USB cards are already a reality; current USB smart cards tunnel ISO-7816 protocol within USB to maintain legacy interfaces as required by Java Card. But native USB support offers much more features and performance, and Java Cards must support this possibility to be competitive with non-Java smart cards.

3.5   Non-communication Problems

There are other scenarios besides communication that require alternate frameworks. Other systemic choices made by the JCRE may need to be overridden for certain applications.

For example, in order to preserve the integrity of data on the card the JCRE requires field updates to be atomic. This places a burden on some applications that do not require such data integrity. Such applications could explicitly rely on Java Card's transaction mechanism when data integrity is required. An alternate framework could relax this requirement allowing higher performance applications.

4   Attempted Solutions

A couple of solutions to work around the protocol limitations of the ISO 7816-4 framework have been attempted. However, each solution had some specific drawbacks.

4.1   Java Card 1.0

An early implementation of Java Card [4] provided byte-level APIs from the framework to the card applications. This allowed the application to read or write bytes from the serial port as desired. It did not presume an ISO-7816 command structure; instead, the card application was responsible for parsing the incoming bytes.

While flexible enough to handle many kinds of serial frameworks, ISO-7816 or otherwise, this approach has one major drawback: any flaw in an applet could potentially make the card unusable if that applet were set to run by default. Unfortunately, handling protocols other than ISO-7816 absolutely required having the applet that handled this protocol selected by default.

Additionally, the applet entry point for Java Card 1.0 was the static main method which made the applet feel more Java like and made off-card simulation more straightforward.

4.2   Adding an Entry Point Method to JC2.1

With the advent of Java Card 2.1 and binary interoperability, scaling the Java Card 1.0 style solution was an obvious candidate. However, adding a 'static' entry point method (such as main) involves changes to the standard Java Card converter and/or addition of a custom component to indicate the new entry point method. This requires additional standardization of export files for binary interoperability and complicates CAP file parsing to determine the new entry method.

5   Framework-based Solution

The solution proposed in this paper is to permit alternative frameworks to be loaded and selected by the JCRE to handle applications that cannot be handled under the JCRE framework. An alternative framework could provide new communication interfaces to allow an applet the flexibility needed for certain kinds of applications, while still allowing backward compatibility for current applications that depend on the JCRE framework.

The proposed solution follows a fairly simple chain of logic:
1. Some applets must be directly involved in the low level aspects of the communications in order to handle special communication protocols. It is not enough to pass a communications buffer to the applet; indeed, it may be impossible to establish communications unless the applet intervenes to handle the communications using a communications protocol other than ISO-7816.
2. Backward compatibility is based on detecting an ISO-7816 style communication versus a different communications protocol. Knowing when a packet is ISO-7816 is straightforward; ISO-7816 is unique in that it sends exactly 5 bytes of data and waits for an acknowledgement. But even some ISO-7816 packets may be intended for handling within the new framework, particularly packets from certain legacy terminals that use a command structure that is not compatible with Java Card 2.1.
3. If a Java Card 2.1 ISO-7816 packet is detected, it can be routed to the JCRE framework to ensure backward compatibility

Note that this shows how a new framework could be backward compatible with Java Card 2.1. However, it is up to the implementer of a new framework to ensure that this compatibility is achieved, by routing appropriate packets (i.e. Java Card 2.1 packets) to the JCRE. In some cases, the new framework might be fundamentally incompatible with conventional ISO-7816 types of terminals. For example, a framework intended for use with a different kind of terminal might not be able to even provide a legacy ATR without interfering with the protocol of the new terminal.

5.1   Specifying and Loading a New Framework

A new framework is specified by writing an applet much like a conventional applet, except that it implements different APIs as needed, such as those needed to handle a different communications protocol. When such APIs need low level access to the hardware, the APIs may be implemented using a combination of native code to provide low level functionality, with Java code exposing this functionality to applications.

For example, a smart card application that needed to control the exact timing of when serial bytes are sent might need an API with a `sendBytes(buffer,length)` method, which immediately transmits the specified bytes of data on the serial port using RS-232 protocol. A smart card application intended to handle Wiegand protocol would need an even lower level protocol, where the exact state of the serial line is controlled by the application at all time. Such an application might need an API with a `setSerial(state)` method, which immediately sets the state of the serial line to 0 or 1. An API that provided precise timing could also be useful in either application, such as a `wait(time)` method, which waits a specified number of milliseconds. Using these two methods, an application could precisely control the smart card output to handle protocols other than RS-232.

The native parts of the APIs must be loaded into the card in a card specific manner. The Java part of the new framework can be loaded in much the same way as a conventional applet. A flag in the CAP file header could indicate that this file is a framework applet, rather than a conventional applet, so it could be triggered accordingly. Appropriate security measures would need to be taken to authenticate and to authorize the alternative framework, since an alternative framework could impose a security risk, depending upon the low level APIs exposed.

5.2   Selecting a New Framework

Once a new framework has been successfully loaded, it can be specified as the default framework in the same manner that the JCRE currently uses to specify the application that is selected by default After the selection is made, the new framework will gain control after the next reset before the answer to reset is made. In fact, it is the responsibility of the new framework to provide an answer to reset, if one is required for the current environment.

A standard entry point is needed for new frameworks. The applet class could be extended to add a new entry point method, in much the same manner as the process-Toolkit entry point method was added for the GSM 0319 Java Card API [6]. This avoids the problems associated with a static entry point as discussed in section 4.2.

5.3   Deselecting a New Framework

When a new framework is running, the new framework can provide mechanisms to temporarily or permanently deselect the new framework and return control to the JCRE. Note that it is up to the framework developer to provide these mechanisms.

To avoid the problem of card lockup discussed with regard to historical solutions, a hardware means must be provided to return control of the card to the JCRE. Thus even if a new framework is loaded that intentionally or inadvertently is unable to return control to the JCRE, this hardware means can be used to recover the card. This hardware function could involve some special manipulation of the reset line, which is detected during card start-up, and resets the card to the JCRE framework. This is not intended to be an end user function, and should not be able to be accidentally triggered by a user. This mechanism is primarily intended for developers, to keep them from locking cards while debugging new frameworks, and for issuers of cards with new frameworks, who need to update or replace the new frameworks.

It is anticipated that many new frameworks will provide Java Card 2.1 backward compatibility. In this case, the new framework temporarily deselects itself and invokes the JCRE framework, which handles the legacy application. This could be triggered by detection of a ISO-7816 protocol command by the unique characteristics of the ISO-7816 header. Or it could be a user command in the new framework which temporarily selects the JCRE framework.

Permanently deselecting the new framework could be accomplished by temporarily deselecting the new framework, and then using a JCRE command to specify a different default framework. Or the new framework itself could implement a command which permanently deselects the framework.

6   Applications

Two applications are presented which illustrate the use of alternative frameworks. The first application shows how even when an ISO-7816 host framework is in use, the JCRE can be too constraining. In this case, specific timing of ISO-7816 commands is need to test compliance with PC/SC requirements. The second application details an extreme example of handling a framework that is not even compatible at the serial level.

6.1   PC/SC Reader Compliance Test Cards

In order to test whether a smart card reader was fully compliant with PC/SC specifications [8], it was not enough to just perform a functional test of commands. The PS/SC specifications called for specific timing requirements which had to be tested. In order to test this timing, commands needed to be sent from the card to the reader at minimum and maximum timing, to ensure that the reader works at both ends of the timing specification. In addition, the ATR was slowed down so that bytes were sent at the worst case timing specified, and some tests involved sending the ISO-7816 reset work waiting time command at maximum allowable intervals to ensure that the reader does not time out.

Test cards for PC/SC reader compliance were created using vintage Cyberflex cards based on the Java Card 1.0 API [4]. This framework allowed the precise timing of bytes sent to and from the reader to be controlled. In effect, the Java Card 1.0 framework was just a pass through, which allowed the application to send bytes directly to the RS-232 controller. This is illustrated in Figure 3.

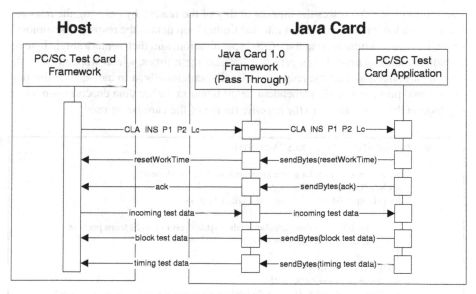

Figure 3. Java Card 1.0 Pass Through Framework

Note that this card potentially suffered from the problem that any applet selected as default could potentially lock the card. Therefore, code was added to test for a special command that would reset the default framework, as illustrated in Figure 4. This code was positioned so that it was the first code that executed upon the receipt of any command, in order to minimize the chance that code executing prior to this segment could lock the card. But there was still risk that an earlier piece of code could permanently lock the card, which is why a hardware based mechanism such as that described in section 5.3 is a superior solution to the locking problem.

```
if (APDUbuffer[1] == SET_DEFAULT_FRAMEWORK)
{
        //Escape from PC/SC test framework
        Execute((short)0, (byte)0);
        bReturnStatus = ST.SUCCESS;
}
```

Figure 4. Escaping to the Default Framework.

A common requirement of the test suite is that the precise timing of the bytes to the serial port had to be controlled to fully test the reader timing. One such test is illustrated in Figure 5.

The test in Figure 5 stresses the timeout ability of the reader, by delaying the response for an extended length of time. An internal timing loop delays the response by almost 7 seconds, the maximum time in the PC/SC specification, and then sends a single byte requesting additional time. This is repeated for sLength times, which is specified by the host in the command, then the response is finally sent. Ideally, a framework for this purpose would provide a card independent delay function, rather than depend upon a timing loop in the applet tuned to the specific timing of the card being used.

```
if (APDUbuffer[1] == TEST_RESTART_TIME)
{
        // Reuse ackByte buffer to send the work waiting time byte
        ackByte[0] = (byte)0x60;
        for (sTemp = (short)0; sTemp < sLength; sTemp++)
        {
                for (delay = (short)0; delay < (short)160; delay++); // 23 loops per 0.1s
                sendBytes(ackByte,(byte)0x01);
        }
        ackByte[0] = pbuffer[1];
        sendBytes(ackByte,ACK_SIZE);
        for (bTemp = (byte)0; bTemp < (byte)sLength; bTemp++)
        {
                dbuffer[bTemp] = bTemp;
        }
        bReturnStatus = sendBytes(dbuffer,(byte)sLength);
}
```

Figure 5. Controlling Precise Timing of Serial Bytes

6.2   Wiegand Protocol

Wiegand protocol [7] is a standard protocol used for certain classes of devices, particularly those associated with physical security, such as building entry. Rather than transmit data at a precisely described rate, as in the case of RS-232, it is a self clocking protocol, which intermingles the clock and data signal on a single serial line. Support of such a protocol clearly requires very low level serial control.

Figure 6 illustrates how a framework specifically designed to handle the Wiegand protocol could potentially hide the complexity of the serial modulation by providing application APIs at a very high level, with methods such as `authenticate` or `sendIdentity`. Alternatively, the framework could provide simple byte array transfer mechanisms, leaving it up to the application to determine the exact content of the messages, similar to what was provided in the Java Card 1.0 API. In either case, the framework must understand and provide the precise timing required for the Wiegand protocol.

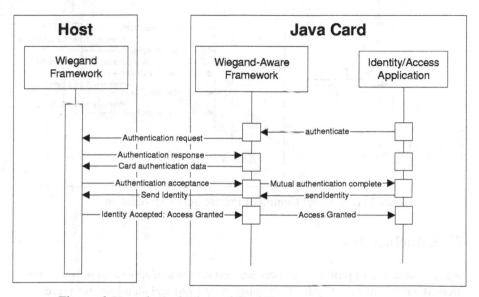

Figure 6. Hypothetical Wiegand Card Framework

Another option is a framework which provides very low level serial control to the applet itself. Such a framework would enable applets to handle Wiegand protocol, as well as other low level protocols such as Manchester (the level 0 protocol most often used for Ethernet traffic).

To use this framework, the applet must control the precise timing of the edges of the serial protocol, so it is imperative that such a framework also include card independent timing functions. Such a framework is illustrated in Figure 7.

The framework illustrated in Figure 7 provides two methods to assist in data transmission: a method to set the serial port to the desired logical value, and a method used to provide precise timing. (It is presumed that similar methods are provided for reading from the serial port as well.) The applet modulates the serial port by setting it to alternate logical values, separated by precise time delays. Thus a waveform of arbitrary characteristics can be created and transmitted from the card to the host. Although such a framework is clearly very flexible, it is also very processor intensive, and realistically could not be expected to handle very fast data transmission without low level support.

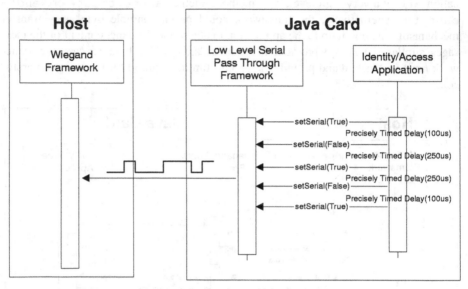

Figure 7. Low Level Control of Precise Serial Modulation

7   Conclusion

We have described a problem that prevents certain kinds of applications from being addressed by current Java Cards. After considering historical solutions, we present a solution that is compatible with existing Java Cards. A flexible invocation mechanism will enable diverse host frameworks to be support, enabling a wider range of Java Card based solutions.

References

[1]   Sun Microsystems Inc., Java Card 2.1.1 Specification. //java.sun.com/products/JavaCard/
[2]   ISIO-7816, Information Technology - Identification cards - integrated circuit cards with contacts.
[3]   Zhiqun Chen. Java Card Technology for Smart Cards: Architecture and Programmer's Guide, Addison-Wesley Publishing, June 2000.
[4]   Cyberflex Pre-Release Developers' Series. Programmer's Guide, Schlumberger, May 1997.
[5]   Yi-Bing Lin, Imrich Chlamtac, Wireless and Mobile Network Architectures, John Wiley & Sons, October 2, 2000.

[6]   GSM 03.19 V7.0.1, Digital cellular telecommunications system (Phase 2+); SIM API for Java Card, DTS/SMG 090319N, ETSI Secretariat, F-06921 Sophia Antipolis, Cedex - France, //www.etsi.org

[7]   Wiegand Card Reader Interface Standard, SIA AC-01, Security Industry Association, Alexandria, Virginia, October, 1996.

[8]   PC/SC Workgroup Specifications 1.0, Parts 1-8. http://www.pcscworkgroup.com/

ElectroMagnetic Analysis (EMA): Measures and Countermeasures for Smart Cards

Jean-Jacques Quisquater and David Samyde

Université catholique de Louvain, UCL Crypto Group,
Laboratoire de microélectronique (DICE),
Place du Levant 3, B-1348 Louvain-la-Neuve, Belgium.
E-mail: {jjq,samyde}@dice.ucl.ac.be
URL: http://www.dice.ucl.ac.be/crypto

Abstract. A processor can leak information by different ways [1], electromagnetic radiations could be one of them. This idea, was first introduced by Kocher, with timing and power measurements. Here we developed the continuation of his ideas by measuring the field radiated by the processor. Therefore we show that the electromagnetic attack obtains at least the same result as power consumption and consequently must be carefully taken into account. Finally we enumerate countermeasures to be implemented.

Keywords: electromagnetic and power analysis, tamper resistance, SEMA, DEMA, SPA, DPA, smartcard.

1 Introduction

The measurement of the consumption of a cryptographic processor (smartcard) provides data on its activities. Handling of a bit with 1 and a bit with 0 involves different energy, so the electromagnetic field can be another vector of information. Any movement of electric charges is accompanied by an electromagnetic field. The currents going through a processor can characterize it according to its spectral signature.

This idea is a generalization of Kocher's idea presented in 1996. His idea laid the foundations of the power analysis. Actually power analysis includes Simple Power Analysis (SPA) and Differential Power Analysis (DPA) [2,3]. However the electromagnetic analysis wants to be more general. The Timing attack developed by Kocher and its practical implementation by Koeune, are limited in the analysis to mono-dimensional data processing. In the same way the DPA attacks or second order DPA use a two-dimensional matrix to visualize the correlation during the treatment [4]. The results from the Electromagnetic Analysis can be treated as the previous ones, but they also hold a three-dimensional information linked to the volume.

I. Attali and T. Jensen (Eds.): E-smart 2001, LNCS 2140, pp. 200-210, 2001.

Smart cards are particularly concerned [5]. They are protected against many non intrusive attacks but they cannot detect a listening material. Moreover, they emit a lot of information because memory accesses are frequent. The dimensions of the chip are directly linked to the emissions of all kind, and a lot of noises are generated by calculations and processor's actions.

For example, the Haming weight can be deducted during the loading time of the data bus. Each " 0 " implies the use of a specific quantity of energy, it is then possible to calculate the number of " 1 " in the data and to deduce the weight. SPA can allow such a measurement, and so does EMA.

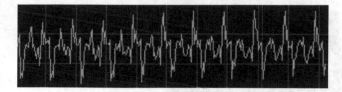

Fig 1 : Few rounds of a DES execution.

In a synchronous processor, the modifications linked to the evolution of the clock characterize the system [6]. The transfers on the bus have a consumption proportional to the number of bits which change between two cycles. So the electromagnetic analysis is strongly dependent on the architecture of the chip, and the knowledge of the internal circuitry of the processor facilitates the work.

2   Context

For a few years the electromagnetic radiation of the electric devices has been taken into account. The standards for electromagnetic radiation are present in order to at least allow the peaceful coexistence of various devices at the same place.

All the electronic devices containing electronic components are sensitive to outside disturbances [7]. However they are themselves disturbing elements in some cases. Thus an office computer can interferer with a radio receiver. We decided to base on this idea to investigate the study of the electromagnetic field emitted by processors during their work.

It appears that this radiation is directly connected to the current consumption of the processor. The electromagnetic field lets informations on the activities of the chip flee. The spectral signature is architecture dependant. However some behaviors are identical from a processor to another. For example an access memory that activates the load pump results in a specific peak in the electromagnetic spectrum and is directly linked to the control of the oscillator.

3   Principles

The principle is relatively simple. Indeed we placed a sensor sensitive to the electromagnetic field near of the processor. Such a sensor must be placed under the smart card, in the very close field . This device is a simple flat coil, so the variations of the electromagnetic field induce a current at the bounds. This current betrays directly the field radiated by the chip.

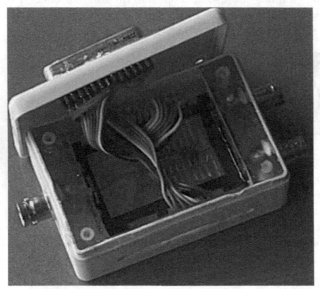

Fig 2 : The false reader with 2 coils.

The electromagnetic field can be decomposed in two primary components : an electric field and a magnetic one. The electric field fails for low frequency (less than 10 MHz) but carries different informations than the magnetic one. From 10 MHz to 80 MHz the magnetic component is not filtered by the bondings wires. Of course the current influences the magnetic part.

3.1   How does it work ?

Microcontrolors actually used in the cards are synchronous. Consequently it implies that the internal operations are cadenced on internal clocks [8]. So their spectral signature contains two kinds of components. The narrow bands are directly linked to a periodic process and the signals with broad band are due to an asynchronous or random activity.

This first kind of working is the essential cause of radiations. Because an asynchronous activity has a lower level of emission. The difference of level is around 30 decibels. In the processor the clock provides a frequency of operation based on a wave of fixed frequency, few submultiples of this frequency are used. As the signals are trapezoidals, their spectrum contains many harmonics of the central frequency.

3.2 The Faraday cage

In order to facilitate the attenuation in terms of noise reduction, we built a Faraday cage with 5 layers, therefore we could carry out the measurements in a favorable environment. Roughtly, we used copper to stop the electric component of the field, and mu-metal to strongly reduce the other orthogonal component. Actually for using EMA the chip must not be isolated from its noisy environment.

3.3 The measurement chain

The system, set up to acquire information and digitalize the electromagnetic field emitted, is very simple. In the case of a smartcard, a false card is inserted in the reader as a real one would be. This copy of a card (with the contacts at the same place) can brings out the control signals. So they were transmitted to our reader towards a traditional smartcard connector. Of course the card under measure is placed in the second reader which contains the flat coils. Under the connector with contacts for the real card, three coils are present. Two of them are 3 millemeters under the micromodule and are positioned as a ISO and AFNOR, and the largest one is in central position. In this manner the radiation emitted by the chip must cross one of the three coils. The total diameters of the coils do not exceed 2 centimeters. There is a connector on the side of the reader to connect a spectrum analyser or an oscilloscope. Provided with this equipment, a simple measure with the spectrum analyzer makes it possible to perceive an order of magnitude of the field radiated by the chip.

4 Actual state of the work

The work shows that the coil must be non adapted. Global results are better if the quality factor of the coil is poor. It allows to measure the global field.

EMA has been tested on a PC processor, it works perfectly, the electromagnetic spectrum is just wider. As a natural spectrum stops at 80 MHz because of the bondings wire, a pentium's spectrum is higher than 100 MHz. The radiation diagram of the chip is particular and specific for each processor. We are actually working on a motorized table, to move the sensor above the chip. The main idea is to use stepper engines to control the screws, so we will set the position of the sensor with a micrometric precision.

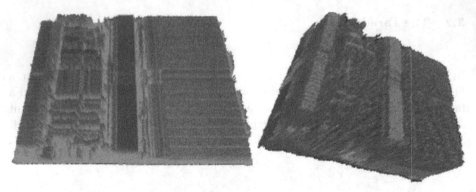

Fig 3 : Two 3D signatures of the same smartcard processor.

Thus the utility of the EMA analsysis is elsewhere it resides in sent on the power wires and poorly radiated in the close field.

5 Optimisations

5.1 Sensors

Several separate sensors were tested. Indeed a differential measurement established by covering of the measured zones provides good average results. Techniques of signal processing allows reduction of the noise and bring EMA closer to a differential measurement. All the treatments for DPA [9] are possible with EMA since this analysis includes at least the same information.

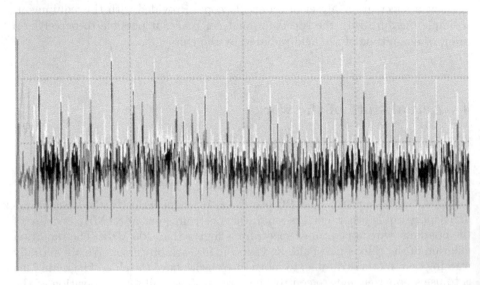

Fig 4 : EMA vs PA (x=frequency, y=decibels). EM noise level is 30 dB under PA one.

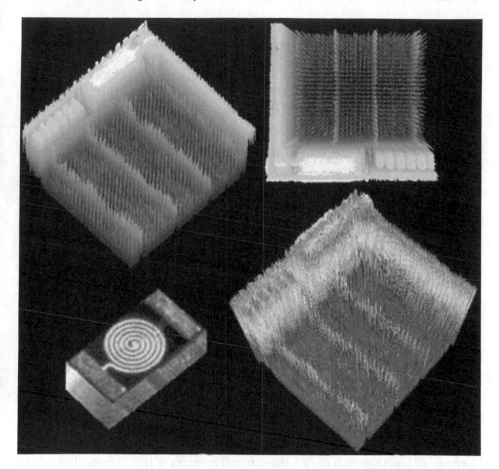

Fig 5 : A 40 micrometers sensor and three view of the same FM signature. The power rails are very easy to distinguish.

In the case of a javacard, a simple applet can make it possible to maximize the few field radiated in cases. Indeed, while making periodic instructions or actions (memory access, I/O), we could manage to reveal particular electromagnetic signatures.

6   CounterMeasures

If the countermeasures are purely hard, they must be mixed with the circuit. Because if the two spectral signatures are too separate on the chip, it is possible to isolate one of them.

Noise addition can be an elegant way for disturbing EMA. If the attacker cannot build a dictionary for each instruction used in the processor, it can become very hard to reverse all its codes.

Countermeasures to strongly slow down or stop the electromagnetic analysis are multiples they can be considered under several angles: the designer can try to block the information leakage, he can reduce it to a non measurable form, he can manage to change the possibilities of correlation, or can quite simply modify the architecture. These protection measures should not preferably installation to the detriment of consumption [10].

6.1   Reduction of the electromagnetic field

The first of commonplace countermeasure consists in using the metal levels that build the chip, in order to reduce the radiated field. Moreover, the metals used in processors in the upper layers are either Aluminium or Copper. Such metals are not known to be excellent ferromagnetic metals. Their presence is enough to strongly reduce part of the electromagnetic field but does not stop its two components. Information available not being the same one for the electric field and the magnetic field if only one of the two components and decreased, it can always have significant losses of information. It is also important to note that the standardized thickness of the smartcards prevents from the quantity of plastic coating the processor. So it is not possible to reduce the radiation using strong metal plates.

6.2   The Faraday cage

A simple way to block the electromagnetic field radiated by the card seems to be to imprison it in a Faraday cage. The construction of a Faraday cage around the processor concerns a non commonplace exercise. However the card has connection requirements for the external contacts of the micromodule, so the Faraday screen cage could not be perfect. Such an operation is realizable, but it is necessary whereas each hole bores in the shielding of the cage is accompanied by a guide of wave having a length eight times higher than its diameter. It is quite obvious that such a realization is conceivable but requires deep modifications of the manufacturing process. Moreover the existence of such a cage will not prevent the attackers from trying to bore it or to introduce a reason to leak.

6.3   Design for very low consumption

One of the important directions [11] in current research in micro-electronics relates to the reduction of consumption. The techniques used are multiple, one of them for example uses the silicon installation on insulator. SOI thus allows to decrease the current consumed by the processor [12], it thus reduces the radiated electromagnetic field. The use of such process would also make it possible to obtain in certain fields of the more interesting achievements by their computing power increased (smart cards without contacts, memories,). the releases of heat per Joule effect will be also reduced [13].

6.4   Asynchronism

Synchronous processor are those which maximize the electromagnetic field. The clock allows the flip-flop to resynchronise the signal and of the reamplify it. The clock is based on a trapezoidal signal including many harmonics. This results ends by multiple lines in the spectrum of the electromagnetic field. It is then very easy to distinguish the fundamental one from the harmonics, in the same way the internal clocks synchronized on the principal signal are visible. An elegant solution with all these problems of measurement of the electromagnetic field lies in the use of asynchronous processors. Indeed the asynchronous processors not including a clock to give rhythm them [14], their electromagnetic signature is strongly reduced. As much the synchronous processors has lines fine and precise in their electromagnetic signature, as much the asynchronous processors have signatures with very broad band with a reduction by 20 to 30 db of the background noise.

6.5   Dual Line Logic

In order to reduce the electric transitions which betray their number and their presence on the power line and in the electromagnetic field near. It is possible to try to balance these transitions. If each transition carried out commutates as much current of a power towards a mass and conversely, the sum of the exchanged currents is null, and the local field is touched [15]. Dual line logic allows such an improvement. Each wire is replaced by two wire transporting each one information, and both of them provide the desired state. It is quite obvious that there are four possibilities of coding and that a designer who really wants to scramble the data will commutate wire not modifying the information transported, it is possible if the two significant states are the opposites one of the other.

6.6   New architectures

The force of EMA lying in the principle of locality, it would be desirable to block this principle in order to counter this attack [16]. To block the principle of locality is however not commonplace thing for that requires to spread out the design of the macro blocks of a chip over all its surface [17]. The first problem which occurs is then a problem of current at exit of the doors. The wire traversing the long processor being on the micrometric scale, the logical doors are obliged to have very powerful amplifiers. It is for that that it seems more judicious to build a new architecture blocking the principle of locality. A distributed parallel architecture could indeed block locally the principle of locality, if the whole of significant calculations is distributed. By exposing its configuration at the request of the software such an architecture would damage EMA. The architecture related to the RAW project [18] of MIT Laboratory for Computer Science seems to be appropriate for such a request. The possibilities and the advantages seem very numerous indeed, in order to block the measurement of current the designer can decide to use calculating units to this end and obliges them to calculate random data. Moreover the software can impose a complete reconfiguration between each use of the cryptographic units. The faults tolerance of such an architecture seems also very interesting, since calculation can be carried out in parallel in completely duplexed form and that only the majority result can be taken into account.

6.7   Modifications of the chip

The solution patented by Schlumberger which consists in separating the chip into half chips and to assemble them face to face to prevent the attacks intrusive can seem good. However in a more general way the easy ways lying in a physical cutting of the processor in order to block the leak or to reduce the losses, seems quite expensive compared to the measurement techniques at very low cost to collect the data. The design of a chip must integrate the concept of local field during its creation and the sensors for these electromagnetic field can undoubtly still reduce of size. Wanting to reduce the field without increasing physically the consumption and the currents traversing the power is not seemed a commonplace spot.

7   Perspectives

The use of preamplifiers and very low noise differential amplifiers, will make it possible to raise the signal level quite strongly. By using the locality principle proper to EMA [19], and taking in account all the problems which are referred to it, such as bondings wires and their own field, it appears possible to us to analyse the work of the processor but especially to extract the data specific to certain parts of the chip.

The use of an array of sensors could allow the creation of a map of the chip. As this array can move around the processor, the map could be tri-dimensional.

8   Conclusion

Actually this attack is not better than the power consumption attack. But as the electomagnetic field can be observed in a local part of the processor, it seems to open the sensibility of new attacks. We mean that the current measurement must be global if the attack is non intrusive, EMA can be more precise.

Countermeasures are purely hard against power consumption, it seems very difficult to defeat electromagnetic analysis, except if the circuit and its countermeasures are overlapped. On the opposite way, as each instruction has a specific electromagnetic signature, it is possible to build a dictionary and to reverse a part of the code.

As the processor contains very specific or regular parts, their spectral signature is characteristic, so if the processor has a memory or a grouped data bus, it is an advantage for EMA.

References

[1] R. Anderson and M. Kuhn, *Tamper resistance - A cautionary note,* Proc. of the Second USENIX Workshop on Electronic Commerce, 1996, pp 1-11.

[2] P.N. Fahm and P.K. Pearson, *IPA: A new class of power attacks,* Proc. of CHES'99 (C.K. Koc and Chr. Paar, eds), Lecture Notes in Computer Science ,vol.1717, Springer-Verlag, 1999, pp. 173-186.

[3] P. Kocher, J. Jaffe and B. Jun, *Differential power analysis,* Advances in Cryptology - CRYPTO'99 (M.J. Wiener, ed.), Lecture Notes in Computer Science, vol. 1666, Springer-Verlag, 1999, pp. 388-397.

[4] *Power analysis of the key scheduling of the AES candidates,* The Second AES Conference, March 22-23, 1999, pp. 115-121.

[5] T.S. Messerges, E.A. Dabbish, R. Sloan, *Investigations of Power Analysis Attacks on Smartcards.*

[6] *Low cost attacks on tamper resistant devices,* Proc. of International Workshop on Security Protocols 1997 (Paris, France) (M. Lomas et .al, ed.), Lecture Notes in Computer Science, vol. 1361, Springer-Verlag, 1997, pp. 125-136

[7] *Towards sound approaches to counteract power-analysis attacks,* Proc. of CRYPTO'99 (M.J.Wiener,ed.), Lecture Notes in Computer Science, vol. 1666, Springer-Verlag, 1999, pp. 398-412.

[8] J-S. Coron, *Resistance against differential power analysis for elliptic curve cryptosystems,* Proc. of CHES'99 (C.K. Ko and Chr. Paar, eds), Lecture Notes in Computer Science, vol. 1717, Springer-Verlag, 1999, pp. 292-302.

[9] J-S. Coron, P. Kocher, and D. Naccache, *Statistics and secret leakage,* Financial Cryptography 2000 (FC'00), Lecture Notes in Computer Science, Springer-Verlag.

[10] E. Biham and A. Shamir, *Differential fault analysis of secret key cryptosystems,* Proc. of CRYPTO'97 (Burton S. Kaliski Jr., ed), Lecture Notes in Computer Science, vol.1294, Springer-Verlag, 1997, pp. 513-525.

[11] D. Boneh, R.A. DeMillo, and R.J. Lipton, *On the importance of checking cryptographic protocols for faults,* Proc. of EUROCRYPT '97 (W.Fumy, ed), Lectures Notes in Computer Science, vol.1233, Springer-Verlag, 1997, pp. 37-51.

[12] E. Hess, N. Janssen, B. Meyer, T. Schutze, *Information Leakage Attacks against Smart Card Implementations of Cryptographic Algorithms and Countermeasures,* Proc. of Eurosmart 2000, pp. 55-63.

[13] A. Neve, D. Flandre, J-J. Quisquater, *Feasibility of Smart Cards in Silicon-On-Insulator (SOI) Technology,* Usenix workshop on Smartcard Technology, (Smartcard'99), Usenix Association.

[14] O. Kommerling, M. Kuhn, *Design Principles for Tamper-Resistant Smartcard Processors* Proc. of the USENIX Workshop on Smartcard Technology (Smartcard'99), pp. 9-20. Usenix Association.

[15] K.P. Slattery, J.P. Muccioli, T. North, *Modeling the radiated Emisssions from Microprocessors and other VLSI Devices,* IEEE 2000 International Symposium on Electromagnetic Compatibility.

[16] J.P. Muccioli, T. North, K.P. Slattery, *Characterization of the RF Emissions from a family of Microprocessors using a 1GHz TEM cell,* IEEE 1997 International Symposium on Electromagnetic Compatibilty.

[17] J.P. Muccioli, M. Catherwood, *Characteristics of Near-field Magnetic Radiated Emissions from VLSI Microcontroller Devices,* EMC Test and Design, November 1993.

[18] A. Agarwal, *Raw Computation,* Scientific American, August 1999.

[19] J-J. Quisquater and D. Samyde, *A new tool for non-intrusive analysis of smart-cards based on electro-magnetic emssions, the SEMA and DEMA methods*, Presented at the rump session of EUROCRYPT'2000.

Information Leakage Attacks
against Smart Card Implementations of the
Elliptic Curve Digital Signature Algorithm

Tanja Römer and Jean-Pierre Seifert

Infineon Technologies Corporation
Security & ChipCard ICs
Technical Innovations, D-81609 Munich, Germany
{Tanja.Roemer,Jean-Pierre.Seifer}@infineon.com

Abstract. In this article we will be concerned with a polynomial-time attack against the ECDSA, which computes the secret key of the ECDSA if a few bits of the ephemeral-key from several ECDSA-signatures are known. The number of needed bits per signature is 12, if one has access to an ideal lattice basis reduction algorithm computing the nth successive minimum of a lattice with rank n. The aforesaid bits of the ephemeral-key can be obtained from insecure ECDSA implementations by so called side-channel-attacks like Timing, Simple-Power-Analysis, Differential-Power-Analysis, Electromagnetic or Differential-Fault attacks. Our attack combines a recent idea of Howgrave-Graham and Smart with an old lattice attack against linear congruential pseudo-random number generators due to Frieze, Hastad, Kannan, Lagarias und Shamir. In contrast to Howgrave-Graham and Smart, our approach enables the exact determination of the number of needed (side-channel) bits and uses an easier lattice problem making the attack very practical.

Keywords: Cryptanalysis, ECDSA, Lattice, Lattice basis reduction, LLL, side-channel-attacks, successive minimum.

1   Introduction

The ECDSA *(Elliptic Curve Digital Signature Algorithm)*, see for, e.g., [JM], is a digital signature algorithm whose security is based on the discrete logarithm problem for elliptic curves (abbreviated as ECDLP for Elliptic Curve Discrete Logarithm Problem) and is derived naturally from the DSA which in turn is based on the El-Gamal signature algorithm. For a thorough introduction into the DSA and the El-Gamal signature we refer the reader to [MvOV].

Under slight modifications and assuming the random oracle assumption Bellare et alii [BPVY] have shown that the security of the ECDSA can be reduced to the ECDLP. Excluding insecure elliptic curves the ECDLP needs in general exponential time to be solved, see for, e.g., [BSS]. Thus, practically the ECDSA cannot be broken by solving the ECDLP.

I. Attali and T. Jensen (Eds.): E-smart 2001, LNCS 2140, pp. 211–219, 2001.

However, it is well known that knowledge of the ephemeral-key k of the ECDSA breaks the system. Moreover, choosing the ephemeral-key k uniformly at random is as well very important, which is due to Bellare et alii [BGM].

This article describes a novel attack against the ECDSA, which is a combination of classical cryptanalysis and a side-channel attack. Instead of attacking directly the secret key d we use lattice methods to attack the randomly chosen k_i from several card signatures. For this purpose the attack assumes that we can learn through a side-channel some bits of the the aforesaid randomly chosen ephemeral-keys k_i corresponding to the card signatures. Our attack is based on an idea of [HGS] and using methods from the geometry of numbers according to [FHK$^+$] we can improve the attack of [HGS] substantially while also extending their attack to the elliptic curve variant of the DSA. For a recent survey on lattice methods in cryptography we refer to [NS].

Gaining knowledge of some secret bits of a smart card is in insecure implementations possible by exploiting methods relying on side-channel attacks such like Timing, Simple-Power-Analysis, Differential-Power-Analysis, Electromagnetic or Differential-Fault attacks. For a thorough description of these attacks we refer to [HJMS] and [CKN].

2   Definitions

We now give a brief introduction into basic terms of the lattice theory and elliptic curves and refer the reader for detailed introductions to [Kan,Lov,BSS,Kob99,Men].

$\mathbb{R}^m$ denotes the m-dimensional real Euclidean vector space and e_i the ith unit vector in $\mathbb{R}^m$, $\langle \cdot, \cdot \rangle$ the canonical scalar product in $\mathbb{R}^m$ and $\|v\| := \sum_{i=1}^{m} v_i^2$ for $v \in \mathbb{R}^m$ the Euclidean norm. A *lattice* L is a discrete additive subgroup of the $\mathbb{R}^m$ with $L := \{y \in \mathbb{R}^m \mid y = a_1 b_1 + \cdots + a_k b_k, \, a_i \in \mathbb{Z}\}$, $b_1, \ldots, b_k \in \mathbb{R}^m$ linear independently over $\mathbb{R}^m$ and $k \leq m$. $[b_1, \ldots, b_k]$ is called a *basis* of the lattice L. The i^{the} *successive minimum* $\lambda_i(L)$ of a lattice L is the smallest positive real number r, such that there exists i linear independent vectors $v_1, \ldots, v_i \in L$ of maximum length r, i.e., $\lambda_i(L) = \min_{\text{l.u. } v_1,\ldots,v_i \in L} \max_{j \in \{1,\ldots,i\}} \|v_j\|$.

An elliptic curve (in affine coordinates) over a finite field $\mathbb{K}$ is a set $E(\mathbb{K})$ of points (X, Y) satisfying an equation of the form

$$Y^2 + a_1 XY + a_3 Y = X^3 + a_2 X^2 + a_4 X + a_6, \quad a_i \in K,$$

together with a point at infinity $\mathcal{O}$. The set $E(K)$ is an abelean group wrt. addition $+$, where $\mathcal{O}$ is the neutral element, see for, e.g., [BSS]. The order of a point $P \in E(K)$ is the smallest natural number n with $nP = \mathcal{O}$. The ECDLP is given by the following problem. For two given points P and Q on an elliptic curve find the smallest natural number d satisfying $Q = dP$. For a general elliptic curve the ECDLP is only known to be solvable in exponential time.

3 The ECDSA

We now give a brief introduction into the ECDSA, for a thorough description we refer to [JM]. Moreover, for simplicity we assume in the following that we are using a prime field $\mathbb{K} = \mathbb{F}_p$, i.e., p is a prime greater than 2. However, our attacks works also fine over fields of the form $\mathbb{F}_{2^m}$.

We consider the situation where Alice wants to send a signed message m to Bob. Firstly, Alice chooses her public key $(E(K), P, n, Q)$ and as well a private key $d \in [1 : n-1]$. Here, $E(\mathbb{K})$ is an elliptic curve over $\mathbb{K}$ and P a point of prime order n on the curve $\mathbb{K}$ with $Q = dP$ and $n \mid |E(K)|$.

To sign the message $m \in \mathcal{M}$ from an appropriate message space $\mathcal{M}$, Alice now chooses uniformly at random a number $k \in [1 : n-1]$, the so called *ephemeral*-key. Hereafter, Alice computes $kP =: (x_1, y_1)$, $r := x_1 \bmod n$ and as well $s := k^{-1}(h(m) + dr) \bmod n$, where $h : \mathcal{M} \to \mathbb{K}$ denotes an arbitrary cryptographic hash-function. Alice now sends Bob the message m and the corresponding signature (r, s).

In order to verify the signature (r, s) of the message m, Bob computes with the public key $(E(K), P, n, Q)$ of Alice as a first step $w := s^{-1} \bmod n$. Then, Bob computes $u_1 := h(m)w \bmod n$, $u_2 := rw \bmod n$, $u_1 P + u_2 Q =: (x_0, y_0)$ and $v := x_0 \bmod n$. Finally, to check the authenticity of the signature (r, s), Bob checks that $v = r$ holds.

As already said above, the security of the ECDSA is based on the ECDLP and indeed under slight modifications and assuming the random oracle assumption ([BPVY]) its security is reducible to ECDLP. Thus, excluding insecure elliptic curves the ECDSA cannot be broken by solving the ECDLP in theory.

In the next section, however, we will sketch a new practical lattice attack on the ECDSA which tries to reconstruct the secret key d from short ephemeral-key fragments, i.e., by using only some bits of several keys k generated by several card signatures.

4 The Attack

We consider the scenario, where Alice's public key is given by $(E(K), n, P, Q)$ and her secret key by d. Moreover, we assume that we have signed l messages m_i, $i = 1, \dots, l$, and obtained their corresponding card signatures (r_i, s_i), $i = 1, \dots, l$. Now, we want to compute the ephemeral keys k_i, $i = 1, \dots, l$, chosen uniformly at random by Alice for every single signature (r_i, s_i), $i = 1, \dots, l$. After having computed the ephemeral keys k_i, $i = 1, \dots, l$, we directly can compute Alice secret key d.

From the ECDSA-signature equation

$$s_i := k_i^{-1}(h(m_i) + dr_i) \bmod n, \quad i = 1, \dots, l,$$

we get

$$s_i k_i - dr_i = h(m_i) \bmod n, \quad i = 1, \dots, l.$$

Substituting in these l equations with the $l + 1$ variables k_i, $i = 1, \ldots, l$, and d the variable d by $r_l^{-1} s_l k_l - h(m_l) r_l^{-1} \bmod n$ yields the system

$$s_i k_i - r_i r_l^{-1} s_l k_l = -r_i h(m_l) r_l^{-1} + h(m_i) \bmod n, \quad i = 1, \ldots, l - 1.$$

Renaming again the variables yields another system of equations

$$b_{ii} k_i + b_{il} k_l = d_i \bmod n, \quad i = 1, \ldots, l - 1$$

with only $l - 1$ equations and l variables $k_1, \ldots, k_l$. However, this underdetermined system has naturally no unique solution. Nevertheless, it is known that a unique solution exists and indeed can be computed quickly if some small fraction of the bits of the $k_1, \ldots, k_l$ is known, see for, e.g., [FHK$^+$].

Wlog. let $\log n$ the bitlength of the k_i, $i = 1, \ldots, l$. If, now, the most significant t bits of the k_i are known, we can write the k_i as

$$k_i = k_i^{(1)} + k_i^{(2)},$$

where the $k_i^{(1)}$ are all known, and $|k_i^{(2)}| \leq n2^{-t}$ holds. Applying this partial knowledge about the k_i's to the aforesaid system of equations and again renaming the coefficients we get the following system of equations:

$$a_{ii} k_i^{(2)} + a_{il} k_l^{(2)} = c_i \bmod n \quad \text{with } |k_i^{(2)}| \leq n2^{-t}. \tag{1}$$

Thus, we have obtained an underdetermined system with the variable constraint $|k_i^{(2)}| \leq n2^{-t}$ where t denotes the number of known most significant bits of the k_i's. To solve this system we use the following theorem.

Theorem 1. *Let*

$$\sum_{j=1}^{l} a_{ij} x_j = c_i \bmod p \tag{2}$$

a system with $a_{ij}, c_i \in \mathbb{Z}$, $i = 1, \ldots, s$, p prime and $s \leq l$, and

$$L = \left\{ y \in \mathbb{R}^l \;\middle|\; y = \sum_{i=1}^{s} v_i (a_{i1}, \ldots, a_{il})^\top + v_{s+1} p e_1 + \cdots + v_{s+l} p e_l, \; v_i \in \mathbb{Z} \right\}$$

a lattice in $\mathbb{R}^l$ satisfying $\|x\| \leq p\lambda_l^{-1}(L)2^{-1}$, then there exists at most one solution x for this system. If the a_{ij}, c_i and p are all known for all i, j, then there exists an algorithm which computes for fixed l in polynomial time the solution x or proves that there is no solution.

Proof. The proof of the theorem follows mainly the ideas given in [FHK$^+$]. The idea is to construct from the underdetermined modular system of equations a system of equations with l equations and l variables over $\mathbb{Z}$. Naturally, such a system has at most one solution. We note that the proof will explicitly construct the unique solution, provided that a solution exists.

We start with the recently presented algorithm due to Blömer [Bl], which computes for the given lattice L l linearly independent vectors

$$w_1, \ldots, w_l \in L$$

with $\|w_i\| = \lambda_i(L)$ for $i = 1, \ldots, l$. Its running time is $3^l \cdot l! \cdot s^{O(1)}$, where s denotes the size of the lattice. Thus, for fixed l it is a polynomial-time algorithm. As the vectors $w_1, \ldots, w_l$ are linearly independent lattice vectors we know that there exists some integral $l \times (s + l)$ matrix M satisfying

$$
\begin{pmatrix} w_{11} & \cdots & w_{1l} \\ \vdots & & \vdots \\ w_{l1} & \cdots & w_{ll} \end{pmatrix} = M \begin{pmatrix} a_{11} & \cdots & a_{1l} \\ \vdots & & \vdots \\ a_{s1} & \vdots & a_{sl} \\ p & \cdots & 0 \\ \vdots & \ddots & \vdots \\ 0 & \cdots & p \end{pmatrix}.
$$

Now, multiplying both sides of the system (2) from left with this matrix M, we get a new modular system

$$\sum_{j=1}^{l} w_{ij} x_j \equiv c_i' \bmod p, \quad i = 1, \ldots, l. \tag{3}$$

Clearly, every solution x of (2) is by construction also a solution of (3). Now, considering an $x \in \mathbb{Z}^l$ satisfying

$$\|x\| \leq \frac{1}{2} p \lambda_l^{-1}(L),$$

we get that

$$\left\| \sum_{j=1}^{l} w_{ij} x_j \right\| \leq \|w_i\| \cdot \|x\|$$

$$\leq \lambda_i(L) \cdot \frac{1}{2} p \lambda_l^{-1}(L)$$

$$\leq \lambda_l(L) \cdot \frac{p}{2} \lambda_l^{-1}(L)$$

$$\leq \frac{p}{2}.$$

Therefore, choosing the c_i' for $i = 1, \ldots, l$ such that $|c_i'| < p/2$, ensures that an integral solution $x \in \mathbb{Z}^l$ of the system

$$\sum_{j=1}^{l} w_{ij} x_j \equiv c_i', \quad i = 1, \ldots, l, \tag{4}$$

over $\mathbb{Z}$ will also be an unique solution of the system (3) satisfying $\|x\| \leq \frac{1}{2}p\lambda_l^{-1}(L)$. This is due to the fact that the aforesaid system (4) has at most one solution over $\mathbb{Z}$. Consequently, our starting system (2) has at most one solution satisfying $\|x\| \leq \frac{1}{2}p\lambda_l^{-1}(L)$. $\square$

Now, in order to determine the unknown fraction of the k_i, i.e., $k_i^{(2)}$, we will apply the former theorem to the above equation system (1). However, the applicability of Theorem 1 requires

$$|k_i^{(2)}| \leq n\lambda_l(L)^{-1}2^{-1}l^{-1/2}.$$

With the subconstraint $|k_i^{(2)}| \leq n2^{-t}$ for the unknowns $k_i^{(2)}$ this means that one needs to know

$$t = \log \lambda_l(L) + 1 + \frac{1}{2}\log l$$

bits of every k_i. Therefore, the number t of known bits in advance only depends on $\lambda_l(L)$. Luckily, if the coefficients a_{ij} are chosen uniformly at random, one can show that with high probability

$$\lambda_l(L) < 5\sqrt{l}\varepsilon^{-1/l}n^{1-l-1/l}$$

is satisfied, where $\varepsilon > 0$ is an arbitrarily small positive constant. This will be shown in the following theorem whose proof combines ideas from [FHK$^+$] with latest lattice research due to [Ba].

Theorem 2. *Let n be a prime, $\varepsilon > 0$ and*

$$L := \{y \in \mathbb{R}^l \mid y = \mathbb{Z}a_1 + \ldots + \mathbb{Z}a_{l-1} + \mathbb{Z}ne_1 + \ldots + \mathbb{Z}ne_l\}$$

a lattice in $\mathbb{Z}^l$, where $a_1 := (a_1, 0, \ldots, 0, a_l), \ldots, a_{l-1} := (0, \ldots, 0, a_{l-1}, a_l)$ are randomly chosen in $\mathbb{Z}^l$. Then, with probability $\geq 1 - \varepsilon - O(1/n^{(l-1)/l})$ it holds that

$$\lambda_l(L) \leq \left(\frac{\pi^{l/2}}{\Gamma(\frac{l}{2}+1)}\right)^{1/l} l\,\varepsilon^{-1/l}\,n^{1-(l-1)/l}.$$

Proof. As an abbreviation we define for the basis

$$B := (a_1, \ldots, a_{l-1}, ne_1, \ldots, ne_l)$$

of the lattice L the so called span(B) as

$$\text{span}(B) := \{y \in \mathbb{R}^l \mid y = \mathbb{R}a_1 + \cdots + \mathbb{R}a_{l-1} + \mathbb{R}ne_1 + \cdots + \mathbb{R}ne_l\}.$$

According to Kannan [Kan] the lattice dual to the given lattice L is given by

$$L^* := \{z \in \text{span}(B) \mid \forall y \in L : \langle z, y \rangle \in \mathbb{Z}\},$$

which means particularly that

$$L^* = \{z \in \mathbb{R}^l \mid \forall y \in L : \langle z, y \rangle \in \mathbb{Z}\}$$
$$= \{z \in \tfrac{1}{n}\mathbb{Z}^l \mid \langle z, a_i \rangle \in \mathbb{Z}, i = 1, \ldots, l-1\},$$

and moreover also that

$$nL^* = \{z \in \mathbb{Z}^l \mid \langle z, a_i \rangle \equiv 0 \bmod n, i = 1, \ldots, l-1\}.$$

Thus, we see that for a randomly chosen point $z \in \mathbb{Z}^l$ we have

$$\Pr_{z \in_U \mathbb{Z}^l}[\langle z, a_i \rangle \equiv 0 \bmod n] = \frac{1}{n}$$

for every $i = 1, \ldots, l-1$, which in turn implies that

$$\Pr_{z \in_U \mathbb{Z}^l}[z \in nL^*] = \left(\frac{1}{n}\right)^{l-1}.$$

Let $S_R(o) := \{x \in \mathbb{R}^l \mid \|x\| < R\}$ the usual open sphere with radius R around the origin $o := (0, \ldots, 0)$ and denote by $G_R(o) := |S_R(o) \cap \mathbb{Z}^l|$ the number of $\mathbb{Z}$ lattice points within $S_R(o)$. From the above we are now able to infer that

$$\Pr_{z \in_U \mathbb{Z}^l}[S_R(o) \cap nL^* = \emptyset] = \left(1 - 1/n^{l-1}\right)^{G_R(o))} \geq 1 - G_R(o)/n^{l-1}.$$

Thus, we see that

$$\lambda_1(nL^*) \geq R \quad \Longleftrightarrow \quad \lambda_1(L^*) \geq \frac{R}{n}$$

holds with probabilty $\geq 1 - S_R(o)/n^{l-1}$. Due to Walfisz [Wa] the number $G_R(o)$ is for $R \to \infty$ given by

$$G_R(o) = \frac{\pi^{l/2}}{\Gamma(\frac{l}{2}+1)} R^l + O\left(R^{(l-1)}\right).$$

Choosing now

$$R := \left(\frac{\pi^{l/2}}{\Gamma(\frac{l}{2}+1)}\right)^{-1/l} \varepsilon^{1/l} \, n^{(l-1)/l}$$

yields for $n \to \infty$ that

$$G_R(o) = \varepsilon \, n^{(l-1)} + O\left(n^{(l-1)^2/l}\right),$$

from which we conclude that

$$\lambda_1(L^*) \geq \frac{R}{n} \geq \frac{6}{25} \sqrt{l} \, n^{(l-1)/l-1} \, \varepsilon^{1/l}$$

holds with probability $1 - \varepsilon + O(n^{-(l-1)/l})$. If we now apply the so called transference bound

$$\lambda_1(L^*) \cdot \lambda_l(L) \leq l$$

due to Banaszcyk [Ba], we finally get our promised result

$$\lambda_l(L) \leq \frac{l}{\lambda_1(L^*)} \leq \frac{25}{6} \sqrt{l} \; n^{1-(l-1)/l} \; \varepsilon^{-1/l}$$

$$\square$$

If we yet put together all the results we have so far, we get that with

$$t \geq \frac{1}{l} \log_2 n + \log_2 l + \frac{1}{l} \log_2 \varepsilon + 3.06$$

known bits of of the randomly chosen k_i we are able to recover the rest of the k_i. The goal is now simultaneously maximizing the probability $1 - \varepsilon + O(n^{-(l-1)/l})$ and minimizing the number t of needed bits in the k_i. We simply set $\varepsilon := 0.01$ and investigate the two functions

$$f_1(n, l) := \frac{1}{l} \log_2 n + \log_2 l - \frac{1}{l} \log_2(0.01) + 3.06$$

$$f_2(n, l) := \epsilon + O(n^{-(l-1)/l})$$

concerning local minima and maxima. However, for f_2 we need to consult Walfisz [Wa] for the hidden constants in the O resulting from $G_R(o)$. Precise determination of these constants and searching for local minima and maxima results finally in a probability of 0.99 and 12 known bits of the k_i if we assuming that n is a 160-bit prime.

Thus, we have proved that with only 12 known bits of every k_i, $i = 1, \ldots, 50$, the ECDSA can be broken in practice. We stress, that these are proven worst-case bounds, whereas in practical experiments we needed much less than 12 bits. Moreover, our attack can be extended to cover even the case when the known bits are somewhere located within the k_i's.

5   Summary

Again, lattice methods have been used to show that a secure proven signature method like the ECDSA can be broken under some circumstances. This implies, that it is very important to protect hard- and software implementations of the ECDSA on smart cards very carefully against side channel attacks in order to avoid any information leakage of secret data to a potential attacker.

References

Ba.   W. Banaszcyk, "New Bounds in Some Transference Theorems in the Geometry of Numbers", *Mathematische Annalen* Vol. 296, pp. 625-635, 1993. 216, 218

BGM.   M. Bellare, S. Goldwasser, D. Micciancio, "Pseudo-random number generation within cryptogrphic algorithms. The DSS case", *Proc. of CRYPTO '97*, pp. ?-?, LNCS Vol. 1294, Springer Verlag, 1997. 212

BSS.   I. Blake, G. Seroussi, N. Smart, *Elliptic Curves in Cryptography*, Cambridge University Press, 1999. 211, 212

Bl.   J. Blömer, "Closest Vectors, Successive Minima, and Dual HKZ-Bases of Lattices", *Proc. of 27th ICALP*, pp. ?-?, LNCS Vol. 1835, Springer Verlag, 2000. 215

BPVY.   E. Brickell, D. Pointcheval, S. Vaudenay, M. Yung, "Design validations for discrete logarithm based signature schemes", *Proc. of PKC 2000*, pp. 276-292, LNCS Vol. 1751, Springer Verlag, 2000. 211, 213

CKN.   J.-S. Coron, P. Kocher, D. Naccache, "Statistics and secret leakage", *Proc. of Financial Cryptography 2000*, Springer LNCS, vol. ?, pp. ?-?, 2000. 212

FHK+.   A. Frieze, J. Hastad, R. Kannan, J. Lagarias, A. Shamir, "Reconstructing Truncated Integer Variables Satisfying Linear Congruences", *SIAM J. Comp.* Vol. 17, pp. 262-280, 1988. 212, 214, 216

HJMS.   E. Hess, N. Janssen, B. Meyer, T. Schütze, "Information leakage attacks against smart card implementations of cryptographic algorithms and countermeasures", *Proc. of EUROSMART-Security-Conference 2000*, pp. 53-64, 2000. 212

HGS.   N. Howgrave-Graham, N. Smart, "Lattice attacks on digital signature schemes", Technical Report HPL-1999-90, HP Labs, 1999. 212

JM.   D. Johnson, A. J. Menezes, "The Elliptic Curve Digital Signature Algorithm (ECDSA)", Technical Report CORR 99-34, Dept. of C&O, University of Waterloo, 2000. 211, 213

Kan.   R. Kannan, "Algorithmic Geometry of Numbers", *Ann. Rev. Comput. Science* Vol. 2, pp. 231-267, 1987. 212, 216

Kob94.   N. Koblitz, *A Course in Number Theory and Cryptography*, Springer Verlag, 1994.

Kob99.   N. Koblitz, *Algebraic Aspects of Cryptography*, Springer Verlag, 1999. 212

Lov.   L. Lovasz, *An Algorithmic Theory of Graphs, Numbers and Convexity*, SIAM, 1986. 212

Men.   A. J. Menezes, *Elliptic Curve Public Key Cryptosystemes*, Kluwer Academic Publishers, 1993. 212

MvOV.   A. J. Menezes, P. van Oorschot, S. Vanstone, *Handbook of Applied Cryptography*, CRC Press, 1993. 211

NS.   P. Nguyen, J. Stern, "Lattice Reduction in Cryptology: An update", *Proc. 4th Algorithmic Number Theory Symposium*, pp. ?-?, LNCS Vol. 1838, Springer Verlag, 2000. 212

Wa.   A. Walfisz, *Gitterpunkte in mehrdimensionalen Kugeln*, Polish Scientific Publishers, Warsaw, 1957. 217, 218

Use of Biometrics for User Verification in Electronic Signature Smartcards

Bruno Struif

GMD, Rheinstr. 75, D-64295 Darmstadt, Germany
bruno.struif@darmstadt.gmd.de

Abstract. If a smartcard provides security functions such as electronic signature creation, valuables such as electronic money and/or sensitive data such as medical data, then the smartcard has to verify that it is used by the legitimate cardholder. For this purpose, the user has usually to present a PIN. Since smartcards become more and more powerful, it is feasible to implement on-card matching algorithms allowing to perform a biometric user verification in the smartcard.

1 Legal Background for Electronic Signatures and Signer Verification

In 1999, the EU has published the "EU Directive 1999/93/EC of the European Parliament and the council of 13 December 1999 on a Community framework for electronic signatures [1]".

In this Directive, the use of "Secure Signature Creation Devices (SSCD)" for the creation of Qualified Electronic Signatures is described. The most important instance of such an SSCD is a smartcard which is able to compute an electronic signature using the Signature Creation Data (= signature key) of the signer. It is required, that the Signature Creation Data shall be protected against misuse and - further more - that there should be a unique link between a qualified electronic signature and the signer as shown in fig. 1.

In order to promote the use of electronic signatures, CEN Working Agreements (CWA) has been worked out within the context of the so-called E-Sign Workshop. Two documents are of special interest for smartcards: "CWA Security Requirements for Signature Creation Applications" [2] und "CWA Secure Signature Creation Devices" [3].

Two types of signer verification methods are possible:

- knowledge based signer verification
- biometric signer verification

The first verification method requires the presentation of a Personal Identification Number (PIN) or password. The second verification method requires the presentation of a physiological or behavioural biometric feature.

I. Attali and T. Jensen (Eds.): E-smart 2001, LNCS 2140, pp. 220-227, 2001.

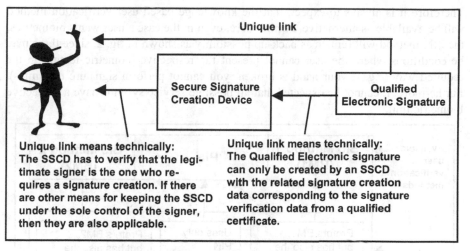

Unique link

Secure Signature Creation Device

Qualified Electronic Signature

Unique link means technically:
The SSCD has to verify that the legitimate signer is the one who requires a signature creation. If there are other means for keeping the SSCD under the sole control of the signer, then they are also applicable.

Unique link means technically:
The Qualified Electronic signature can only be created by an SSCD with the related signature creation data corresponding to the signature verification data from a qualified certificate.

Fig. 1. Linkage of a Qualified Electronic Signature to the Signer

2   Usage of Biometrics in Electronic Signature and other Smartcard Applications

The biometric industry has developed a great variety of products using different kind of biometrics:

- Fingerprint
- Face recognition
- Voice pattern
- Signature dynamics
- Iris pattern
- Hand geometry
- key stroke
- ...

Due to the complexity of matching algorithms and their requirements with respect to program storage, data storage and CPU capacity, it is not yet possible to implement matchers for all kind of biometrics in today's smartcards. Matchers for fingerprint verification has been successfully implemented, matchers of other biometric methods will follow. In the EU study [4], more details are presented.

In applications designed for a greater portion of the population, the usage of biometrics cannot be enforced. Biometric methods are not suitable, nor applicable to any signer, or more general, to a user in the following cases:

- rejection due to personal reasons;
- cultural incompatibility;
- absence of the respective biometric feature;
- insufficient characteristics of the respective biometric feature;
- abnormal characteristics of the respective biometric feature.

Therefore it is always to expect, that the knowledge based user verification method will be available as alternative. Furthermore, even in the case a user wants biometrics, the PIN method will remain as back-up possibility as shown in fig. 2, since there may be conditions where the user cannot present the respective biometric feature in the required way (e.g. if your hand is broken, you cannot perform signature dynamics). Furthermore, it cannot be expected that all possible service systems have a respective biometric unit.

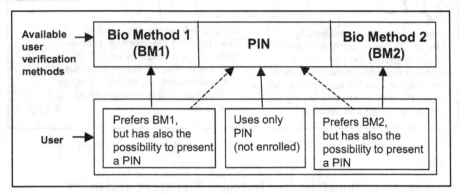

Fig. 2. User verification methods and user preference

Since an enrolled user will usually prefer to present the biometric feature, if possible, he might have even a greater problem to remember a PIN rarely used. A solution to this problem can be to store all PINs in a protected device (e.g. in the handy, in a palmtop or a dedicated PIN storage device), so that the user has only to remember *one* PIN.

3   Biometric User Verification in Smartcards

If biometric user verification is provided, then a work sharing between service system and smartcard takes place in the way, it is shown in fig. 3. The biometric reference data have to be stored in the smartcard either
- when personalizing the smartcard using biometric reference data captured in a separate enrollment process before or
- when the smartcard is delivered to the user in an authorized service center (e.g. a bank).

4   Standardisation Issues

In order to enable interoperability, standards for various topics are needed.

4.1   Interindustry Commands for Biometric User Verification

Interindustry commands for knowledge based user verification have been specified in ISO/IEC 7816-4 "Interindustry commands for interchange [5]" (VERIFY command)

and in ISO/IEC 7816-8 "Security related interindustry commands [6]" (commands CHANGE REFERENCE DATA, ENABLE/DISABLE VERIFICATION REQUIRE-MENT and RESET RETRY COUNTER). In ISO/IEC 7816-11 "Personal verification through biometric methods [7]" the usage of the VERIFY command has been extended to support those biometric user verification methods, which work with static features from the viewpoint of the smartcard (e.g. fingerprint, signature dynamics[1]). For dynamic biometric methods, which needs to retrieve a challenge from the card to which the user has to react on (e.g. voice recognition, if several words have been enrolled), the commands GET CHALLENGE and EXTERNAL AUTHENTICATE have been extended for biometric usage.

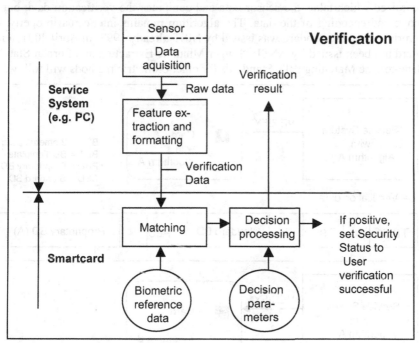

Fig. 3. Work sharing between service system and smartcard with on-card matching

4.2   Biometric Information Data Objects

Prior to sending e.g. a VERIFY command to the smartcard, the service system must know whether

- the user is enrolled and if,
- the biometric type
- the biometric feature (e.g. which finger is enrolled)
- the conventions for the biometric verification data.

---

[1] The smartcard receives only the biometric verification data and cannot recognize whether these data have been produced on the basis of an action or just presentation of the respective biometric feature.

Biometric information data objects will be defined in ISO/IEC 7816-11 in compliance with the Common Biometric Exchange File Format [8].

4.3   Biometric Data

The service system has to perform the feature extraction and the encoding of the biometric verification data in the way required by the smartcard. If this is not possible, then service system and smartcard are incompatible with respect to biometric user verification. For interoperability it is therefore mandatory, to standardize the biometric verification data seen at the interface. Not the algorithm itself has to be standardized which takes the sensor data and computes the verification data, but the structure and encoding of the data. The algorithm remains intellectual property. For fingerprints, the first standard was issued by NIST already 1993. In April 2001, a new standard has been issued by ANSI: "Finger Minutiae Extraction and Format Standard for One-to-One Matching [9]". Standards for other biometric methods will follow.

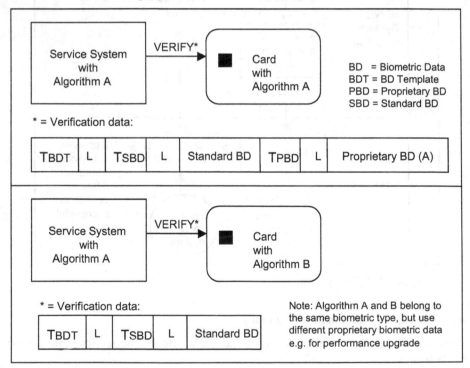

Fig. 4. Usage of standardized and proprietary biometric data

The ANSI standard on Minutiae encoding is not applicable for smartcards without adaptation. Therefore it is expected that on the ISO level a New Work Item will be initiated possibly by ANSI. Biometric verification data may be split in a standardized part and in a proprietary part e.g. for achieving a better performance, see fig. 4.

4.4   Cryptographic Security Issues

Several biometric methods uses biometric data which cannot be considered as secret, i.e. they use "public verification data", e.g. fingerprints or facial data. It is obvious that e.g. the minutiae data cannot be simply presented to the card using the VERIFY command. They have to protected e.g. by a cryptographic checksum whereby the key used may be established in an authentication procedure with key exchange to avoid replay attacks (see fig. 5).

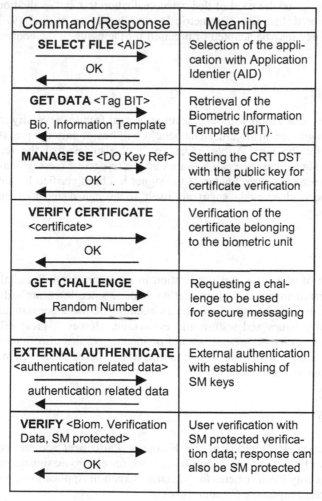

Command/Response	Meaning
SELECT FILE \<AID\> → ← OK	Selection of the application with Application Identier (AID)
GET DATA \<Tag BIT\> → Bio. Information Template	Retrieval of the Biometric Information Template (BIT).
MANAGE SE \<DO Key Ref\> → ← OK .	Setting the CRT DST with the public key for certificate verification
VERIFY CERTIFICATE \<certificate\> → ← OK	Verification of the certificate belonging to the biometric unit
GET CHALLENGE → ← Random Number	Requesting a challenge to be used for secure messaging
EXTERNAL AUTHENTICATE \<authentication related data\> → ← authentication related data	External authentication with establishing of SM keys
VERIFY \<Biom. Verification Data, SM protected\> → ← OK	User verification with SM protected verification data; response can also be SM protected

Fig. 5. Example of a command sequence, where the biometric verification data are protected by a cryptographic checksum

Also the new ANSI standard X9.84 [10] points out, that cryptographic security mechanisms are needed in the context of biometrics.

4.5   Testing and Evaluation

Especially in the field of electronic signature smartcards, evaluation according to ITSEC or Common Criteria is required. The evaluation assurance level depends e.g. on the quality of the electronic signatures which shall be created by the respective card. If the signature creation data (i.e. the signature key) shall be protected by biometric user verification, then the respective biometric verification method is also subject of evaluation. Aspects of testing and evaluation are rather new in the field of on-card matching and the need of dedicated evaluation test and evaluation documents has to be explored. In UK a "Biometric Device Protection Profile" [9] is under development, which may be adapted or precised for the usage in the context of on-card matching.

5   Benefits

Biometric user verification will become an important feature especially in the context of electronic signature smartcards. The benefit will be not only the provision of more convenience for the user. A big advantage will also be, that the receiver of an electronically signed message can be sure that the respective message has been really signed by the respective cardholder, if the signer has been verified by biometrics and this fact has been added by the smartcard itself to the signed signature attributes in an unforgeable way.

6   Outlook

The provision of biometric user verification in smartcards is still a challenge to the industry, research institutes and evaluation bodies, since there are still some open issues as outlined with respect to implementation of the algorithm itself, cryptographic security issues and testing and evaluation. However, great efforts will be made to achieve quick progress. It should be mentioned, that also fingerprint sensors and complete fingerprint verification modules, which can be integrated in a smartcard, are under development.

References

1. EU Directive 1999/93/EC of the European Parliament and the council of 13 December 1999 on a Community framework for electronic signatures
2. CWA Security Requirements for Signature Creation Applications, April 2001
3. CWA Secure Signature Creation Devices
4. Scheuermann, D., Schwiderski-Grosche, S., Struif, B.: Usability of Biometrics in Relation to Electronic Signatures. EU Study 502533/8, September 12, 2000 (see www.sit.gmd.de/SICA/projects/bio_sig.html)
5. ISO/IEC 7816-4: 1995 - Interindustry commands for interchange
6. ISO/IEC 7816-8: 1999 - Security related interindustry commands
7. ISO/IEC 7816-11 (Committee Draft 2001) – Personal verification through biometric methods

8. NISTIR 6529 – Common Biometric Exchange File Format (CBEFF), January 3, 2001
9. ANSI B10.8 – Finger Minutiae Extraction and Format Standard for One-to-One Matching, April 24, 2001
10. ANSI X9.84 – Biometric Information Management and Security, March 27, 2001
11. Biometric Device Protection Profile, Draft issue, January 15, 2001

Programming Internet Smartcard with XML Scripts

Pascal Urien

Bull CP8 R&D - 68 routes de Versailles - BP 45
78431 Louveciennes CEDEX – France
Pascal.Urien@Bull.net

Abstract. This paper describes an innovative architecture for an internet smartcard. We believe that a communication stack approach, in which a smartcard is used as an usual internet node (running well defined server and client applications) is the best way for adapting smartcards to internet applications. Our experimental smartcard is organized around an XML script parser, which is invoked from an embedded web server. XML scripts have access to all embedded resources, and manage connections to remote internet servers.

1 Introduction

A communication stack approach aims at using smartcards as an usual network node. In this context smartcards run internet server and client applications (which are defined by internet RFCs). They include an Http server, every embedded resource is identified by an URL; they are able to exchange information with remote internet servers according to various protocols. Communication with embedded objects is performed thanks to XML messages, in order to support emerging distributed architectures, like SOAP.

1.1 Motivation

Smart cards are generally recognized as the best device to insure safe data storage, and to process cryptographic algorithms (encryption / decryption , certification...). But until now, no high level interface has been specified for smart cards. The ISO 7816 standards only define a set of low level commands (APDUs), which typically perform writing orders, reading orders, or cryptographic functions invocation.

Therefore, a software component working with a smartcard must generate specifics APDUs which are needed for achieving a particular service. In order to improve inter-operability, some tentatives have been done to describe this translation in XML syntax, according to a particular grammar (SML - smartX Markup Language [17]).

I. Attali and T. Jensen (Eds.): E-smart 2001, LNCS 2140, pp. 228-241, 2001.

But a dedicated SML parser (named *application process*) must be plugged in standard web browsers which don't natively support this feature.

For several years, there is an increasing trend to use Internet anywhere, and from any terminals (*ubiquitous Internet*). This need is increasing, due to the exponential growth of the net economy. Internet Protocol is the *de facto* standard for data exchange (*IP overall*). In particular, web browsers are becoming a standard man machine interface, which exchange electronic documents, using HTML or XML languages.

For example XML documents are made up of storage units called entities, which are identified by URLs and transported by HTTP protocol. Therefore a smartcard supporting HTTP protocol and including a web server is natively adapted to XML technologies. As a consequence embedded resources are identified and named by URIs (Unified Resource Identifier).

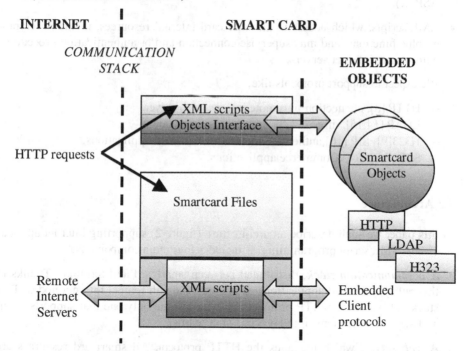

Fig. 1. XML programming concept

1.2 Embedded XML Parser

An other critical issue is identification and execution of embedded procedures. More generally the basic problem is to interact with smartcard objects. There is a trend in distributed architecture (like CORBA) to exchange data between objects, according to non-proprietary transfer syntax like XML.

As an illustration the SOAP protocol, an XML based protocol, has been designed for information exchange in a distributed environment (like Internet network).

It consists of three parts: an *envelope* that defines a framework for describing what is in a message and how to process it, a *set of encoding rules* for expressing instances of application-defined data types, and a *convention* for representing remote procedure calls and responses.

We believe that an embedded XML parser, interpreting XML encoded messages carried in HTTP requests, is a right approach for using smartcard in distributed environment. Smartcard implements HTTP protocol, and its objects are invoked through XML messages. We shall distinguish two kinds of embedded resources (figure 1),

- Various file, like HTML or XML documents, images or mobile code (APPLET, ASP …).

- XML scripts, which access to all smartcard internal resources, including crypto-graphic functions, and may supervise connection and/or authentication procedures with remote internet servers.

We expect to support protocols like,

- HTTP [8], connection to remote internet web server.
- LDAP [14,15], directory for smartcard management.
- H323[9], SIP [16],authentication features in VoIP applications.
- SSL [7,8], for eCommerce applications.

1.3 Architecture

In this paper we shall describe an architecture (figure 2) supporting internet applications and XML script programming. It includes four main components,

- *A communication stack*, distributed between smartcard and terminal. Thanks to this entity embedded applications exchange data with remote internet nodes. This stack is based on SmartTP protocol [5], which is the only one that supports client and server applications in today 8 bits smartcards.

- *A web server*, which manages the HTTP protocol. All smartcard resources are identified by URLs.

- *An XML script parser* which is the central point of our internet smartcard. It has access to every embedded resources and manages one or two internet sessions.

- *A file System Interface*, which supervises files operations (reading, writing) and is in charge of all authentication procedures.

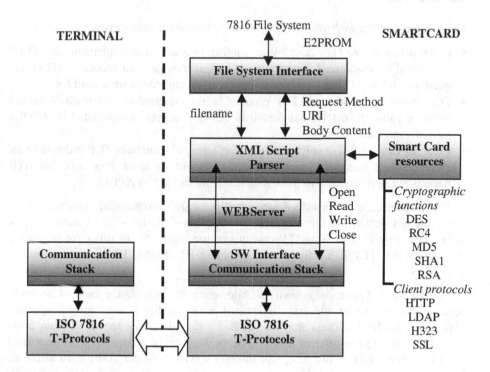

Fig. 2. Software Architecture

2 Communication Stack

The goal of a communication stack (figure 3) is to exchange information between smartcard and the internet network. It is distributed between terminal and smartcard, because this device is quite different from a classic computer,

First, it doesn't include a communication board, in order to send and receive data from network. This resource must be located outside the smart card, in a terminal to which the card reader is connected.

Second, communication protocols (ISO 7816 T=0 or T=1) are not full duplex, terminal sends a command and smartcard produces a response. For that reason a simple protocol like SLIP (serial line IP), which requires a bi-directional serial link, can't work with a 7816 chip.

2.1 State of Art

Several (web) server architectures have been proposed for smartcards,

- *HTTP proxy server* [1] . A software running in a terminal implements an HTTP server and is customized for each smartcard; it translates an incoming HTTP request as a set of APDUs which select and read an embedded smartcard file.
- *TCP server* [2], a subset of TCP protocol is implemented in smartcard. A tunnel software running in terminal forwards TCP/IP packets encapsulated in APDUs to/from smartcard.
- *Protocol gateway* [3], a software located in terminal translates TCP protocol in an other protocol transport, named SmartTP (Smart Transfer Protocol). SmartTP packets are sent/received to/from smartcard and carried by APDUs.

Client features, e.g. embedded smartcard software's exchanging data with a remote internet server, are more complex to define and design. This functionality is today only supported by SmartTP communication stack [5], in this case smartcard shares terminal TCP/IP configuration, including IP address, DNS server, gateway, web proxy,...

We believe that *protocol gateway* architecture is the best choice for IPv4 network, because the number of addresses is limited, and mobility is not really supported. However a fix IPv4 address may be suitable for applications in which smartcards work in the same geographical IP sub-network. If mobility is required then smartcard must implement DHCP protocol, and internet service provider (ISP) must affect an IP address to each smartcard; these two constraints are not realistic with today ISP capabilities and smartcard computing capacities.

IPv6 uses 128 bits addresses, which implies that their number is quite infinite; therefore it seems to be the future way for smartcard application naming. But because smartcard is a mobile object the support of *mobile IP* will be mandatory.

2.2 Socket

In network, a smartcard application is located by two parameters,

- A Network Service Access Point, NSAP, which is *the network address associated to a smartcard*. This parameter can be an IPv4 or IPv6 address in the internet network or a phone number in the GSM network.

- A Transport Service Access Point, TSAP, which is *the name of an embedded application*. In TCP/IP architecture a port number (between 0 and 65535) identifies a specific application (for example the well known port value 80 is associated to a web server).

We call *socket*, the couple NSAP:TSAP which identifies a smartcard embedded application.

2.3 Channels

A logical channel is a session between two applications, one of them is located in a smartcard (SC) and the other in a remote network node (NET). It's identified by two sockets, SC_NSAP:SC_TSAP and NET_NSAP:NET_TSAP.

Typically channel #0 is affected to a session between card web server and an external client (web browser …), a second channel (#1) is available for a session with a remote internet server.

2.4 Marks

We call *payloads*, data which are sent and received by the terminal to/from the network. Payloads, which are coming from the network are stored in one or more reception queues, located in the terminal, in order to be sent when possible toward smartcard.

Because terminal and smartcard need to exchange additional information, a *header* is added to the payload, and then these data (header + payload) are transported according to a 7816 protocol. Terminal and card exchange *stack protocol data unit* (SC_PDU) which are made up with a payload (network data) and a header. Conceptually a SC_PDU is always sent over a smart channel.

A header may include a channel name (SC_NSAP:SC_TSAP - NET_NSAP:NET_TSAP) associated to its payload and other information, that we call *marks*. We manage five marks in order to exchange data over a channel,

- BLOCK.
  - This mark is issued by a sorting terminal stack (TSS) to notify that no more payload will be sent until the reception of a CS_PDU addressed to this channel.
  - This mark is produced by smartcard stack (CSS) to indicate that a channel want to send data again.
- READY, when no particular event is associated to a payload, CS_PDU includes a READY mark.
- OPEN, this mark indicates a new channel creation.
- CLOSE, this mark notifies a channel deletion.
- NACK, this mark is produced by CSS in order to delete a channel and then to send an other CS_PDU. The terminal response is a CS_PDU including a CLOSE mark, addressed to the channel which had issued the previous NACK mark.

2.5 Application Interface

Smart card applications work with the communication stack through a software interface, according to well known open/connect read/recv write/send close/shutdown paradigm, used in UNIX systems to manipulate files or TCP/IP sockets.

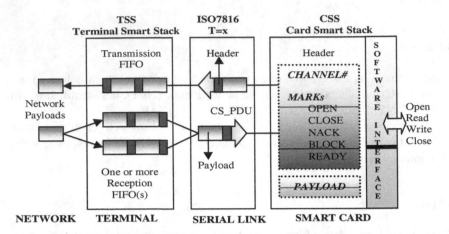

Fig. 3. Smartcard communication stack

3 HTTP Server

An HTTP client sends a request to the server in the form of a request method, URI (Unified Resource Identifier – typically a file name and its path), followed by a Mime-like message containing requests modifiers, client information and a possible body.

An HTTP daemon processes an incoming message, checks its validity and extracts the following basic information:

- The request method, typically GET or POST.
- The associated URI.
- An optional body content.

When a complete HTTP request has been received, associated parameter are passed to the script parser, which then is in charge of the current session management over channel zero.

4 File System Interface

Basically smartcard file is a memory (E2PROM) block, characterized by a base address a length and a maximum size (for writing operations). The *file system interface* (FSI) associates a name to this object (a file is a *named memory area*), manages its attributes and supervises all access pr ocedures.

This module performs all operations which are necessary for adapting an 7816 file system in order to support an *UNIX like* naming scheme; although it should be noticed that sophisticated file system can be implemented in Java language. FSI manages authentication processes that are compatible with HTTP protocol. It is invoked,

- From an HTTP message, incorporating a request method, an URI and an optional body content. If a file is protected by an authentication procedure, FSI typically generates an HTML page including a form, in order to get all elements needed by authentication process (for example login and password).
- From an XML script, in order to read or modify a smartcard file. If a script attempts to perform a forbidden file operation, FSI internally produces an error message, and script execution is aborted.

In our full Java FSI implementation, files are identified by a name (up to 255 characters) and are located in logical partitions, protected by passwords. A file may support reading and/or writing operation; it is either *public* or *protected* according to its partition lock value; an optional HTTP header specifies file MIME type (for example text image or applet). There are two types of files, static files or scripts, which are similar to executable files.

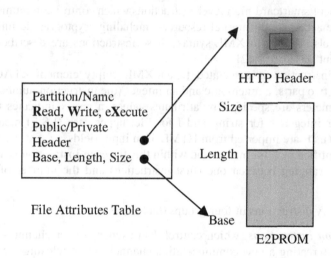

Fig. 4. File System

5 XML Script Parser

Script parser is the key point of our experimental smartcard. Once an incoming HTTP request has been checked by the web server, all further card operations are supervised by this software component.

5.1 Motivation

There are two main motivations for organizing an internet smartcard around a central XML parser,

- First reason is flexibility, XML script offers a high level description of services which are offered by smartcards. Embedded resources are described by specific DTD, what guaranties that *well formed* scripts can be correctly executed.
- Second reason is supporting an open object distributed architecture. Embedded object messages are expressed in XML syntax, which is independent from any smartcard operating system.

5.2 Implementation

This module managed an HTTP session over channel #0, and an optional second channel (#1), created from a script instruction (<Open_1/>. At any time, if HTTP session is closed script execution is aborted, and smartcard control is passed back to the web server which is then ready for processing next HTTP session.

A script is a set of smartcard high level instructions which control communication sessions and have access to all internal resources, including cryptographic functions and client protocols. Thanks to XML syntax, these instructions are described by a data type document (DTD) [11,12].

A smartcard instruction is associated to an XML empty element <TAG.../>, which is made of two parts, a mnemonic and an integer (the instruction number).

Optional parameters are specified by attributes values, a prefix indicates the attribute type, i for integer, s for string and f for file; upper case (I,S,F) mean that attributes values (i,s,f) are imported from HTML form input fields.

A script is identified by a file name, and within this file each instruction is associated to an index, ranging between one (first instruction) and the number of script instructions.

We shall classify instructions in four groups (table 1):

- *Communication instructions*, which control data exchange over channels (#0 or #1), like open (creating a new communication channel), close (closing a communication channel), send (data transmission over a communication channel), recv. (data reception over a communication channel). Data reception is always associated to a reception protocol (Ptcol), like
  - Raw reception (#0), data are received until channel closing
  - ASN1 protocol (#1), incoming data block is encoding according to Abstract Syntax Notation 1.
  - HTTP protocol (#2).
- *Control instructions*, which allow script programming, like call, jump , if.
- *Files instructions*, which control files operations, like copy (adding data to file) or cat (appending data to file).
- *Resources instructions*, which access to all available card resources (functions, network protocols ...), like add (adding an integer to a file content).

Table 1. Example of XML script instructions

Instruction	Description	Attributes		Example
		1st	2nd	
Send_0	Sending data over a channel iCh	sf	i	`<Send_0 f="file" iCh="1"/>` `<Send_0 s="Hello" iCh="0"/>`
Open_1	Open channel#1 and connect it to an internet server	sf		`<Open_1 s="host:80"/>` `<Open_1 S="Host">`
Close_2	Close channel #1			`<Close_2/>`
Recv_3	Data reception over ch#1 according to iPtcol	f	i	`<Recv_3 f="file" iPtcol="0"/>` `<Recv_3 f="file" iPtcol="2"/>`
Copy_11	Copy data in a destination file fD	sf	f	`<Copy_11 s="Hello" fD="file"/>` `<Copy_11 f="source" fD="Dest"/>`
Cat_12	Append data to a destination file fD	sf	f	`<Copy_12 s="Hello" fD="file"/>` `<Copy_12 f="source" fD="dest"/>`
Add_20	Source+Destination => Destination	if	f	`<Add_20 i="1000" fD="balance"/>` `<Add_20 f="x" fD="balance"/>`
Call_7	Call a script	s		`<Call_7 s="pme"/>`
Jmp_8	Jump to a script instruction	i		`<Jump_8 i="5"/>`
If_9	If a file content is >= jump to an instruction	f	i	`<if_9 f="balance" i="5">`

5.3 Executing a script

Let's consider a simple script named *pme* which adds an integer value to a file variable named *Balance*. This script uses an input parameter *Money* which is imported from an html form input field. Following the addition procedure, an html page is dynamically built in order to display the result. This page is sent over the communication channel #0.

```
<pme>
<Add_20 I="Money"  fD="Balance"/>
<Send_0 f="Header"  iCh="0"/>
<Send_0 f="Balance" iCh="0"/>
<Send_0 f="Trailer" iCh="0"/>
</pme>
```

Fig. 5. A pme script

This script is executed from an HTTP request using either GET method, *http://127.0.0.1:8080/pme?Money=+1000*, or POST method produced by an HTML form (figure 6).

```
<html><body><H1>PME</H1>
<FORM METHOD=POST ACTION=/pme>
<INPUT VALUE=ADD TYPE=submit>
<INPUT NAME=Money>
</FORM></body></html>
```

Fig. 6. Invoking a smartcard script (pme)from an HTML form

5.4 Sending a Message to a Smartcard XML Script

An XML script can be sent to smartcard in order to be internally processed, in this case it acts as an XML encoded message which interacts with smartcard objects.

```
<Add_20  f="In"  fD="Balance"/>
<Copy_11  f="Balance"  fD="Out"/>
```

Fig. 7. Modified pme script.

For example we can slightly modify our *pme* script, so that an input (file) variable *In* is added to the balance content; operation result is copied in a file named *Out* (Figure 7). The next step is to send, encapsulated in an URL, an XML script identified by the prefix X?x,

```
             http://127.0.0.1:8080/X?x=<Copy_11 s="+1000" fD="In"/>
             <Call_7 s="pme"/><Send_0 f="Out" iCh="0"/>
```

This message invokes the pme script with the *In* value set to +1000 and transmits the return value over channel #0.

5.5 Modeling Network Interaction

Script may interact with remote internet servers, like for example a LDAP server (ils.microsoft.com:389). First step is the creation of a new session over channel #1,

```
                <Open_1 s="ils.microsoft.com:389"/>
```

Upon success, a request message, stored in a file (*Out*) is sent to remote node,

```
                <Send_0 f="Out" iCh="1"/>
```

Script then waits for an incoming response, of which length is determined according to a known protocol, like ASN1 for LDAP messages,

```
                <Recv_3 f="In" iPtcol="1">
```

An interaction with a remote server consists of one or several message exchanges, which are eventually processed by additional script instructions. Script ends a connection by executing the <Close_2/> instruction.

6 JavaCard Implementation

6.1 Architecture

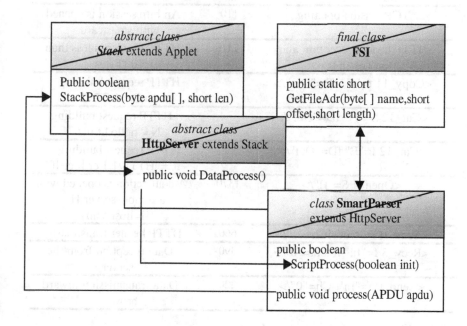

Fig. 8. JavaCard Software Architecture

Our software architecture (figure 8) is made up four Java classes. An abstract class named *Stack* implements the SmartTP protocol, all incoming APDUs are processed by the StackProcess method.

Data which are received from logical channels are forwarding, by invoking method DataProcess() to an abstract class *HTTPServer*. HTTP method type (Get or Post), URI and optional body content are extracted from an incoming HTTP request. When a complete message has been received and checked, all further incoming information are transmitted via ScriptProcess() method toward the *SmartParser* class.

SmartParser is in charge to analyze the incoming URI, it uses FSI services (in particular *GetFileAdr* method) to determine if a valid file (an E2PROM block) is associated to this URI. If the requested file is an XML script, its content is interpreted on a per instruction basis.

The code size may be as small as 6.5 Kb (in bytes code units), but obviously it is proportional to the number of supported script instructions and is dependent of FSI complexity (in term of security features for examples).

6.2 Performances

Action	Time ms	Comments.
TCP session opening	110	An http session is opened with smartcard
HTTP header reception and processing	710	HTTP Header is less than 100 bytes
<Copy_11 f="G" fD="Out"/>		HTTP request building G="GET /"
<Cat_12 S="N" fD="Out"/>		HTTP request building N="hello.html"
<Cat_12 f="E" fD="Out"/>		HTTP request building E="HTTP/1.1 cr lf cr lf'
<Open_1 S="H"/>	1370	A connection is opened with a remote server H (H=host.com)
<Send_0 f="Out" iCh="1"/>	660	HTTP header transmission
<Recv_3 f="In" iPtcol="0"/>	390	Data reception from the server
<Send_0 f="In" iCh="0"/>	220	Data transmission toward browser

Table 2. Performances example

Table 2 shows timing measurements observed at script execution which includes seven instructions. This test script has two input parameters H (for host name) and N (for page name); its function is to open an HTTP session with a remote host (H), and then to transmit information, stored in *In* file back to the browser. The HTTP request is built in the *Out* file, and script is launched from the following URL,
http://127.0.0.1:8080/g?H=host.com&N=hello.html.

7 Future Work

We planned to investigate security aspects, for example by supporting additional features like script signature and user authentication.

8 Conclusion

We have realized an experimental internet smartcard which is fully programmed by XML scripts. Code size and executing times show that this approach is realistic even with today existing 8 bits JavaCard. Although we think that security requirements need further studies, we believe that this innovative architecture will facilitate smartcard integration in internet applications, in which electronic documents use XML syntax.

References

[1]   Jon Barber "The Smart Card URL Programming Interfcace", Proceedings of Gemplus Developer Conference (GDC' 99), Paris, France, 21-22 June 1999.

[2]   J. Rees and P. Honeyman, "Webcard: a Java Card web server," Proceedings of. IFIP CARDIS 2000, Bristol September, 2000.

[3]   Pascal Urien - "Procédé de communication entre une station d'utilisateur et un réseau, notamment de type internet, et architecture de mise en œuvre" brevet déposé le 13 août 1998, N° d'enregistrement 98 10401, N° de publication 2 782 435.

[4]   Pascal Urien, "Carte à puce internet & Objets mobiles embarqués" OCM'2000 Ecole des Mines de Nantes, 18 mai 2000.

[5]   Pascal Urien " Internet Card, a smart card as a true Internet node", Computer Communications, volume 23, issue 17pp 1655-1666- October 2000.

[6]   Pascal Urien, Hayder Saleh, Adel Tizraoui "Internet Card, a smart card for internet", Protocols for Multimedia Systems (PROMS) Cracow Poland, October 22-25 2000.

[7]   Pascal Urien, Hayder Saleh, Adel Tizraoui "SSL dans une carte à puce" Journées Doctorales Informatique et Réseaux, JDIR'2000, Ministère de la Recherches, Paris, 6-8 novembre 2000.

[8]   Alan O Freier, Philip Karlton, Paul C. Kocher "The SSL Protocol Version 3.0" Internet Draft, March 1996, available at http://home.netscape.com/eng/ssl3/ssl-toc.html.

[9]   T Berners Lee & All "Hypertext Transfer Protocol - HTTP/1.1" - RFC 2068 - January 1997.

[10]   International Telecommunication Union (ITU) Recommendation H323, "Packet-based multimedia communication systems", October 1997.

[11]   Extensible Markup Language (XML) 1.0 (Second Edition), W3C Recommendation 6 October 2000.

[12]   Extensible Style sheet Language (XSL) Version 1.0, W3C Candidate Recommendation 21 November 2000.

[13]   Simple Object Access Protocol SOAP, http://msdn.microsoft.com/xml/c-frame.htm?/xml/general/soapspec.asp

[14]   RFC 1777, " The Lightweight Directory Access Protocol", LDAP version 2, March 1995, http://www;ietf.org/rfc/rfc1777.txt

[15]   RFC 2251, "The Lightweight Directory Access Protocol", LDAP version 3, http://www;ietf.org/rfc/rfc2251.txt

[16]   RFC 2543, "SIP: Session Initiation Protocol," - March 1999.

[17]   Xavier Lorphelin "Internet and Smart Card Application Deployment" July 1999 http://www.smartcardcentral.com/technical/articles/jsource/article9907.pdf

Public-Key-Based High-Speed Payment (Electronic Money) System Using Contact-Less Smart Cards

Hideo Yamamoto[1], Tetsutaro Kobayashi[1], Masahiro Morita[2] and Ryuji Yamada[1]

[1] NTT Information Platform Laboratories,
1-1, Hikarinooka, Yokosuka, Kanagawa, Japan
hideo@alsace.isl.ntt.co.jp
kotetsuryu@isl.ntt.co.jp
ryu@isl.ntt.co.jp
[2] NTT Communications Corporation,
1-6, 1-Chome, Chiyoda-Ku, Tokyo, Japan
hiro.morita@ntt.com

Abstract. Contact-less smart cards are very convenient in use and are expected to expand the application fields of electronic money; they will accelerate the penetration of all electronic money services. Contact-less smart cards have limited capabilities and so it is difficult for them to perform complicated operations such as public key cryptographic processing. Moreover, the usage style of contact-less smart cards makes it difficult to guarantee the consistency of the transaction. To answer these questions, we have developed a high-speed payment processing system. Based on the elliptic curve digital signature algorithm, the proposed system reduces the processing time and the amount of data that needs to be transmitted. We describe a typical implementation that uses pre-computation. Also described here is a transaction mechanism that ensures processing consistency in the face of the unstable operating environment of contact-less smart cards.

1 Introduction

Smart cards are becoming extremely popular; over 800,000,000 units were shipped in the fiscal year of 2000 [1]. Its application fields are expanding from communication and finance, to public transportation, electronic authentication, and administration services.

In the finance field, there are already several electronic money schemes offering commercial services like MONDEX [2], Geld Karte [3], Proton [4], and Visa Cash [5]. In Japan, NTT has been investigating electronic money schemes. We have demonstrated our schemes in commercial trials. Internet Cash [9] is the electronic money trial service for virtual shops on the Internet, and Super Cash[10] is a large scale electronic money trial service; customers can use the electronic money in real shops, vending machines, and virtual shops on the Internet.

I. Attali and T. Jensen (Eds.): E-smart 2001, LNCS 2140, pp. 242-254, 2001.

In the public transportation field, such as railroad, subway, and bus companies are investigating the introduction of smart cards for ticket gating. The transportation card called OCTPUS [6] was put into service in September of 1997 in Hong Kong. About 7 million OCTPUS cards have been issued, and customers can use them for a wide range of transportation services, such as trains, subways, buses, and ferries. In Japan, the East Japan Railway Company has decided to introduce the same type of transportation card, called SUICA (Super Urban Intelligent CArd) [7], in metropolitan Tokyo in 2001.

These public transportation-gating cards are contact-less because they simplify the operations and increase the customer's convenience. Instead of inserting the card into a card reader/writer; customers can pass through the gates simply by waving the cards close to the reader/writer, even if the card remains in a wallet.

Most of the electronic money schemes, including NTT's electronic money, are built on public key cryptographic systems and use contact-type smart cards for their certainty and safety. Electronic money schemes may offer conventional cash features, such as user anonymity, person–to-person transferability, but the most important features are the certainty of the payment process and the prevention of malicious use. The financial institutions that have been investigating the contact-type smart cards have demanded the high security traditionally only possible with public key cryptographic systems. It has been assumed that security far outweighed processing speed.

From the customer's point of view, however, the use of contact-less smart cards sounds very attractive. The trick is to be able to offer the same security and functionality as regular contact–type smart cards.

This paper introduces a high-speed electronic money payment system that uses contact-less smart cards; it offers excellent security and reliability based on a public key cryptographic system. Its performance is certainly practical, a complete payment cycle can be completed within 0.4 seconds.

2   Application of the Contact-Less Smart Card of Electronic Money

2.1   Electronic Money Scheme

In electronic money schemes, money is stored as electronic value in the smart cards. This electronic value should be transferred when making a payment such as paying a conventional bill.

Various electronic money schemes or services has been proposed and introduced, and they have features such as virtual shop/real shop support, smart card (off-line) type/server-access type, open-loop circulation type/closed-loop circulation type, etc [13].

NTT's electronic money scheme has the following features.

– **Payment scheme for real shops:** The ability to use electronic money at real shops, such as kiosks and convenience stores is the key to popularizing electronic money.

- **Smart card based:** Smart cards are tamper-resistant devices, and offer high security and high convenience.

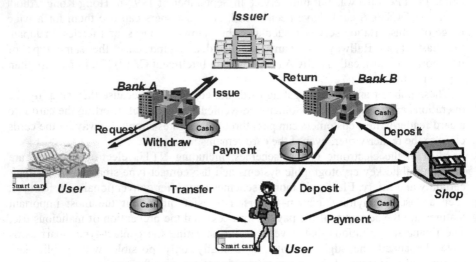

Fig. 1. Basic scheme of NTT's electronic money system

- **Payment can be accomplished without accessing the server systems:** NTT's electronic money scheme allows the user to use off-line electronic money payment, and the shop to store electronic money data in a non-tamper-resistant storage device such as a database.
- **High security and reliability**: NTT's electronic money scheme uses electronic signatures to prevent illegal usage such as eavesdropping, overspending, counterfeiting, copying, and alteration.

2.2   Contact-Less Smart Cards

Application using contact-less smart cards have been advanced focusing on the field, which needs rapid processing, such as payment at the fare gate.

Contact-less smart cards remove the need to insert the card into the reader/writer in using; the user simply waves the card close to the reader/writer, the card can even be kept in his wallet. In addition, since no physical contact is needed, maintenance of the reader/writer is easy and durability is high.

The contact-less smart card is excellent not only in terms of user-friendliness but also technically. For example, a communication speed between smart card and reader/writer is improved as compared with a contact smart card. The basic communication speed of a contact smart card, based on ISO7816 [14], is 9600bps. That of a contact-less smart card, based on ISO14443 [15], is 106Kbps, and two communication signal interfaces, Type-A and Type-B, are standardized.

3   Problems in Implementing Contact-Less Smart Card

To expand the use field of contact-less smart cards, we must prepare the certainty of the payment process and prevent illegal usages, such as eavesdropping, overspending, counterfeiting, copying, and alteration; for this purpose we adopt electronic signatures.

In order to realize a contact-less smart card that offers secure and high speed electronic payments, it is necessary to solve the following problems.

3.1   The Problem of Processing Time

The use of a contact-type smart card requires it to be inserted into a reader/writer. Since the mechanical functions of insertion and ejection take time, processing time did not have to be fast.

The purpose of the contact-less smart card is to improve user convenience so speed I critical. The contact-less smart card can operate only in a magnetic field that emitted from reader/writer. Considering that the user will wave the card over the reader/writer, the process must be completed while the card moves a magnetic field; the processing time must be less than 1 second. This leads to the second problem.

3.1.1   The Problem of Communication Time

In order to accelerate payment processing by taking full advantage of the high communication speeds of contact-less smart cards, it is important to reduce the size of data transmitted and to reduce the need for block chaining.

By adopting a contact-less smart card, the communication speed between the card and the terminal improves. In general, however, the communication buffer of a contact-less smart card is small compared to that of a contact-type smart card. Data that exceeds communication buffer size is transmitted in several steps[1]. We call such data transmission block chaining.

In electronic money systems based on public-key cryptography, it is necessary to transmit a lot of data, such as signatures and certificates. It is important to reduce the size of data transmitted and to reduce the need for block chaining.

3.1.2   The Problem of Signature Generation Time

In our electronic money system, ESIGN [16] and RSA [17] were adopted as public-key cryptographic systems. In order for a smart card to create the signatures like RSA, it must use a specialized cryptographic co-processor. It is difficult for contact-less smart cards to use such co-processors because their power consumption is high. Current chip technology makes it difficult for a contact-less smart card to supply enough electronic power to the co-processor; the power is supplied from the reader/writer by microwave transmission.

For example, in the case of RSA, the key length is usually 1024 bits. In that case, we need to perform 1024 bit-long integer calculations. This demands a co-processor

---

[1] This is the feature of the T=1 protocol.

with high clock speeds, 5MHz or more [10]. It is clear that we need a way of shortening the signature generation time without requiring the use of a co-processor.

3.2   The Problem of Guaranteeing Payment Completion and Data Consistency

Our existing electronic money system completes the transfer of electronic money by passing messages between the card and the read/writer. The failures of the communication path between the two of them during a transaction can serious impact the integrity of the card's contents.

A smart card, which has a CPU, is a kind of microcomputer. Unlike a regular microcomputer, a smart card does not contain its own power source. Inadvertent or malicious power interruptions can cause destruction of the stored data structure. Therefore, problems that arise when updating of the data may cause the loss of electronic money.

Our existing electronic money system uses various management techniques to support practical use [9]. For example, in order to prevent the loss of electronic money, the card itself is mounted in the reader/writer in such a way so as to prevent power interruptions and transmission errors.

The user of a contact-less smart card can move freely with the smart card. Therefore, the occurrence of transmission errors and power interruptions are greatly increased.

It is necessary to enhance the management software on the system side to cope with this problem.

4   Implementation Methods for Realizing the Security of Contact-Less Smart Cards

We adopted the following approaches to achieve adequate security and payment speed in contact-less smart card system.

4.1   Elliptic Curve DSA

We selected the ECDSA (Elliptic Curve Digital Signature Algorithm) for signature generation. The elliptic curve DSA has the following merits.

4.1.1   Less Data is Transmitted:

The ECC (Elliptic Curve Cryptosystem)[2] provides the highest strength-per-bit of any cryptosystem known today. This means that smaller key sizes yield equivalent levels of security. To achieve reasonable security, RSA should employ 1024-bit modulus, while a 160-bit modulus should be sufficient for ECC [18]. The smaller key size means that signatures and certificates are smaller. Less data needs to be transmitted between the card and the terminal so communication times are shorter.

---

[2] ECDSA is the elliptic curve analogue of DSA

4.1.2   Performance:

ECC, in which F_{2^m} is selected as the underlying finite field, can be implemented very efficiently, and offers high performance on smart cards [19][20][21]. Most of the computation for ECC takes place at the finite field level, and the algorithm can be implemented in available ROM, so no co-processor is required to perform signature generation[3].

4.2   Pre-computation to Shorten Signature Generation Time

The Elliptic Curve Digital Signature Algorithm (ECDSA) and ESIGN algorithms can be divided into two parts: the message independent portion and the message dependent portion. By using this division, we can greatly shorten the signature generation time [26].

The signature generation algorithm of ECDSA is as follows.

$$\text{Generate random number } k \tag{1}$$

$$R = (R_x, R_y) = kP \tag{2}$$

$$r = R_x \bmod n \tag{3}$$

$$s = k^{-1}(h(m) + xr) \bmod n \tag{4}$$

Where $P(P_x, P_y)$ is the base point, n is the base point order, x is the private key, r is the first signature parameter, s is the second signature parameter, and m is the message.

In the above algorithm, steps (1), (2), (3), and the following step can be done at any time and are independent of the message begin signed. Thus, in advance of signature generation, the set of values $(r, k1, xr')$ can be calculated.

$$k1 = k^{-1} \bmod n \tag{5}$$

$$xr' = xr \bmod n \tag{6}$$

At the time of signature generation, we simply calculate for the remaining values as shown below.

---

[3] The contact-less smart card, which has DES and T-DES accelerator, can perform ECC more high speed because the addition operation over a filed r_{2^m} can be perform by XOR operation.

$$\text{Generate hash value } h(m) \tag{7}$$

$$s = k1(h(m) + xr')\bmod n \tag{8}$$

We used this technique, whereby the message independent portion is processed beforehand and the results $(r, k1, xr')$ are stored in the smart card's non-volatile memory area. The remaining portion (steps (7) and (8)) is processed at the time of signature generation, whereupon both results are combined. This technique dramatically reduces signature generation time.

4.3   Introduction of Efficient Resending and Transaction Mechanism

Our existing electric money system uses a re-sending mechanism in case for the transmission failures. This mechanism, stores the data needed to reconstruct the response to the terminal, such as payment challenge data, in non-volatile memory before transmission. When the smart card receives the payment request that has same payment challenge data as previous request, it reconstructs the response using stored data, and resends the response.

Furthermore, in order to guarantee the consistency of the data updated by the whole smart card, we implemented a transaction management mechanism. The smart card maintains a commit buffer in non-volatile memory that stores the original contents of updated data until the transaction is finished. Should a transaction fail before completion, the data associated with the transaction are restored to their original values held in the commit buffer.

The problems of the mechanism described above include too many write operations to non-volatile memory and the overhead of managing data updates.

In order to reduce these processing times, we adopt a method that guarantees the completion of the entire electronic money payment process and the consistency of data while requiring fewer writes to non-volatile memory.

First, in order to avoid the overhead associated with managing data updating, all data to be updated (include the data required to reconstruct the response to the terminal) is unified and managed in one area (we call this area the log). This removes the need manage different data update operations separately, only the updating state of the log.

To update the log atomically, we need two non-volatile memory areas that store the latest log and previous log. When we update the log, the latest log is copied to volatile memory, and each set of data log is updated appropriately on volatile memory. When updating (transaction) is completed, the log on the volatile memory area is copied to the previous log.

This transaction mechanism protects against such events as power loss in the middle of a transaction because no change is made to the latest log.

This mechanism is suitable for smart card implementation. Most smart cards use EEPROM for non-volatile memory, and RAM is used for volatile memory. EEPROM has a write-access time of about 7 milliseconds which is approximately 10,000 times slower than RAM [25]. Accordingly, reducing the number of writes that need to be made to EEPROM is very effective in minimizing the processing time.

5   Implementation and Results

We implemented an electronic money application using a commercial smart card and the techniques described in this paper.

5.1   Experiment Overview

The experimental environment is detailed in Table 1 and the electronic money payment sequence is shown in Fig. 2. The smart card used in this implementation, is a commercially available smart card that supports the both interface: contact and contact-less (Type-B interface). With ECDSA, $F_{2^{163}}$ is selected as the underlying finite field. SHA-1 is adopted as the hash function. To authenticate the terminal, we use Triple-DES.

Table 1. Experiment environment

Smart Card	
CPU	16bit (core 8bit), 3.39MHz
RAM	1.2KB
EEPROM	16KB
Interface	Dual Interface (contact/contact-less)
Contact-less Smart Card Reader/Writer	
To Smart Card	106Kbps (Type-B contact-less)
To Terminal	115Kbps(RS-232C)
PC terminal	
CPU	PentiumIII 800MHz
RAM	256MB
OS	Windows98

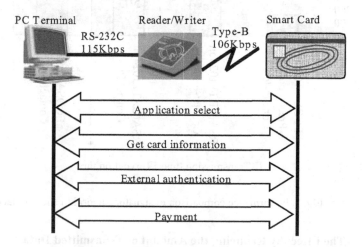

Fig. 2. Sequence of electronic money payment

5.2   Results

In our implementation, the complete payment processing time is about 0.4 seconds. This time covers creating the payment challenge on the PC, command sequence in Fig. 2, and payment verification on the PC.

Table 2 and Fig. 3 compare the processing time for the electronic money payment portion as realized by RSA and ECDSA, and between the contact and contact-less modes. The performance of RSA is an estimated value assuming that the communication speed is 9600bps(contact) and 106Kbps(contact-less), and the signature generation performance (RSA 1024bit with CRT) is referred for the technical newsletter of RSA laboratories [17].

Fig. 3 shows that the performance of our contact-less smart card offer excellent performance, better than that of a smart card with an RSA co-processor and contact-less interface.

Table 2. Performance comparison of signature algorithms and interfaces

	Transmission time	Execution time
ECDSA 163bit+ Pre-computation Contact-less I/F	23ms	138ms
RSA(CRT) 1024bit Contact-less I/F	40ms	330ms
RSA(CRT) 1024bit Contact I/F	503ms	330ms

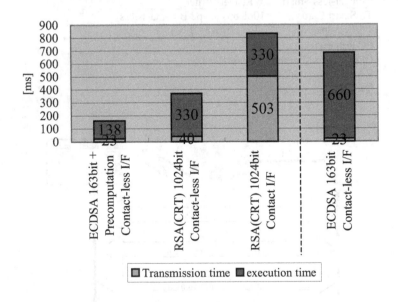

Fig. 3. Performance comparison of signature algorithm and interfaces

5.2.1   The Effect by Reducing the Amount of Transmitted Data

In our electronic money system, the smart card returns the signature and user public-key certificate as its response.

We estimated the block chaining number and transmission time, the results are shown in Table 3. This estimation assumes that the size of the communication buffer is 254 Bytes (contact) and 127 Bytes (contact-less).

Table 3 confirms that the block chaining number is reduced the smaller volume of transmitted data. This minimizes the transmission time.

Table 3. Comparison of transmission time

	Size of response	Block chaining	Transmission time
RSA(with CRT) 1024bit Contact I/F	310 Bytes	2	503ms
RSA(with CRT) 1024bit Contact-less I/F		3	40ms
ECDSA 160bit Contact-less I/F	141 Bytes	2	23ms

5.2.2   The Effect of Pre-computation

The impact of the pre-computation technique on signature generation performance is shown Table 4.

In our implementation, the signature generation process involves just one addition and one multiplication. As a result, the signature generation time is shortened by 93%.

When we use the pre-computation technique, the pre-computed values must be erased after each payment to prevent disclosure of the private key. In our implementation, the pre-computed values are computed and stored during the electronic money loading.

Table 4. The effect of pre-computation

	With pre-computation	Without pre-computation
Signature generation time	38 ms	522 ms

5.2.3   Evaluation of Transaction Mechanism

We prepared four log areas in EEPROM and a pointer that indicates the latest log to implement the method described in section 4.3.

When we refer to the balance in the smart card, we refer to the data in the log indicated by the pointer. In same way, the data required to reconstruct the response to the terminal is found from the indicated log. In our implementation, eight values must be update during payment transaction. The total size of this data can be stored in one page (64byte/page). Our conventional transaction mechanism needs 16 EEPROM writes (to store each values to the commit buffer, and update each value) per transaction. In this implementation, only two EEPROM writes (see Fig. 4) were needed per transaction. Assuming that an EEPROM page-write-access time of 7 milliseconds, processing is shortened from 112ms to 14ms.

252   Hideo Yamamoto et al.

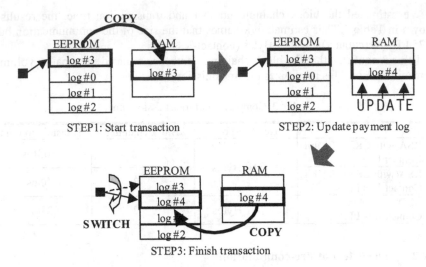

Fig. 4. Transaction mechanism

6   Conclusion

We have realized a high-speed payment system that uses contact-less smart cards. The system can complete an electronic money payment within 0.4 seconds. It will expand the popularity of electronic money systems because it offers the very high-speed processing needed in applications such as public transportation and shop registers.

To confirm the system's feasibility, we implemented it on a dual interface smart card, which means that conventional smart card reader/writers can also be used. Although contact-less smart card reader/writers are currently expensive, their price is expected to fall. Contact smart card reader/writers will probably remain cheaper and so will be used in the home. For example, electronic money loading could be done at home using the contact interface, while payments at shop counters could be done using the contact-less interface.

The system's high-speed signature generation technique and high-speed transaction mechanism are not restricted to electronic money payment; they can be applied to other smart card applications. We are going to apply this technology to other applications that need the security offered by public-key cryptography, such as electronic tickets and personal forms of identification.

Acknowledgment

The authors would like to thank all the members of this project, especially Mr. Seiji Tomita, Mr. Masayuki Hanadate and Mr. Takuo Nishihara, our group leader, with their earnest discussions and important comments on this paper. Also special thanks to Mr. Matsumoto, to give us the opportunities to investigate this study.

References

1. Gartner Dataquest Inc. Worldwide Chip Card Vender shipments in 2000. http://www4.gartner.com/5_about/press_room/pr20010514b.
2. Mondex International. Mondex electronic cash. http://www.mondex.com/.
3. Stadtsparkasse Dortmund. GeldKerte. http://www.spkdo.de/.
4. Banksys, Proton. http://www.banksys.be/en/.
5. Visa International. VisaCash. http://www.visa.com/.
6. Moribatake, H et al. Hierarchical electronic cash scheme. In the proceedings of the 1998 Symposium on Cryptography and Information Security, SCIS'98.1D, 1998.
7. Okamoto, T., and Ohta, K. disposable zero-knowledge authentication and their applications to untraceable electronic cash. In the proceedings of the 7th conference on Theory and Application of Cryptographic Techniques, Lecture notes on Computer Science, No. 435, pp.481-496, Springer-Verlag, 1990.
8. Okamoto, T., Kawahara, H., and Koyama, K. NTT's public key cryptosystem and electronic money system. In the proceedings of Certicom Public Key Solutions'98, 1998.
9. Morita, M et al. InternetCash: An electronic money trial service over the Internet. In the proceedings of the International conference on Computer Communication 1999.pp. 508-515. 1999.
10. NTT Communications. Super Cash. http://www.s-cash.gr.jp/.
11. OCTOPUS. http://www.erg.com.au/transit/projects/Hong_Kong.pdf.
12. SUICA. http://www.jreast.co.jp/suica/index.html.
13. Sudou, O., Gotoh R. Densi Money. CHIKUMA SHOBO Publishing Co., Ltd, 1998.
14. ISO JTC1/SC17. Information technology - Identification Cards – Integrated Circuit Cards with Contacts. ISO/IEC 7816
15. ISO/IEC FCD 14443-2 part 2: Radio frequency power and signal interface. 26th March 1999.
16. Fujioka, A. Okamoto, T. and Miyaguchi, S. ESIGN: An Efficient Digital Signature Implementation for Smart Cards. In the Proceedings of Advances in Cryptology – EUROCRYPT. 1991.
17. RSA Security Inc. CryptoBytes Performance Comparison of Public-Key Cryptosystems. Volume 4, Number 1. http://www.rsa.com/rsalabs/cryptobytes/index.html.
18. A Certicom White Paper. REMARKS ON THE SECURITY OF THE ELLIPTIC CURVE CRYPTOSYSTEM. September 1997. http://www.certicom.com/research/wecc3.html.
19. A Certicom White Paper. The Elliptic Curve Cryptosystem for Smart Cards. May 1998. http://www.certicom.com/research/wecc4.html.
20. Adam D. Woodbury., Daniel V. Bailey., Christof Paar. Elliptic curve cryptography on smart cards without coprocessors. In the proceedings of the IFIP CARDIS. 2000.
21. Kobayashi, K., Kobayashi, T., and Morita, H. An Optimum Smart-Card Implementation for Elliptic Curve Schemes. In the proceedings of the Symposium on Cryptography and Information Security 1999.

22. Michael Rosing. Implementing ELLIPTIC CURVE CRYPTOGRAPY. Manning Publications Co, 1999.
23. A Certicom White Paper. CURRENT PUBLIC-KEY CRYPTOGRAPHIC SYSTEMS. April 1997. http://www.certicom.com/research/wecc2.html.
24. Morita, M., Akashika, H., and Nishihara, T. Rapid processing of electronic money payment. In proceedings of the Symposium on Cryptography and Information Security 2000.
25. W. Rankl & W. Effing. Smart Card Handbook 2nd Edition. John Wiley & Sons, LTD, 2000.
26. Bruce Schneier. Applied Cryptography second edition. John Wiley & Sons, Inc, 1996.

Author Index

Lecture Notes in Computer Science

For information about Vols. 1–2104
please contact your bookseller or Springer-Verlag